Law in Australian Society

What is the 'rule of law'? How do laws get made? Does our legal and political system achieve justice for all Australians equally? Designed for beginners as well as non-law students, this textbook provides a comprehensive and accessible guide to understanding Australia's system of law and government.

Law in Australian Society explains legislation and case law, courts, and the doctrine of precedent. Keiran Hardy examines the roles played by parliaments, politics, and the media. He explains founding principles, including democracy, liberalism, the separation of powers, and federalism. Human rights and justice are highlighted, with an emphasis on First Nations peoples and the law. The book explains criminal responsibility and the justice system, including police powers and the criminal trial. It concludes with case studies of cybercrime and counter-terrorism laws to illustrate law reform in action. This second edition has been fully updated throughout, including recent legislation, cases, and topical issues from Australian law and politics, including from the COVID-19 pandemic and the recent referendum on an Indigenous Voice to Parliament. Each chapter features practical examples, chapter summaries and review questions together with a glossary of key terms.

Concise, accessible and up-to-the-minute, this is a vital guide for anyone seeking to understand Australian law and government.

Keiran Hardy is a Senior Lecturer in the School of Criminology and Criminal Justice at Griffith University and a member of the highly respected Griffith Criminology Institute. He is a recognised expert on counter-terrorism and national security laws and contributes regularly to public inquiries and the media.

"*Law in Australian Society* provides an invaluable entry point for new students and all those seeking to understand the institutions and laws under which we live. In accessible prose, Keiran Hardy demystifies the law and explains its role in contemporary Australia, drawing on recent issues and live debates. A terrific book!"

—**Andrew Lynch**, *Professor & Dean, UNSW Faculty of Law & Justice*

"This highly readable book provides a comprehensive introduction to the law, setting out key concepts using contemporary and engaging examples."

—**Elaine Pearson**, *Asia Director, Human Rights Watch*

"There is a special lauded place in academia for those who possess the skills to distil the complex into the palatable—and this book does exactly that … I commend this book for all those who seek to understand our legal system and strive to study it without undue complexity."

—**David Heilpern**, *Associate Professor and former Magistrate, Dean and Chair of Discipline (Law), University of Southern Queensland*

Law in Australian Society

An Introduction to Principles and Process

Second Edition

KEIRAN HARDY

Routledge
Taylor & Francis Group
LONDON AND NEW YORK

Designed cover image: jasonbennee / Getty Images ®

Second edition published 2025
by Routledge
4 Park Square, Milton Park, Abingdon, Oxon, OX14 4RN

and by Routledge
605 Third Avenue, New York, NY 10158

Routledge is an imprint of the Taylor & Francis Group, an informa business

First edition published by Allen & Unwin 2019
First published by Routledge 2020

British Library Cataloguing-in-Publication Data
A catalogue record for this book is available from the British Library

ISBN: 978-1-032-56021-2 (hbk)
ISBN: 978-1-032-56020-5 (pbk)
ISBN: 978-1-003-43340-8 (ebk)

DOI: 10.4324/9781003433408

Typeset in Vectora LH
by Deanta Global Publishing Services, Chennai, India

For Mum and Dad, who taught me the value of education.

For learning and teaching resources, including videos, quizzes and more, please visit lawinsociety.com.au

Contents

List of figures xv
Acknowledgment of country xvi
Introduction xvii

PART 1: LAW AND ITS INFLUENCES

1 What is law? 3
2 Legislation 19
3 Case law 35
4 Politics 48
5 Media 72

PART 2: RIGHTS AND JUSTICE

6 Founding principles 93
7 Justice 113
8 First Nations peoples and the law 131
9 International law and human rights 155

PART 3: CRIMINAL JUSTICE

10 Criminal responsibility 183
11 Investigation and trial 201
12 Sentencing and appeals 218
13 Cybercrime 235
14 Counter-terrorism 252

Glossary of key terms 271
Index 295

Detailed contents

List of figures xv
Acknowledgement of country xvi
Introduction xvii

PART 1: LAW AND ITS INFLUENCES

1 What is law? 3

1. Law in daily life 3
2. What is law? 5
3. Sources of law 7
4. Branches of law 9
5. Law and society 14
6. Law and employment 16
Discussion questions 18

2 Legislation 19

1. What is legislation? 19
2. How is legislation made? 21
A. Process for approving Bills 22
B. Committee stage 24
3. Where can I find legislation? 25
4. How do I read legislation? 27
A. Citation 27
B. Parts, divisions, sections 28
C. Elements of the law 30
D. How do judges read legislation? 31
5. Regulations 33
Discussion questions 34

3 **Case law** **35**

1. What is case law? 35
   A. Precedent 37
   B. Court hierarchy 38
   C. Jurisdiction 40
2. Where can I find case law? 41
3. How do I read case law? 42
   A. Citation 42
   B. Catchwords 44
   C. Material facts and *ratio* 44
   Discussion questions 47

4 **Politics** **48**

1. What is politics all about? 48
2. Houses of parliament 50
   A. House of Representatives 51
   B. Senate 54
3. Political parties 61
   A. Labor party 62
   B. Liberal Party 63
   C. National Party 65
   D. The Greens 65
   E. Minor parties 66
   F. Independents 67
4. Ministers 68
5. Your vote matters 70
   Discussion questions 71

5 **Media** **72**

1. Media ownership 72
2. The media as 'fourth estate' 77
3. Media bias 83
4. Social media and misinformation 85
   Discussion questions 88
   Notes 89

PART 2: RIGHTS AND JUSTICE

6 Founding principles **93**

1. Liberalism 93
2. Democracy 95
3. Federalism 98
   - A. Shared lawmaking powers 99
   - B. Local government 101
   - C. Advantages and challenges 102
4. Separation of powers 104
5. Rule of law 108

Discussion questions 111
Notes 111

7 Justice **113**

1. What is justice? 113
2. Due process 120
3. From retribution to rehabilitation 122
4. Access to justice 124
5. The role of government 127

Discussion questions 128
Notes 129

8 First Nations peoples and the law **131**

1. Justice 131
2. Sovereignty 134
3. Settlement and federation 137
   - A. Settlement and *terra nullius* 138
   - B. To Federation and beyond 139
4. *Mabo* and native title 141
5. Constitutional recognition 144
   - A. 1967 referendum 145
   - B. Expert panel 146
   - C. Voice to Parliament 148

Discussion questions 151
Notes 152

9 International law and human rights 155

1. International law 155
   - A. Branches and sources 156
   - B. United Nations 159
2. Human rights 164
3. Rights protection in Australian law 168
   - A. The Constitution 168
   - B. Judicial review 170
   - C. Statutes and committees 172
   - D. Models for change 174

   Discussion questions 177
   Notes 177

PART 3:CRIMINAL JUSTICE

10 Criminal responsibility 183

1. What is a crime? 183
2. Types of crime 187
   - A. Homicide 187
   - B. Assault 187
   - C. Property offences 190
   - D. Drug offences 191
   - E. Other offences 192
   - F. Summary and indictable offences 192
3. When is someone guilty of a crime? 193
   - A. Physical and fault elements 193
   - B. Inchoate and accessorial liability 195
   - C. Defences 196
   - D. Young offenders 199

   Discussion questions 200
   Notes 200

11 Investigation and trial 201

1. Discretion 202
2. Police powers 203
   - A. Searches 203
   - B. Questioning 204
   - C. Arrest 205
   - D. Charge 206

E. Misuse of police powers 207
3. Bail 208
4. The criminal trial 210
A. Pre-trial 210
B. Summary trials 211
C. Jury trials 212
D. Evidence 214
E. Witnesses 215
Discussion questions 216
Notes 217

12 Sentencing and appeals **218**

1. Punishment and sentencing 218
A. Types of punishment 218
B. Purposes of punishment 219
C. Principles of sentencing 220
D. Aggravating and mitigating factors 221
E. Evidence 222
F. Instinctive synthesis 224
G. Mandatory minimums 225
H. Sentencing Indigenous offenders 226
I. Imprisonment and parole 228
2. Appeals 229
A. Appeals and the court hierarchy 229
B. Appeals against conviction and sentence 230
C. The High Court 232
D. Benefits and limits 232
Discussion questions 233
Notes 234

13 Cybercrime **235**

1. What Is cybercrime? 235
2. Cyber-enabled crime 238
A. Fraud 238
B. Identity theft 239
C. Sexting and revenge porn 240
D. Cyberbullying 242
3. Cyber-dependent crime 243
A. Criminal hacking 243

B. Denial of service 245
C. Malware 247
Discussion questions 249
Notes 250

14 Counter-terrorism **252**

1. Australia's legal responses to terrorism 252
2. What is terrorism? 254
3. Offences 256
A. Preparatory offences 256
B. Terrorist organisations 257
C. Declared areas 259
D. Advocating terrorism 259
E. Hate symbols 260
4. Powers 260
A. Control orders 260
B. Preventative detention orders 261
C. ASIO questioning warrants 262
D. Special intelligence operations 263
E. Metadata 263
F. Encryption 264
G. Citizenship stripping 265
5. Lessons 265
A. Scrutinise laws properly 265
B. Protect human rights 266
C. Protect media freedom 267
Discussion questions 268
Notes 269

Glossary of key terms 271
Index 295

Figures

1.1	Branches of law	10
2.1	Citing legislation	20
2.2	Process of enacting a Bill	24
2.3	Structure of legislation	28
2.4	Screenshot of legislation from AustLII	29
3.1	Court hierarchy	38
3.2	Citing case law	43
3.3	Medium-neutral citation	44
3.4	*Mabo* judgment from AustLII	45
4.1	Example House of Representatives ballot paper	53
4.2	Comparing the House of Representatives and Senate	54
4.3	Example Sample Senate Ballot Paper: Voting Above the Line	57
4.4	Example Sample Senate Ballot Paper: Voting Below the Line	58
4.5	Executive branch of government	69
6.1	Section 51 of the Constitution	100
6.2	Levels of government in Australia	102
6.3	Separation of powers	106
7.1	Equality vs equity	116
9.1	Universal Declaration of Human Rights	166
11.1	Stages of the criminal justice process	202
12.1	Appeals hierarchy	230

Acknowledgement of country

I acknowledge the traditional owners of the land on which this book was written: the Kombumerri peoples of the Yugambeh language group, on the lands we call the Gold Coast.

I pay respect to their elders, past and present, and extend that respect to all Aboriginal and Torres Strait Islander peoples.

I acknowledge that the Australian legal system described in this book is a recent addition—some 120 years ago—to a rich history of First Nations law, culture and connection with country extending back 65,000 years and more.

Introduction

This book teaches you about Australia's legal system and how it relates to politics, government and society. You should keep in mind three themes while reading it.

First: the law is constantly changing. When I started law school, I expected to memorise rules and cases and be tested on my knowledge of them. But there was no memorising, and I was surprised that many of the rules were different to those my sister had learned, while studying only a short time before me! What was the point, then, in learning different rules if they would soon be out of date? As my torts lecturer told me, learning about the law means understanding and analysing rules, knowing how to read and interpret them, and applying them to new and different situations—whatever the specific rule may be—not memorising them and applying them mechanically. Indeed, many of the mechanical tasks associated with legal research are increasingly being done by artificial intelligence. In our rapidly changing world, it is crucial to consider how and why laws change, the legal system as a whole, and whether elements in that system create or undermine fairness for everyone in society. It is especially important to think about what the law ***should*** be—not only what it ***is***—when thinking about evolving threats and technologies. Those skills will not be replaced by computers anytime soon.

Second: there are some things that do not change. Of course, that sounds like it contradicts the first point, but our legal system combines fundamentals that have not changed in more than 100 years, with specific rules that change from one day to the next. The fundamentals play a significant role in determining the specific rules we have in place from time to time. Australia's **Constitution**—the founding document of our nation—came into force on 1 January 1901. Changing the text of the Constitution is very

Constitution: Australia's founding legal document, which came into force 1 January 1901

difficult. It must be done at a **referendum**: a national vote on whether the text should be changed. There have only been 8 successful referendums in more than 120 years. In October 2023, a referendum to establish an Indigenous **Voice to Parliament** was unsuccessful. The Voice was to be an advisory body that allowed representatives of our First Peoples to speak to the federal parliament (our main lawmaking body) on issues affecting their communities. Sometimes, changes to the law that do not happen are the most fundamental.

Referendum: a national vote on whether to change the text of the Constitution

Voice to Parliament: proposed representative body that would allow representatives of First Nations communities to advise the parliament and executive government

Third: Australia has some glaring gaps in its legal system compared to similar nations. Our Constitution still fails to recognise First Nations peoples, or even to mention them. This sets us apart from countries like New Zealand, Canada and the United States, which have extensive agreements with their Indigenous peoples. In Australia, Aboriginal and Torres Strait Islander peoples were long treated as flora and fauna under the doctrine of ***terra nullius*** ('land occupied by no one'). It was only by 1992, in the famous High Court decision of *Mabo*, that this highly discriminatory idea was overturned. Still, our Constitution does not recognise that Indigenous peoples have been living on these lands for 65,000 years and counting. Our First Peoples experience significant disadvantage compared to the rest of the Australian population, including higher rates of infant mortality and significantly higher rates of imprisonment. Indigenous people make up less than 4% of the Australian population, but 33% of our prison population. Constitutional recognition and a Voice to Parliament would not automatically fix these and other symptoms of colonisation. But they would take significant steps towards respecting and repairing Australia's relationship with its First Peoples.

***Terra nullius*:** legal fiction that allowed Britain to settle Australia (means 'land belonging to no one')

We also have no codified human rights protection at the national level. **Human rights** are core protections that all human beings should be afforded to respect their dignity and wellbeing. The lack of national human rights protection in Australia again sets us apart from our closest partners. You might be able to name something from the US Bill of Rights—like pleading the fifth, or protections for free speech—but these were not written into our own Constitution. Canada's Charter of Rights and Freedoms, the UK's Human Rights Act, and New Zealand's Bill of Rights Act are other examples. Indeed, Australia is the only democratic country that does

Human rights: core freedoms that all human beings should be afforded to respect their dignity and wellbeing

not have some form of codified national human rights protection. This is not something we want to be known for on the global stage.

Lacking human rights protections has significant flow-on effects for the rules, offences and powers that make up our legal system. For example, Australia's counter-terrorism laws impact on many different human rights, including those to liberty, privacy, and the right to silence. People can be placed under house arrest without a criminal trial or put in prison if they refuse to answer questions put to them by our domestic spy agency. You can read more about these laws in the final chapter of this book. It would not be possible to enact laws like these in countries with strong human rights protections.

It is striking that our Constitution does not mention First Nations peoples or human rights, but it mentions the Queen of England more than 50 times. It even mentions lighthouses, beacons, buoys, telegraphs, telephones, postal services, fisheries and fermented liquids—but not Indigenous peoples or human rights. How is that possible? The Constitution is an historical document, its text can only be changed with a referendum which rarely succeed, and the King of England is still our **head of state** (the highest representative in a system of government). Australia is a constitutional monarchy: a system of government where a King or Queen's power is limited by a constitution. We are not a **republic**: a system of government ruled only by the people's representatives. A referendum to create a republic failed in 1999. Still, it is hard to read the Constitution and feel like it speaks to contemporary Australia. What does it say about the society we live in, and want to live in, that the founding legal document of our legislation has these two major gaps?

Head of state: the highest representative in a system of government

Republic: a system of government with a head of state that represents the people

Based on these key themes, you can keep in mind three questions while reading the chapters to come:

1. How can Australia ensure it has the best laws in place to deal with evolving threats and technologies?
2. Does a constitution from 1901 represent the Australia we are today and want to be in the future?
3. How can Australia best recognise First Nations peoples and protect human rights, to ensure we have a fair legal system for all?

By the end of this book, you will know enough about Australian law and politics to think of some answers to these big questions.

The book is divided into 3 parts.

Part 1 introduces you to the law and its influences. Chapter 1 explains what law does, what it is, where to find it, and how it relates to the society we live in. Chapters 2 and 3 explain legislation and case law. Chapter 4 delves into politics and elections. Chapter 5 explores the important role that the media plays in shaping public debate.

Part 2 covers rights, theories and justice. Chapter 6 explains core ideas underpinning our system of law and government, including liberalism, democracy, and the separation of powers. Chapter 7 explores different meanings of justice. Chapter 8 focuses on First Nations peoples and the law. It explains ***terra nullius***, ***Mabo***, native title, sovereignty, and the Voice referendum. Chapter 9 discusses international law and protections for human rights.

Part 3 focuses on criminal justice. Chapter 10 explains criminal responsibility and different types of offences. Chapters 11 and 12 explore the process of criminal justice, from investigation through to bail, trial, sentencing, and appeals. Chapters 13 and 14 conclude with case studies in two key areas of law reform: cybercrime and counter-terrorism. These chapters build on what you have learned throughout the book. They reinforce the idea that the law is not a set of fixed rules. Rather, the legal system must continually adapt and evolve to changing threats and other events in society.

Public law: area of law that tells us about Australia's system of law and government

State: term used in political philosophy that refers to the national government of a country

Together, these chapters teach you about public law and criminal law. **Public law** is the 'law of government'. It tells us about relationships between the **state** (government) and its citizens. It tells us about the structure of our legal system and its fundamental features, including the Constitution, parliament and the courts. Public law overlaps with politics—or at least some knowledge of Australian politics helps substantially with understanding it. Its fundamentals are part of any 'civics' education, but public law addresses more complex legal questions as well.

Criminal law: area of law that tells us when someone breaches the rules of society and should be punished

Criminal law also governs relationships between the state and citizens. Fundamentally, it tells us when someone breaches the rules of society and should be punished for it. When someone is thought to breach a criminal law, the state brings a case against them. If the person is found guilty, they face criminal punishment, which is often but not always imprisonment.

Chapter 1 briefly explains **private law**, which governs relationships between individuals. Private law is also called civil law. It includes contract law and property law, which tell us (for example) what happens when we buy something from a company and transfer ownership. This book does not address those sorts of legal questions. Private law topics still tell us about law and society, but they require their own treatment, and are not usually covered in depth in introductory law courses.

Private law: area of law that governs relationships between individuals, and between individuals and companies

A key aim of this book is to pitch the material at a genuinely introductory level. Lawyers have a well-earned reputation for making things sound complex. This can make learning about the law difficult. Complexity in the law helps to ensure fair outcomes. But this should not deter anyone who wants to learn about how laws are made, what justice means, when someone is guilty of a crime, how we could achieve greater protection for human rights, or other fundamental questions about law and society. You can learn a lot about these important questions without dissecting case law and legislation.

Questions about law and society are relevant to students from wide-ranging degrees beyond law, including criminology, human services, psychology and allied health. Indeed, they are questions that everyone in a democracy should understand, think about and be heard on. Resources for learning about them must be accessible to people from varied backgrounds, including first-year university students, mature-age students with diverse professional experience, people for whom English is a second language, high school students studying legal studies—or anyone wanting to learn more about how Australia 'works' as a country. Law plays a major role in that daily functioning.

The chapters speak to these wider audiences by assuming no prior knowledge, defining key terms alongside the content, summarising key points and posing questions for discussion and review. The references are kept to a minimum, and geared where possible towards sources that are easy to find online and easy to read. This does not mean the content is not challenging, as all learning should push the boundaries of what you know and how you think.

By the time you read the final chapters, you will have the knowledge and skills required to think critically about law reform in those two key areas. I hope you might then apply what you know to other areas of study or interest. If I can achieve that, even for a proportion of readers, I will be proud that the book has extended legal education to a wider audience.

KEY POINTS

- This book teaches you about the fundamentals of Australia's legal system and how it relates to politics, government and society.
- Laws change constantly, but the fundamental features of our legal system, like the Australian Constitution, have stayed largely the same since 1901.
- The book is divided in 3 parts: (1) law and its influences, (2) rights and justice, and (3) criminal justice.

DISCUSSION QUESTIONS

1. How can Australia ensure it has the best laws in place to deal with evolving threats and technologies?
2. Does a Constitution from 1901 represent the Australia we are today and want to be in the future?
3. How can Australia best recognise First Nations peoples and protect human rights, to ensure we have a fair legal system for all?

Part 1
Law and its influences

Chapter 1
What is law?

In this chapter, you will learn about:

- What law does and what it is
- Sources and branches of law
- Law and society

It is difficult to think of an aspect of society that law does not influence. In this chapter, you will learn about what law does and how it shapes your everyday life. You will learn what law is, how it changes over time, and where to find it. Law reflects society's morals and values, and it can shape them in turn. It will also influence your employment, no matter which job you choose.

1. LAW IN DAILY LIFE

You may have never hired a lawyer or set foot in a courtroom, but law still influences your behaviour and the things you interact with every day. From the time you get up in the morning until you go to bed, law shapes your life in countless ways, even if the rules and their effects are not obvious.

Do you live in a rented apartment? You would have signed a **lease**: an agreement that governs the relationship between a tenant who lives on and uses the property, and a landlord who owns it. Has your air conditioning ever broken in the heat of summer? Have you found mould after rain, or had water dripping down from an apartment above? Who needed to fix it and how quickly did it need to be done?

Lease: agreement that governs the relationship between a tenant who lives in a property and a landlord who owns it

DOI: 10.4324/9781003433408-2

Are you engaged to be married or living with a long-term partner? It does not sound very romantic, but marriage is a union of two individuals recognised under law, which triggers rules relating to taxation, emergency medical decisions and inheritance. Some of those rules apply to de facto partners (generally, those who have been living together for more than two years). None of those rules apply if you are not living with your partner or have been living together only for a short time.

Metadata: data about communications, including the time, location and length of phone calls between two devices

Have you browsed the Internet today, or called a family member? Laws govern the types of data that are collected about you and how long they are kept by service providers. Every time you make a phone call, your provider keeps **metadata** about where and when you made the call, who you called, how long you spoke for and the devices that you used. That data will be kept for two years. Not because you did or are likely to do anything wrong, but because laws enacted in response to terrorism mean that service providers must keep metadata on all their customers, in case police or our domestic spy agency needs it to assist with a terrorism investigation.

Contract: legally binding agreement

Did you buy something online? Perhaps after seeing an advertisement on TV? If you did, you entered into a **contract**—a legally binding agreement—to purchase those goods. The advertisement followed rules about the types of content that can be shown at different times of day and night (mostly to protect children). Maybe you saw a gambling ad and placed a bet on your favourite sporting event? Even stricter rules apply to those advertisements, including the warnings that must be given every time they are shown.

Have you binge-watched a violent or romantic show? Classification rules determine the levels of violence and sexual activity that can be shown to viewers. Did you have a few drinks while watching it? Then you could not drive your car to get dinner, or you would lose your licence, so maybe you ordered delivery instead. You entered into another contract to purchase the food, possibly through a third-party company to deliver it, but there are even more rules behind the food itself and how it was prepared. Employees can work only so long without breaks, and they must be paid at least the minimum wage. Restaurants must comply with food and safety regulations to make food for the public.

If something goes wrong in any of these situations, the law can help to fix it. Lawyers and courts are not always needed. If your online shopping never arrives, you might send an email to complain; the shop could apologise and offer a refund or free express shipping to make up for the delay. Technically, there might have been a **breach** of contract—a failure to meet the terms of the agreement—but there is no point paying lawyers to sort it out. But if more money is involved or anyone is harmed, the law will play a bigger role. A court can then issue a **remedy**—such as the payment of money as compensation—to help address any loss or harm.

Breach: fail to meet a legal requirement

Remedy: a court order designed to offset harm or loss

These are just a few examples, but they are enough to see how law influences many aspects of our lives. This does not mean you need to know everything about how the law works. You can turn on light switches without being an electrician and use your computer without being a programmer. It would not be useful or even possible to learn and think about every law that shapes your life (or, if you did, there would not be much time left to live it). But it is useful to understand that law plays a crucial role in how societies function, and that we are all subject to its many requirements.

Law's impact on our daily lives was most obvious in 2020 and 2021, when we all faced restrictions during the height of the COVID-19 pandemic. Most of us would never have thought we would be required to stay within a 5km limit, wear a face mask outside, or be vaccinated before entering our favourite café. In the name of public health, everyone was required to make these sacrifices—but they were not just asked of us, there were laws behind every one of them.

If you were over 18 in 2023 and an Australian citizen, you would have also voted in the referendum on an Indigenous Voice to Parliament. That vote was unsuccessful, but it is possible that an advisory body based on the proposal may be created in the future. A referendum gives every Australian the chance to have their say on whether the text of our Constitution should be changed.

2. WHAT IS LAW?

If law does so many different things, what is it, exactly?

Law is a body of rules that regulate our behaviour. To **regulate** behaviour means to influence, guide and restrict it. A **rule** is a statement, principle or instruction

Law: a body of rules found in legislation and case law that regulate behaviour

Regulate: to guide and restrict behaviour

Rule: a statement, principle or instruction that says what someone can, cannot or must do, or how something must be done

that says what someone can, cannot or must do, or how something must be done.

In other words, law tells us:

- what people cannot do;
- what people may do;
- when they can do something;
- what they must do;
- how they must do something.

Rules saying what we cannot do are found in the criminal law. Criminal laws prohibit us from doing things that harm one another or society. They also deter us from breaking the law. For example, a teenager may think about stealing an item from a convenience store, but decide not to because they know they may be punished for stealing it. That is how law can regulate our behaviour just by existing in the background. You will learn more about the criminal law in Chapter 10.

The other categories can be seen in police powers. Laws say that a police officer may arrest someone when certain conditions are satisfied. They also say what an officer must do when they arrest someone and how they must do it (for example, they must use certain words to tell the person that they are being arrested and what they are being arrested for). To **arrest** someone means to take them into police custody to investigate a crime or have a court determine whether they committed one. You will learn more about police powers and the criminal justice system in Chapters 11 and 12.

Arrest: to take a person into police custody to investigate a crime or have a court determine whether they committed one

Least common is for rules to say that we ***must*** do something. It is rare for the law to compel action. Even if someone is dying on the street, the law does not require you to do anything about it. Morally speaking, helping might be the right thing to do, but legally speaking, you can simply walk on by. More commonly, the law says what someone must do if and when they choose to do something. Even in the case of police powers, an officer is not required to arrest someone every time a crime is committed; they can choose to use that power, and if they do, they must follow a series of requirements.

Mostly, the law says what we cannot do and we are otherwise free to live our lives as we choose. This is a core principle underlying societies, like Australia, which are guided by the philosophy of liberalism. You will learn more about liberalism in Chapter 6.

Laws, then, are rules that tell us what we can and cannot do and how we must do things. Less often, they say that we must do something. But laws are not just any rules. A parent can tell a child they cannot stay out past midnight, or that they can play computer games only for one hour after they finish their homework. Those rules could be strictly enforced, and they may come with penalties, like being grounded or denied a weekly amount of pocket money. But they are not laws, and no one else is required to follow them. Laws are formal rules that everyone in Australia must follow.

3. SOURCES OF LAW

Where do we find all the rules that govern society and regulate our behaviour?

There are two main sources of law in Australia: (1) legislation and (2) case law.

Legislation is a document containing legal rules that were approved by a **parliament**: a lawmaking body of elected politicians. You will learn more about legislation in Chapter 2 and more about politics in Chapter 4.

Case law refers to the written reports issued by judges after they resolve disputes in courtrooms. Most of the time, a dispute is between two **parties**, who come before the court to resolve some legal disagreement. A **judge** is a highly experienced lawyer who is appointed to preside over and resolve these disputes. Case law is also called the '**common law**'. This is an old phrase referring to judgments that were 'common' throughout the land of England.

Legislation and case law work in tandem: parliament creates rules in legislation, and judges interpret those rules to resolve disputes. Dividing these tasks is a core aspect of the separation of powers, which you will read about in Chapter 6.

Within the two main categories, there are more specific types. **Regulations** are rules like legislation but they are written by Ministers instead of parliaments. A

Legislation: a document containing legal rules that were approved by a parliament

Parliament: a lawmaking body made up of elected politicians

Case law: collection of judgments published by courts

Party: one of the sides in a legal dispute

Common law: another name for case law

Regulations: legislation made by ministers

Minister: a senior member of government with responsibility over a specific policy area

Secondary legislation: another name for regulations

Subordinate legislation: another name for regulations

Delegated legislation: another name for regulations

Minister is a senior member of government appointed to look after a specific policy area like policing or foreign affairs. Regulations are known as **secondary legislation** or **subordinate legislation**, because the power to make them is given by a main or 'primary' piece of legislation. They are also called **delegated legislation**, because parliaments delegate (hand over) their lawmaking power to a Minister. A more official term is **legislative instruments**, because regulations (and some other rules and determinations made by Ministers) are very similar to legislation.

Regulations provide more detail on what the law means and how it should be used in practice. It is impossible to list all these details in legislation. For example, aviation legislation says that a 'weapon' cannot be taken through an airport security checkpoint, but the regulations specify a longer list of things that qualify as weapons. Regulations are quicker and easier to change than legislation, as Ministers can do it without requiring the approval of a parliament. Lists like these can then be updated more frequently. You will learn more about how legislation is approved in the next chapter.

Tribunal: quasi-court that is part of the executive branch of government

Case law includes tribunal decisions. **Tribunals** are similar to courts, but they resolve less complex disputes on specific topics more quickly. For example, tenancy tribunals resolve disputes between tenants and landlords. To use the example above, if your landlord refused to fix your air-conditioning for a long time, you could take the matter to a tenancy tribunal. The tribunal might require your landlord to complete the repairs as soon as possible and repay a portion of your rent.

The ultimate source of law in Australia is the Constitution. It is a unique piece of legislation. It is actually just one section of a piece of legislation passed by the British parliament. But it is fundamental and different from all other legislation for two reasons: all legislation in Australia must be consistent with it, and the text of it cannot be changed without a referendum. It has existed in nearly the same form since 1901.

There is also international law, which you will learn about in Chapter 9. It is best to think of international law as sitting outside Australian law. It is a source of law that Australian parliaments and courts can look to when making and interpreting laws, but the rules contained in treaties and other international instruments are not strictly part of Australian law unless those rules are recreated in our own legislation. A **treaty** is a formal, written agreement between two or more countries that is governed by international law. It is similar to a contract between countries at the international level. Treaties cover many different topics, including trade matters, access to natural resources, environmental protections, cybercrime, terrorism, and human rights.

Treaty: a formal, written agreement between two or more countries that is governed by international law

4. BRANCHES OF LAW

Legislation and case law cover many different topics, so it is useful to divide them into categories or topic areas. These are often called the 'branches' of law. They can help determine which courts resolve which types of disputes. A court has **jurisdiction** over a matter if it has the power to resolve a dispute on that topic. Most courts have jurisdiction to hear a wide range of cases, but some (like land and environment courts) can hear cases only on specific topics.

Jurisdiction: the geographical area in which laws operate and a court's power to hear different types of cases

Figure 1.1 shows the main branches of law in Australia. The major distinction is between public law and private (or civil) law. Usually, when we talk about public law, we mean the law of government, including fundamental features like the Constitution and parliaments. Broadly speaking, as a branch of law distinct from private law, public law includes any topic area that governs relationships between individuals and the state. For this reason, it includes criminal law and taxation law (even though the financial focus in taxation law seems to fit better in private law).

Private law governs relationships between individuals. This includes interactions between companies, and between individuals and companies. A company is essentially a group of individuals acting together as one legal person. (The word 'corporation' comes from the Latin ***corpus***, meaning body. Individuals unite in one body to form a company and, among other things, enter into contracts.) Private law includes contract law, property law, torts, corporations law, and environmental law. We do not consider private law in detail in this book, but a few examples from the key areas of tort, contract and property law will help you understand some basic principles.

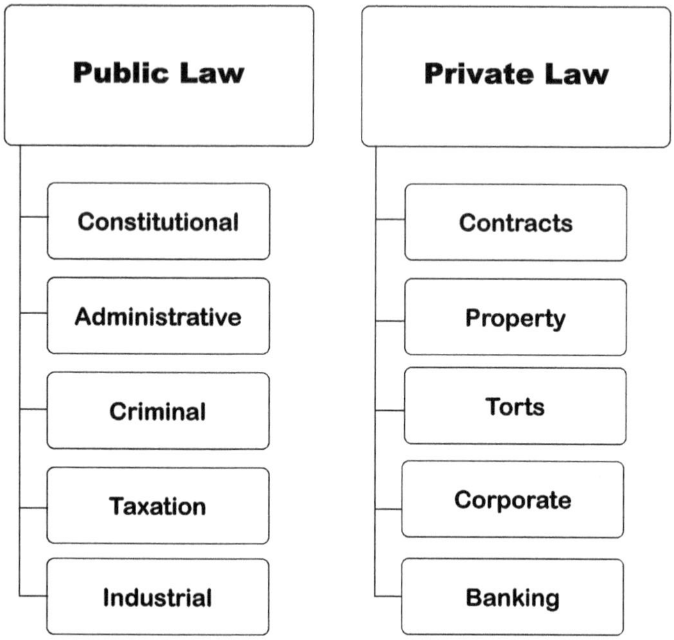

Figure 1.1 Branches of law

Contract law: area of the law that governs agreements between individuals

Contract law governs agreements between individuals. It is easy to spot a contract when they are formal and written, such as a contract for the sale of land. You read the document and decide whether to sign on the dotted line with a lawyer or other witness present. But contracts can also be informal—and they might just be part of a conversation. Imagine you see some second-hand goods advertised on an online marketplace. You call the listed mobile number and agree in a phone conversation with the seller to purchase them. Later that night, you change your mind and do not send them the money. What if the seller wants to enforce the agreement? If you keep refusing and they insist, the matter might end up in court. A court would consider three main things:

(1) whether an offer was made;
(2) whether you accepted the offer;
(3) whether consideration was promised by each party to the agreement.

Consideration is the legal value that each party promises to exchange in a legally binding contract. In this example, you were offering a payment of money;

the seller was offering to transfer title to their goods and possession of them in return.

Consideration: the legal value that each party promises to exchange in a legally binding contract

If the court enforced this agreement, you might think that was unfair. Perhaps you should not be required to buy the goods if you changed your mind. But the same rules would protect you if the seller refused to deliver the goods after you paid for them, or they sold them to someone else in the meantime, and *you* wanted to enforce the agreement.

A **tort** is an unlawful but non-criminal harm. **Negligence** is a common example. Someone is negligent when they cause harm by breaching a duty of care. A **duty of care** is an obligation not to cause foreseeable harm to others. We all have a duty of care to each other, but these duties are most obvious where one person has greater power and responsibility in the partnership: like doctors to their patients, teachers to their students, or shops to their customers. Imagine a shop fails to put up a wet floor sign after cleaning. A customer slips over and breaks their ankle. The shop owner would not be guilty of a crime, but the injured customer could **sue** the company (bring a civil action against them in court). Typically, negligence and other tort claims result in **damages**: the payment of money as compensation to offset the harm caused. The amount of damages would depend on the level of harm. This example would probably be **settled** (agreed) out of court, but damages can be substantial where negligence results in serious injury, permanent disability or death.

Tort: an unlawful but non-criminal harm

Negligence: acts that cause harm to someone by breaching a duty of care

Duty of care: an obligation not to cause foreseeable harm to others

Sue: bring a civil action against someone in court

Damages: payment awarded by a court as compensation

Settle: agree to resolve a legal dispute out of the courtroom, often by one side paying money to the other as compensation

Defamation is another common tort. This is where someone harms another person's reputation by publishing false information. For example, a blogger might claim that a celebrity had an affair or committed a crime, when those things did not actually happen. If the celebrity was hounded by the media as a result and lost opportunities to be paid in new roles, they could sue the

Defamation: when someone harms another person's reputation by publishing false information about them

blogger for damages. Private law often considers whether someone expected to receive some value, and did not receive it because of someone else's conduct.

Torts overlap with crimes: both involve harm being caused to someone. When someone is detained against their will, this could be the crime of kidnapping, or it could be the tort of **unlawful imprisonment**. Unlawful imprisonment can be made out where police detain a suspect for too long or for no lawful reason. **Assault**—contact with another person without their consent—is another crime and tort. Whether it would be heard as a crime or tort (or both) would depend on the harm caused and whether the assaulted person chose to make a separate civil claim. It is quite common for one series of events or circumstances to generate multiple court proceedings based on different lines of argument.

Unlawful imprisonment: tort where someone is detained against their will

Assault: contact with another person without their consent

Property law governs usage and ownership rights. Most often, we think about it in relation to land, houses and other dwellings like apartments. If you are lucky enough to own a block of land and a house on it, you have what is called **Torrens title**, also known as **freehold title**. It is sole registered ownership to the exclusion of all others. **Strata title**, by contrast, is a type of shared-ownership arrangement, usually between the owners of different apartments within the same building. Strata title does not give you ownership of the land you are living on, but you own part of the building and can use the common areas (like the BBQs, gym and swimming pool). As an owner in a strata scheme, you automatically become part of a **body corporate**, which is essentially a committee that manages the property on behalf of its owners. Body corporates have the power to make **by-laws**: rules that specify things that owners and tenants can and cannot do on the common property.

Property law: area of law that governs usage and ownership rights

Torrens title: sole registered ownership of land and property to the exclusion of all others

Freehold title: another name for Torrens title

Strata title: a shared ownership arrangement commonly used in apartment blocks

Body corporate: committee that manages a property on behalf of all owners in a strata title scheme

Property law governs many complex land uses and transfers of ownership rights. For example, a government department might want to purchase a side passage through someone's land to access utilities like gas or water. This can be done through an **easement**: a right to use part of someone's land for a specific purpose without owning it. Or the government might resume (take back) multiple properties to build a highway or metro line. If you have seen the movie ***The Castle***, you would know this must be done, according to the Constitution, 'on just terms' (in other words, for fair compensation).

By-laws: rules made by body corporates that say what people can and cannot do on common property in a strata title scheme

Easement: a right to use part of someone's land for a specific purpose without owning it

Aside from land rights, property law provides general rules relating to title and possession of all items, no matter how small. To have **title** to something means to own it and to **possess** it means to physically control it. If someone searches a beach with a metal detector and finds a missing ring, they will own the ring, which is now in their possession, until someone else (most likely the previous owner) makes a better claim to it.

Title: ownership rights over something

Possess: have physical control over something

Rules about possession also determine when drug offences apply in the criminal law. **Constructive possession** is a principle that applies where someone else possesses a thing that you own. If you can get the thing back whenever you ask for it, the law says it is still technically in your possession. This means a person charged with possessing large amounts of illegal drugs cannot avoid punishment simply because someone else is storing the drugs for them.

Constructive possession: principle that says the owner of goods can still be in possession of goods held by another person

There are too many other aspects of property and private law to address them properly here. However, we will cover one aspect of property law in more detail in Chapter 8. **Native title** is a usage right granted to First Nations peoples that recognises their ongoing connection with land and water according to traditional law and customs. It was first recognised in 1992 by the High Court in its historic ***Mabo*** judgment. Importantly, while native title can grant Indigenous groups exclusive possession over land and water, it does not grant them a legal right to own it.

Native title: property usage right granted to Indigenous groups based on their traditional connection to the land

You have probably started realising from these examples that the lines between different branches of law are not clear-cut. Contract and property law often overlap: leases are legally enforceable contracts that determine property usage rights between landlords and tenants. Torts can also be crimes, and property law shapes parts of the criminal law. Native title is part of property law, but it would be impossible to talk about public law without it. So do not worry if you ever feel confused that different branches of law overlap, because they do! The main distinctions, though, are typically drawn along the lines shown in Figure 1.1. Dividing law in this way helps us to understand the full scope of legal rules in Australia and some of the specific topic areas they cover.

5. LAW AND SOCIETY

It is important to understand that laws on all these topics are not static or fixed. Many laws have existed for a long time, but they are not set in stone. Rather, laws are dynamic: they change frequently. This happens in two ways:

(1) Parliaments enact new laws and change old ones (Chapter 2).
(2) Courts refine legal rules by applying them to new situations (Chapter 3).

The idea that laws change over time can be difficult to grasp. Students often believe that the law is a body of strict, specified rules, and that the purpose of studying law is to learn what those rules are (I thought this myself when I started studying law as an undergraduate). For lawyers, there is some benefit to approaching the law in this way. To argue a case effectively in court, you need to know the current rules in detail. But you still need to know about previous cases, new judgments that are handed down, and changes to legislation that could affect your clients. So it is always important to understand how laws change over time and how new rules are made.

It is okay if this idea does not make much sense now, because legislation and case law are explained in detail in the next two chapters. For now, the point is simply that laws change all the time. For this reason, law tells us about the society we live in, and it can shape society in turn. **Law reform**—when new laws are proposed and made by parliaments—is heavily influenced by different groups and interests. Public opinion, political parties, media reporting, government inquiries, royal commissions, businesses and advocacy groups can all influence the laws that are enacted in parliament. Courts are independent from the other branches of government and they do not propose new laws, so they are not subject to the same sorts of

Law reform: when laws are proposed and made by parliaments

debates and influences. But court cases are still decided within a wider context of government policy, media coverage and public opinion, and they can shape those things in turn.

Law reform that allowed same-sex marriage is an important example that tells us much about Australian society. Before 2017, national legislation defined marriage as being 'between a man and a woman'. Now, marriage is a union of any two people. This was a minor change to the law with major outcomes for people in same-sex relationships. Achieving the change was not easy and took a long time, because different groups in society had very different and strongly held opinions. The government at the time did not support a **conscience vote** on the issue, so every Australian was asked to vote in a postal survey on whether the change should be made. A clear majority (more than 60%) voted in favour, though rates of support differed quite a lot across the country and between urban and regional areas. In the federal parliament, politicians celebrated an historic vote to make same-sex marriage legal, though a small number voted against it and a larger number **abstained** from voting.

Conscience vote: when members of a political party can vote according to their individual views and not party politics

Abstain: decline formally to vote for or against a proposal

Whatever your views on same-sex marriage, the law reform process showed us that views on marriage equality in Australia have changed over time, and also that a significant number of Australians still believe in the traditional institution. Changing the law can be very difficult when a rule has existed for a long time, even if change is wanted by most people. The idea that laws change all the time does not mean that laws change easily as soon as society's morals and values shift. Plenty of laws remain in place even if they are problematic or large numbers of people disagree with them.

In this case and others, changes to the law may also change people's views in turn. Once same-sex marriage has been legal for a longer time, rates of support for it may well be even higher across the country. Perhaps 50 or 100 years from now, no one will even remember the previous version of the law!

Law's ability to change means that governments use it to address many social problems. Law is a tool or mechanism that can be used to prevent harm from being caused to members of the community. This is especially true of criminal laws. Governments have used new criminal laws to counter bikie gangs, cybercrime, 'one-punch' drunken assaults, and terrorism. Before the 9/11 attacks on New York and Washington in 2001, Australia did not have any national laws that made terrorism a crime. Now, we have nearly 100 pieces of legislation to prevent and counter this threat. You can read more about Australia's counter-terrorism laws in the final chapter.

It should be clear by now that law is not simply a list of rules to be learned. It is a fundamental part of Australian society. We could even say that law plays a significant role in creating the society we live in. It says who can be married, whether you own property, and when someone goes to prison. The laws we have in Australia are not a 'given'; there are always important and difficult questions about what the law should be.

Understanding law is critical to understanding how Australia 'works' as a country. This is important for everyone's education, lawyers and non-lawyers alike. Understanding our system of law and government is a fundamental part of being an informed citizen.

This does not mean you need to know how to read case law and legislation in detail. That's a skill that lawyers train many years for and develop over their entire careers. However, after reading this book, you will be familiar with legislation and case law, where to find them, and how to read them. You will understand how laws are made, the importance of the Constitution, and foundational principles like liberalism, democracy, justice and human rights. You will understand the different stages of the criminal justice system, from investigation and arrest through to charge, bail, trial, and sentencing. And you will understand how the Australian government is using law to reduce cybercrime and terrorism. These are two key areas of ongoing law reform here and around the world.

6. LAW AND EMPLOYMENT

Law is also important to you individually as it will impact on your career, regardless of the profession you decide to enter. Governments that introduce new laws can favour very different approaches to your area of employment. Changes to the law could mean you have new or different powers available to use in your job. You may be required to make decisions in a different way, or your department or agency may be subject to a formal inquiry. It is difficult to think of a career that could not be impacted by law in some way.

Imagine you leave university and begin working as a police officer. At first, you might work under a government that believes in giving police strong powers to prevent crime. Following an election, you could find yourself working under a very different government: one that limits police power, improves rights for suspects, and launches an inquiry into police corruption. Your experience of working as a police officer would be very different under those two governments.

Or imagine you become a social worker. You start your job under a government that increases welfare payments and improves employment opportunities for people with disabilities. Following an election, a new government might divert crucial resources from the people you care for daily, meaning they cannot seek out your services. Similar laws could impact on psychology and allied health. Laws could affect registration and training requirements for these and other professions. They determine how much you pay for these qualifications at university, and how many years it will take to pay off your student debt.

Law's reach extends well beyond professions related to justice, health and welfare. You might work for a media or broadcasting company producing local content in Australia, but there is not enough work available because most people watch content from streaming services based overseas. Changes to the law could mean that digital devices, applications, and platforms must show Australian content more often. This could lead to more jobs for local content creators.

Changes to law and policy would cement these different approaches to policing, social work, and media production. They could be made in legislation, regulations, or a court might issue a judgment that changes how an existing power is interpreted. Keeping on top of the changes will become more important the higher you rise in your career, but they impact employees at all levels.

It is not the primary aim of this book to explain how law will impact on your employment. However, the chapters that follow introduce you to Australia's legal system and explain how laws can be influenced by politics, the media, and other groups and interests. This will help you understand the important role that law plays in Australian society.

KEY POINTS

- Law is a body of rules found in legislation and case law that guide and restrict our behaviour.
- You don't need to read case law or legislation in detail to learn about Australia's system of law and government.
- Law tells us about and shape the society we live in. New and changing laws will also impact on your chosen career.

DISCUSSION QUESTIONS

1. Can you think of five things in your day that might be influenced by law?
2. How would you explain the law to somebody who doesn't know what it is?
3. What is the difference between public and private law?
4. What are two ways that law changes over time?
5. How might law impact your future employment?

Chapter 2
Legislation

In this chapter, you will learn about:

- What legislation is and how it is made
- Where to find legislation
- How to read legislation and how judges interpret it

There are two main sources of law in Australia: legislation and case law. This chapter explains the first of these. You will learn what legislation is, where to find it, and how to read it. An important concept is jurisdiction, meaning the geographical area in which legislation operates.

1. WHAT IS LEGISLATION?

Legislation is a document containing rules that have been debated, voted on, and approved by a **parliament**. Parliaments are lawmaking forums made up of members and **senators**: the politicians we vote in at election time to make rules on our behalf. This parliamentary system is the defining feature of our democracy.

There is a parliament in Canberra and a parliament in each state and territory. We often call the parliament in Canberra the '**federal parliament**', but it is actually the division of powers between this central parliament and several state parliaments that is known as a **federal system** of government. You will read more about federalism in Chapter 6. We also refer

Legislation: a document containing legal rules that were approved by a parliament

Parliament: a lawmaking forum made up of elected politicians

Senators: politicians elected to the Senate

Federal parliament: the Australian parliament in Canberra

DOI: 10.4324/9781003433408-3

Federal system: a system of government which has a national government and several state or regional governments

Commonwealth Parliament: the Australian parliament in Canberra

Amend: to change a law

Repeal: to remove or revoke a law

Act: a piece of legislation

Statute: a piece of legislation

Enact: to make a Bill into law

Jurisdiction: the geographical area in which laws operate and a court's authority to hear different types of cases

to the federal parliament as the **Commonwealth parliament**. It represents the joining together ('common wealth') of different states into the single country known as the Commonwealth of Australia.

Parliaments spend most of their time debating and approving legislation. Legislation can create new rules, change existing rules, or remove rules that should no longer apply. Changing an existing rule is known as **amending** the law. Removing or revoking a rule is known as **repealing** a law.

A piece of legislation approved by a parliament is also known as an **Act** or **statute**. When legislation is approved by a parliament and becomes part of the law of Australia, we say the parliament **enacted** it.

For practical purposes, legislation is a document that tells us what the rules are in a topic area. Every statute is named by a title, the year it was enacted, and the parliament that enacted it. The parliament that enacted it tells us the **jurisdiction**; this is the geographical area in which the rules operate. Rules enacted by the federal parliament in Canberra apply all over Australia, whereas rules enacted by a state or territory parliament apply only in that state or territory (otherwise, Queensland could make rules for New South Wales, and vice versa!).

For example, the legislation that sets out the criminal law of New South Wales is shown in Figure 2.1.

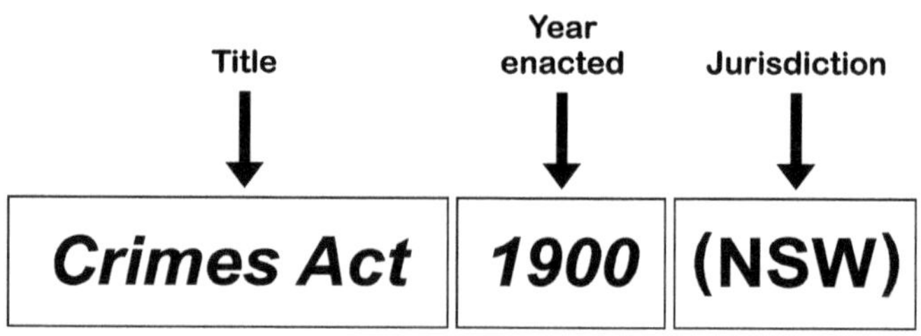

Figure 2.1 Citing legislation

Legislation sets out rules in numbered **sections**. These sections are divided into subsections, sub-subsections and so on (this is partly why laws are so difficult to read). Subsections are indicated with brackets, numbers, small letters and (if the section is long enough) small roman numerals. For example, section 18 of the *Crimes Act 1900* (NSW) creates the crimes of murder and manslaughter:

Section: an individual rule in legislation

18 Murder and manslaughter defined

(1)

(a) Murder shall be taken to have been committed where the act of the accused, or thing by him or her omitted to be done, causing the death charged, was done or omitted with reckless indifference to human life, or with intent to kill or inflict grievous bodily harm upon some person, or done in an attempt to commit, or during or immediately after the commission, by the accused, some accomplice with him or her, of a crime punishable by imprisonment for life or for 25 years.

(b) Every other punishable homicide shall be taken to be manslaughter.

Section 18 has a short title that tells us what it contains. Subsection (1)(a) tells us when a person commits the crime of murder. Subsection (1)(b) tells us an unlawful death ('homicide') that does not qualify as murder will instead be manslaughter (an unintended or negligent death). The penalties for committing murder or manslaughter are set out in additional sections.

2. HOW IS LEGISLATION MADE?

The section above is one small example of the thousands of laws that have been enacted by Australian parliaments. In 2023 alone, the federal parliament passed 122 statutes, each with many specific rules. Many more were passed by the state and territory parliaments.

For legislation to be enacted, there is a specific process the document must go through. Legislation starts off as a Bill, which is essentially a draft version of the final document. A **Bill** is a proposal for a new law to be considered by a parliament. Bills are drafted by specially trained lawyers on advice from members of the government and government agencies.

Bill: a proposal for legislation

Government: political party with a majority of seats in the House of Representatives

Minister: senior member of government with responsibility over a specific policy area

House: chamber in a parliament

Chamber: a large room where legislation is debated

Bicameral: having two chambers

House of Representatives: lower house of the federal parliament

Senate: upper house of the federal parliament

Unicameral: having one chamber

The first step is for the Bill to be introduced into parliament, meaning that it is formally submitted for consideration. Bills can be introduced by any member of parliament, though they are usually introduced by the government. The **government** is the political party that won the majority of seats at the last election. More specifically, Bills are usually introduced by **Ministers**: senior members of government who are responsible for different policy areas. You will read more about political parties, elections and Ministers in Chapter 4.

Most Australian parliaments have two **houses**. These are large rooms, also known as **chambers**, where politicians meet to debate legislation. A parliament with two houses is known as a **bicameral** parliament (meaning it has 'two chambers'). In a bicameral parliament, both houses debate and approve the same legislation according to the procedure explained below. The two houses of the federal parliament are the **House of Representatives** (also known as the lower house) and the **Senate** (also known as the upper house).

All Australian states, except Queensland, have bicameral legislatures. The state houses of parliament are usually called the Legislative Assembly (lower house) and the Legislative Council (upper house). Members of a Legislative Council are called members (not senators, as at the federal level). Queensland, the Northern Territory and the Australian Capital Territory have **unicameral** legislatures, meaning there is only one chamber that debates and approves legislation.

A. Process for approving Bills

The reason we refer to a 'lower' and 'upper' house has to do with the process for approving Bills in parliament. A Bill is usually introduced into the lower house before being passed to the upper house. For the Bill to be approved and become law, it must go through three readings in each house. (In a unicameral legislature, the Bill need only be approved by one house.) **Readings** are the stages of parliamentary debate on the Bill.

Reading: stage of parliamentary debate on a Bill

Each reading is concluded with a vote, and the Bill will only progress to the next stage if a majority of members vote 'yes'. These debates are supervised by the **Speaker**, a member of parliament who is chosen to preside over proceedings and ensure that debate is conducted according to the rules of parliament (known as **standing orders**). The Speaker does not vote on a Bill unless there is a tie, in which case the Speaker has the deciding vote.

Speaker: member of parliament who is chosen to preside over proceedings

Standing orders: rules that specify how parliaments are run

The first reading is typically a formality where members agree to consider the Bill. More substantial debate happens at the second and third readings. At the start of the second reading, the Minister makes a speech to explain the purpose of the Bill and what it contains. This is called a **second reading speech**. Second reading speeches are an important part of the parliamentary record and a useful resource for legal research.

Second reading speech: Minister's speech in parliament which outlines the purpose of a Bill and what it contains

The legislation is then considered in more detail and members suggest amendments (changes) to a Bill before it is approved.

After three readings in the lower house, and a majority 'yes' vote from the politicians, the Bill is 'passed up' to the upper house. After three readings in the upper house and another 'yes' vote, it will become law.

For a Bill to become an 'Act of Parliament' and part of Australian law, it must also be signed by the Governor-General. This is called granting the Bill **royal assent**. The **Governor-General** is the King's representative in Australia. The King is our **head of state**, so all legislation must technically be approved by him. Nowadays this is just a formality, though it remains an important final stage in the lawmaking process.

Royal assent: when the Governor-General signs a Bill to become law

Governor-General: the King's representative in Australia

Head of State: the highest representative of a sovereign state

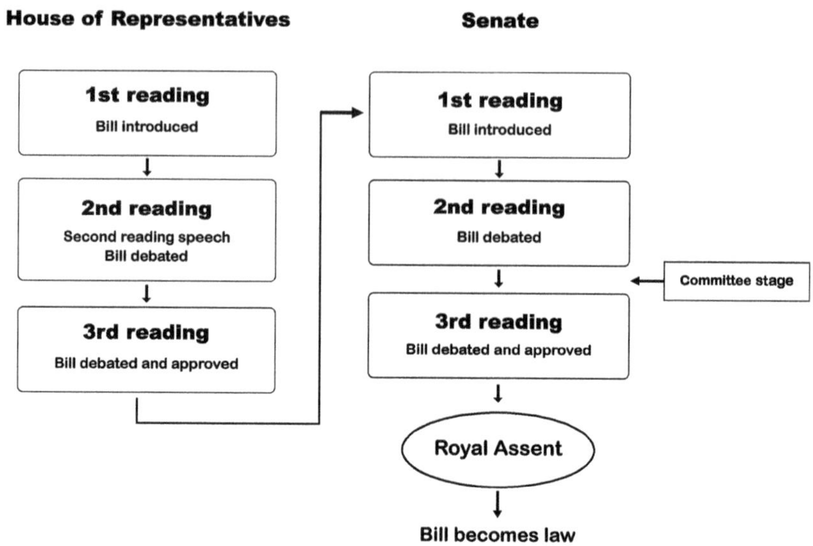

Figure 2.2 Process of enacting a Bill

The entire process for debating and enacting a Bill in parliament can be seen in Figure 2.2. This example refers to the federal House of Representatives and Senate, but a similar process is followed in the states and territories.

B. Committee stage

An important part of this process is the committee stage. Between the second and third readings, a Bill can be referred (sent) to a parliamentary committee for more detailed consideration. A **parliamentary committee** is a group of members or senators who meet separately to examine the Bill in more detail. Some committees are made up of members only from the lower house, some are made up of members only from the upper house, and **joint committees** have representatives from both.

Parliamentary committee: group of members or senators who meet separately to examine Bills in detail

Joint committee: a parliamentary committee made up of members from both houses

To begin the committee stage, parliament assigns the Bill to an appropriate committee (there are many committees with responsibility for different issues). The committee will then advertise a public inquiry and call for written submissions. This is an important part of our democracy, as it gives everyone in Australia the opportunity to contribute to the lawmaking process. You can write to the committee and make your own case as to what you think the law should be. This can be in the form of a letter, a brief written document, or a more substantial report including detailed research. Typically, many submissions come from government agencies, academics, human rights groups, and professional organisations (such as those representing the legal profession).

After a committee receives written submissions, it holds public hearings. Some individuals and organisations are invited to give their submissions in person. This is called 'giving evidence' to the committee or 'appearing as a witness' to a public inquiry, although it is not quite like giving evidence in court. Instead, the committee asks the witness what they think the Bill should contain and what should change before it is approved. The witness answers these sorts of questions and elaborates on their written submission. These hearings are transcribed as part of **Hansard**, the public record of parliament.

Hansard: transcripts of parliamentary proceedings

The committee considers the written and oral submissions, writes up a report, and tables this in parliament. To **table** a document means to formally submit it into the parliamentary record (the phrase comes from the act of laying a document on the table at the centre of the parliamentary chamber). Essentially, the committee is handing the report to parliament, which feeds into the remaining debate. Its recommendations may or may not be incorporated into the Bill, and the rest of the process continues.

Table: formally submit a document into the parliamentary record

3. WHERE CAN I FIND LEGISLATION?

A key component of the rule of law is that laws should be publicly available (you will read more about the rule of law in Chapter 6). Fortunately, this means that legislation is relatively easy to find online. In Australia, the two main places you should look for legislation are AustLII and government websites.

AustLII (austlii.edu.au), the Australasian Legal Information Institute, is a comprehensive online database of Australian and New Zealand law. It is maintained by academics at the University of New South Wales (UNSW) and the University of Technology Sydney (UTS). AustLII includes legislation from all jurisdictions

AustLII: the Australasian Legal Information Institute, an online database of legislation and case law across Australia, as well as related materials like Bills and explanatory memoranda.

Explanatory memorandum: document accompanying a Bill that explains what the Bill contains

An **explanatory memorandum** is a document accompanying each Bill that explains what the Bill contains. This helps with interpreting Bills, which can be very technical and difficult to read. You can search and browse AustLII by title, jurisdiction, year, and keywords.

The federal, state and territory governments each maintain online databases of legislation and related materials. The federal government website can be found at legislation.gov.au. The state government websites can be found at legislation.qld.gov.au, legislation.nsw.gov.au, legislation.vic.gov.au (and so on).

Technically, these government websites are the 'official' version, but AustLII is highly authoritative and arguably easier to navigate. If you need to reference the law for assignments, AustLII is not the equivalent of Wikipedia or other online resources which are possibly unreliable and not typically used in an academic setting. It is highly reliable; you should just make sure when you reference legal materials from AustLII or a government website that you cite the legislation (or case law) you are looking at, and not the website you found it on. These websites are a gateway for finding the law; the law is the thing you should cite.

AustLII is helpful if you prefer to browse a HTML version of legislation. You can click on individual sections and navigate back and forth in your browser. It is easier to copy and paste sections from these pages into your study notes. The government websites are best if you want the most official version, or if you prefer to browse a PDF document, download it, and save it to your computer. You can search the entire PDF for keywords. This is much harder in AustLII, as each section is on a separate webpage.

Consolidated Acts: the current and complete version of legislation

Numbered Acts: legislation listed by the year it was enacted

When navigating these websites, a few terms will be unfamiliar. **Consolidated Acts** are the current and complete version of legislation, including all changes recently made. **Numbered Acts** are the legislation listed by year, including legislation that changed the wording of a previous law. Some numbered Acts are entirely new pieces of legislation, but most of them are amending legislation. This is useful for seeing how the law has developed over time. It is similar to looking at the 'track changes'.

You can also search in any search engine using the title, year and jurisdiction. For most searches, the AustLII and government websites will appear at the top of the results. For example, try searching for 'Crimes Act 1900 NSW' and the first results will be from the NSW government website and AustLII. Browse or search the legislation and see if you can find section 18 (defining murder and manslaughter).

4. HOW DO I READ LEGISLATION?

When reading legislation, you should take note of the title and citation, then browse the overall structure, which is organised into parts, divisions, and sections. You read the sections of the legislation to work out the elements of the law.

A. Citation

To start reading legislation, take note of the title, year, and jurisdiction. The title indicates the topic area. The possible jurisdictions, indicated in round brackets, are as follows:

- Commonwealth (Cth);
- New South Wales (NSW);
- Queensland (Qld);
- Victoria (Vic);
- Western Australia (WA);
- South Australia (SA);
- Tasmania (Tas);
- Northern Territory (NT);
- Australian Capital Territory (ACT).

Here are a few examples from different years and jurisdictions. Which issues do you think this legislation addresses? Which parliament enacted them? See if you can find a copy of them on AustLII, a government website, or via a search engine.

- *Creative Australia Act 2023* (Cth);
- *South Australian Public Health Act 2011* (SA);
- *Police Powers and Responsibilities Act 2000* (Qld);
- *Charter of Human Rights and Responsibilities Act 2006* (Vic);
- *Family Violence Reforms Act 2022* (Tas).

B. Parts, divisions, sections

Part: a group of divisions in legislation

Division: a group of sections in legislation

Once you find a piece of legislation, browse its overall structure and see how it is divided into **parts** and **divisions**. These are like subheadings that organise the legislation into different categories of rules.

Parts are the biggest grouping. They are made up of several divisions. Most legislation begins with an introductory part that defines key words used in the legislation and sets out other general rules.

A division contains the individual sections (or rules), which are numbered sequentially from the beginning to the end of the entire document. We normally refer to a section with the letter 's' (as in, s 16 or s 22). Not all parts are divided into divisions. Smaller parts can just list the individual sections.

It may be confusing at first to understand that a section is an individual rule, whereas parts and divisions group these rules into larger 'chunks' of the document. Figure 2.3 shows you this structure of legislation—from parts down to divisions, and from divisions down to sections and subsections.

Figure 2.4 shows you a screenshot of legislation from AustLII and its main features. This legislation is the *Australian Security Intelligence Organisation Act 1979* (Cth),

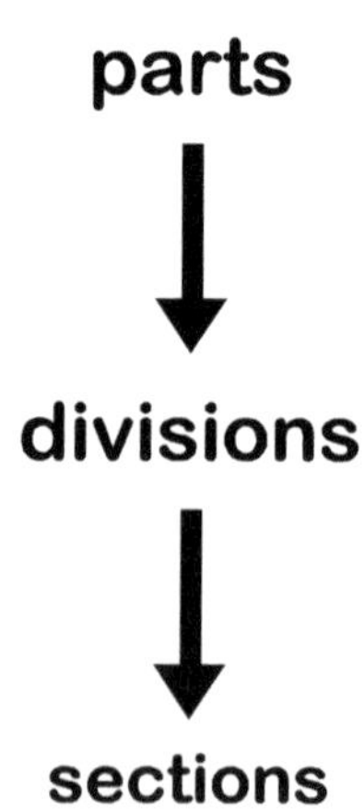

Figure 2.3 Structure of legislation

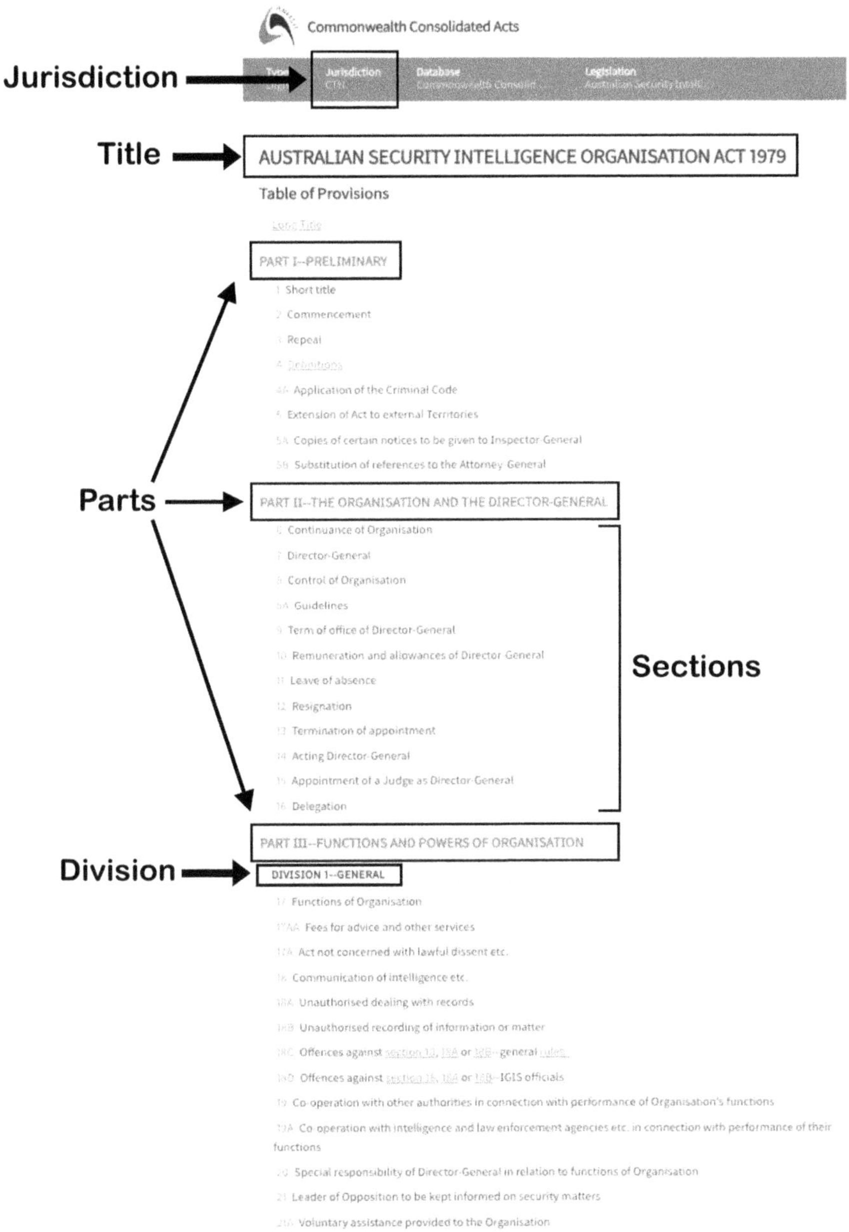

Figure 2.4 Screenshot of legislation from AustLII

which governs Australia's domestic intelligence agency. You will learn more about some of its powers in Chapter 14 on counter-terrorism.

C. Elements of the law

Elements: the components or ingredients of legal tests

Your main task when reading legislation is to work out the **elements** of the law. These are like the components or ingredients of the law. You can think of them as a series of legal tests. They determine how a legal rule should be applied to different fact scenarios that come before a court.

Below, section 18(1)(a) from the *Crimes Act 1900* (NSW) is copied out again, but this time the elements of murder as a criminal offence are bolded.

> **18 Murder and manslaughter defined**
>
> (1)
>
> (a) Murder shall be taken to have been committed where the **act** of the accused, or thing by him or her omitted to be done, **causing** the **death** charged, **was done** or omitted **with reckless indifference to human life, or with intent to kill or inflict grievous bodily harm** upon some person, or done in an attempt to commit, or during or immediately after the commission, by the accused, some accomplice with him or her, of a crime punishable by imprisonment for life or for 25 years.

Essentially, we are stripping out the extraneous words to come up with a formula for defining murder, so we can work out if a person has committed that crime. It is not that the other words are unimportant; in certain cases, some of them might be crucial to the outcome of a case. But this is a useful exercise to craft a general definition of murder that can be applied as a starting point to all cases. Putting the bolded words together into a sentence gives us the following:

> Act … causing death … was done … with reckless indifference to human life, or with intent to kill or inflict grievous bodily harm.

This gets us much closer to a workable definition of murder—something that could be tested in court. Rephrasing this slightly gives us the following definition:

> Murder is an act causing death that was done with intent to kill, intent to inflict grievous bodily harm, or reckless indifference to human life.

We can also present this in a more logical or mathematical format, so that we can clearly see a 'list of ingredients' for murder. For a person to be found guilty of murder, we need the following elements:

1. Act causing death, AND
2. Intention to kill, OR
3. Intention to inflict grievous bodily harm, OR
4. Reckless indifference to human life.

A major part of 'thinking like a lawyer' is to identify elements like these and structure them logically in a way that allows you to apply a rule to specific cases. For example, in an exam or assignment, a common task is to work through a hypothetical fact scenario (essentially, a story made up by your lecturer). You might need to work out whether someone is guilty of murder or another crime.

A formula like this can help you do that. To work out whether the person is guilty, you would work through these elements and determine whether each is satisfied on the facts. When you do this, it is important to note which elements are essential, and which are alternatives. In this example, we need the first element for there to be a murder, but only one of the next three elements. You will learn more about how to categorise these sorts of criminal law elements in Chapter 10.

Learning how to identify elements from legislation is a skill that can take some time to develop. Your lecturers will help you with it, and if you are looking at case law as well, the issues that judges focus on will help you to identify them. For now, you can think of the elements as key words in any section of legislation.

D. How do judges read legislation?

In a courtroom, methods for reading a statute become more complicated. It is rare for a statute to be completely clear on what the rules are. This might sound surprising, as the law is very detailed. However, all words and phrases can be interpreted in different ways, especially when the wording is so complex. And sometimes, laws are simply not drafted clearly. Lawyers also make arguments in court so that legislation can be interpreted to benefit their client. Judges therefore play a crucial role in working out what statutes mean for the purposes of a case.

Statutory interpretation: methods used by judges to determine the meaning of words and phrases in legislation

Statutory interpretation refers to the methods used by judges, based on submissions by lawyers from both sides, to determine the meaning of specific words and phrases in legislation.

Methods of statutory interpretation are clearer now that the overall approach has been clarified in statute. Section 15AA of the *Acts Interpretation Act 1901* (Cth) says:

> In interpreting a provision of an Act, the interpretation that would best achieve the purpose or object of the Act (whether or not that purpose or object is expressly stated in the Act) is to be preferred to each other interpretation.

There are equivalents in each state and territory. Basically, this says that statutes must be interpreted by courts to best achieve the law's purpose. This requires courts to consider parliament's intention in enacting the law. For example, parliament might have enacted a law to prevent crime or protect public health. Taking account of those purposes can influence the meaning given to a word or phrase.

Literal rule: common law rule that said judges should prefer the ordinary or dictionary meaning of a word

Golden rule: common law rule that said judges could substitute another meaning of a word if the literal rule led to an absurd or inconsistent result

Mischief rule: common law rule that said judges could consider the problem legislation was designed to prevent

This approach has developed out of a longer and more complicated common law history. Traditionally, courts would progress through a series of tests, depending on the outcome of each. They would start with the **literal rule**, which favoured the ordinary or dictionary meaning of a word or phrase. The **golden rule** said that the literal meaning should be preferred unless it led to an absurd or inconsistent result. The court could then substitute a better meaning.

The **mischief rule** said that a court could consider the mischief (problem) the law was designed to prevent, but only in cases of absurdity or inconsistency. This was also called the **purposive rule** or approach, as it considered parliament's purpose in enacting the law. Courts were also reluctant to consider materials outside the legislation (known as **extrinsic materials**) unless there was a good reason. Extrinsic materials include government reports, explanatory memoranda, parliamentary speeches, international treaties, or anything else that can assist.

Purposive rule: another name for the mischief rule

The modern approach confirms that the law's purpose can be considered by courts in the first instance, even if the text is clear. This does not mean that literal meanings are ignored, but rather that literal meanings, other sections in the legislation, the purpose behind a statute, and the wider context in which it was enacted, all play a role from the outset in determining what specific words and phrases mean. Modern approaches also view extrinsic materials more favourably from the outset. Section 15AB of the ***Acts Interpretation Act 1901*** (Cth) says that extrinsic materials may be considered to determine the law's purpose or to confirm the ordinary meaning of a word. Extrinsic materials are still less important than text, context and purpose, but they are an important aid that can be used whenever they are needed—not only as a last resort.

Extrinsic materials: materials separate to legislation that can be used to determine its purpose or the meaning of a word or phrase

One specific method of statutory interpretation is known as the **principle of legality**. This is a presumption that parliament did not intend to interfere with fundamental rights and freedoms, unless it did so using clear words. You will learn more about the principle of legality and how it relates to human rights in Chapter 9.

Principle of legality: judicial presumption that parliament did not intend to interfere with fundamental rights and freedoms

5. REGULATIONS

Regulations are legislation made by Ministers instead of parliaments. As discussed in Chapter 1, they are also known as secondary, subordinate or delegated legislation. Regulations usually contain more detail than legislation and they often say how it should be used in practice.

Regulations: legislation made by Ministers

Delegated legislation: another name for regulations

You will not likely spend much time looking at regulations during your degree. However, many jobs will require you to read, understand and use regulations in practice—especially if you work for a government department.

We refer to regulations in a similar way to legislation, with a title, year and jurisdiction. The documents are structured in a similar way to legislation, though the numbered rules are known as 'regulations' instead of 'sections' (for example, we would say 'regulation 12' or 'reg 12' rather than 'section 12').

You can find regulations in a similar way to legislation, by browsing and searching AustLII or the relevant government websites.

KEY POINTS

- Legislation begins as a Bill, which will become law only if it passes through three readings in the lower and upper houses of parliament.
- You read legislation to identify elements that can be used to resolve legal issues. For example, you can read a section of legislation to find out what 'murder' means and whether a person is guilty of that crime.
- Judges use text, context and purpose to work out the meaning of words and phrases in legislation. This is called statutory interpretation.

DISCUSSION QUESTIONS

1. Can you find a copy of the ***Online Safety Act 2021*** (Cth)? What are the some of the headings for its parts and divisions? What are some of the sections about?
2. How does a Bill become an Act of Parliament? Can you draw the steps as a flow chart or diagram?
3. Can you find the Minister's second reading speech for the ***Summary Offences (Prevention of Knife Crime) and Other Legislation Amendment Act 2024*** (Qld)? Why was this legislation introduced, and which two existing statutes did it amend?

Chapter 3
Case law

In this chapter, you will learn about:

- Precedent and the court hierarchy
- Where to find case law
- How to read case law

The second main source of law in Australia is case law. This chapter explains what case law is, where you can find it and how to read it. It explains the court hierarchy and how courts apply rules to new cases through the doctrine of 'precedent'. We revisit the idea of jurisdiction, meaning not only the geographical area in which laws operate, but also the authority of courts to hear different types of cases.

1. WHAT IS CASE LAW?

Case law is the collection of documents issued by courts, which set out the reasons why judges arrived at their decisions in individual cases. Case law is also called the **common law**—an old British term referring to judgments that were 'common' throughout the land. (There are some other meanings given to the phrase common law, but this is the most common way it is used.)

Case law: collection of judgments published by courts

Common law: another name for case law

DOI: 10.4324/9781003433408-4

A **case**, also known as a matter, is when two **parties** (like sides or teams) come before a court to resolve a dispute. This could be a couple arguing over custody of a child, or two companies arguing over a business contract. If someone is accused of a crime, the two parties are the government (known as the **Crown**) and the accused person (known as the **defendant**). We refer to this as an **adversarial system** of justice because the two parties are like 'adversaries': they are in a sort of contest or competition with each other in the courtroom.

Cases are presided over by a **judge** or **magistrate**: an experienced lawyer who is appointed to these high-level positions. Magistrates sit in local courts and judges sit in higher courts. They have slightly different roles, but they both act as a sort of umpire or referee in the courtroom. We say that judges and magistrates are appointed to the **bench**, as they sit in an elevated position at the front and centre of the courtroom.

At the end of a case, a judge writes up a document known as a **judgment**. A judgment is a statement of reasons that explains a judge's decision and how they arrived at it. It is also called their **opinion**, though it is not simply what they thought about the matter. It explains, usually in a long and complex way, how they resolved a dispute by interpreting and applying legal rules.

In some courts, multiple judges might hear the same case. If there are multiple judges, the outcome is determined by what a majority decides. The report of a judge who is 'outvoted' by the majority is known as a dissenting judgment (or just a **dissent**). Where there are multiple judges, some judges will write their opinions together (known as a **joint judgment**) and some will write by themselves. This is often but not always split along the lines of how the judges decided the matter.

Case: legal dispute between two parties in court

Party: one of the sides in a legal dispute

Crown: the government that is prosecuting the defendant in a criminal case

Defendant: the accused person in a criminal trial

Adversarial system: a court system where two parties oppose each other

Judge: a highly experienced lawyer who is appointed to preside over trials and resolve legal disputes

Magistrate: judge in a local court

Bench: the central, elevated platform in a courtroom where the judge or magistrate sits

Judgment: published statement of reasons that explains a judge's decision and how they arrived at it

Opinion: another name for a judgment, or, in evidence law, a belief that something was likely to happen

Dissent: minority opinion of a court

There are specific phrases we use to name judges in a judgment and explain what they decided. We refer to a judge of a supreme court or the High Court of Australia as 'Justice' (or 'Chief Justice' if they have been appointed as the most senior judge on that court). In written text, we indicate this with a 'J' after their last name, 'JJ' where there are multiple Justices, or 'CJ' if they are a Chief Justice.

Joint judgment: when two or more judges write their opinions together

If we want to explain a point made in a judgment, we say that a judge or judges **held** something—not that they said or concluded it (this might sound a bit odd at first, but it becomes second nature when talking about the law). We could say, for example: 'Brennan J held in the famous ***Mabo*** decision that ***terra nullius*** "depended on a discriminatory denigration of indigenous inhabitants"'. If you spoke this or a similar sentence out loud, you would say 'Justice Brennan', not 'Brennan J'.

Held: decided by a judge or judges

It is good practice to refer to individual judges wherever possible, but you can say 'the High Court held … ' or 'the 'Victorian Supreme Court held … ' if you are referring to a general principle outlined by a majority of the judges. So, for example, we could say: 'the High Court held in ***Mabo*** that Indigenous groups can make claims to native title which grant usage rights based on traditional ownership of the land'.

A. Precedent

Judgments feed precedent. **Precedent** is the overarching logic of the legal system. It is a core principle which says that the rule and reasoning used in a previous judgment must be used again when similar cases come before the court. In other words, if two similar disputes come before the court, those cases should be decided in the same way. This promotes consistency and fairness: we do not want a legal system where parties come before a court and receive a different outcome to a similar case from the previous week.

Precedent: core principle of law which says the rule and reasoning used in a previous judgment must be used again when similar cases come before a court

More specifically, precedent says that lower courts must apply the decisions of higher courts in previous similar cases. We refer to this as **binding precedent**,

Binding precedent: rules from previous judgments that courts must follow

Stare decisis: Latin name for the doctrine of precedent (means 'to stand by things decided')

meaning that lower courts must use the reasoning from higher courts: they cannot choose whether to use it or not. The technical term for the doctrine of precedent is ***stare decisis***, which is Latin for 'to stand by things decided'.

B. Court hierarchy

By lower and higher courts, we mean the different levels of court in Australia's legal system. Figure 3.1 sets out the hierarchy of courts in Australia.

Local court: lowest court on the court hierarchy

Magistrates court: another name for the local court

The hierarchy begins at the bottom with **local courts**, which are also known as **magistrates courts**. There are many of these in each state and they hear most cases. In Queensland, there are 130 magistrates courts and they hear close to 95 per cent of the state's case load. Local courts hear disputes involving small amounts of money and minor offences like shoplifting and drink driving.

Local court cases like these are presided over by a magistrate, who determines how the dispute should be resolved or whether the person is guilty. Magistrates can hear cases involving more serious crimes, but they only hear these briefly

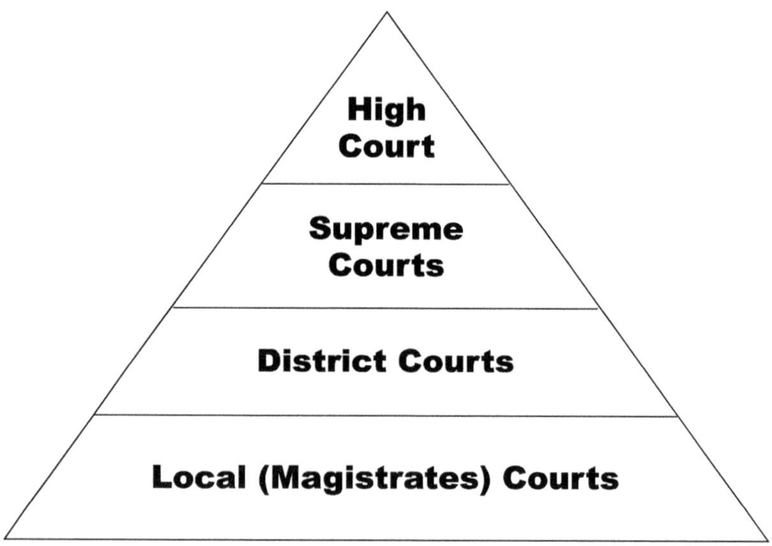

Figure 3.1 Court hierarchy

before 'committing' them to a higher court (you will learn more about committal hearings in Chapter 11).

Next are the **district courts**. These are like regional courts. They are fewer in number than local courts, but there are still many throughout a state (in Queensland, there are 32 district courts). District courts hear cases involving larger amounts of money and more serious crimes such as robbery, rape and fraud. District courts are presided over by a judge rather than a magistrate. In the district court, a jury (not the judge) determines whether a person is guilty of a crime.

District court: court on the second tier of the court hierarchy

The highest court in each state is a **supreme court**. In a supreme court, judges hear cases involving large amounts of money and very serious crimes such as murder and drug trafficking. Supreme courts also hear appeals on legal issues from the district court. An **appeal** happens where there is disagreement about how a case was decided, and the case is taken to a higher court to resolve the issue. You will learn more about appeals in Chapter 12.

Supreme court: the highest court in a state

Appeal: challenge a decision in a higher court

Finally, the High Court of Australia sits at the top of the hierarchy. As its name suggests, the **High Court** is the highest court in Australia. It does not hear disputes over contracts or determine whether someone is guilty of a crime in the same way as the other courts. Instead, it hears appeals on matters of public importance and other complex legal issues that usually involve interpreting the Constitution.

High Court: the highest court in Australia

Following the doctrine of precedent, local courts must follow decisions made by all higher courts. District courts must follow decisions by supreme courts and the High Court, and supreme courts must follow decisions by the High Court. In theory, the High Court is not bound to follow its own previous decisions, though it usually does unless there is a good reason to overrule itself.

Outside this core structure are two federal (national) courts. The Federal Court of Australia hears a wide range of matters arising under Commonwealth law, including native title, bankruptcy, corporations and consumer law issues. The Federal Circuit and Family Court of Australia hears federal, family law and migration law matters. The current court was created in 2021 when the federal circuit and family courts were merged. There are also specialist land and environment courts and many different tribunals. A **tribunal** is a quasi-court that is technically part of the executive branch of government (you will read more about the executive in Chapters 4 and 6). Tribunals hear legal disputes on the basis of fact rather than law. They usually have jurisdiction over specific topic areas (like immigration, tenancy disputes, or review of mental health detention).

Tribunal: quasi-court that is part of the executive branch of government

C. Jurisdiction

Jurisdiction, meaning the geographical area in which laws operate, is important to understanding precedent and the court hierarchy. Judgments from the High Court apply everywhere in Australia, but judgments from one state do not apply in any other state (even if they are from a supreme court).

However, courts in one state can still consider judgments from other states when making their decisions. This is known as **persuasive precedent** (as opposed to binding precedent). They are not required to apply that precedent, but they can draw on it to shape their reasoning.

Persuasive precedent: rules from previous cases that are not binding on courts, but may be considered

In relation to courts, **jurisdiction** has an additional meaning: the power or authority to hear different types of cases. Local courts and district courts have jurisdiction to hear cases with differing levels of seriousness. State supreme courts are organised into a criminal division, which hears cases involving serious crimes, and a civil division, which hears disputes around property, contracts and other financial matters. There is also an appeals division, which hears appeals from lower courts.

Jurisdiction: the area in which laws operate and a court's authority to hear different types of cases

Courts may be acting outside their jurisdiction if they aim to answer questions on areas of law that do not fall within their mandate. It is important that people bringing cases to court know which court has authority to hear their matter.

The High Court has two types of jurisdiction: original and appellate. **Original jurisdiction** is the power to hear cases for the first time, and **appellate jurisdiction**

Original jurisdiction: a court's power to hear a case for the first time

gives a court the power to hear appeals from lower courts.

Appellate jurisdiction: a court's power to hear appeals from lower courts

The High Court sources its original jurisdiction from the Australian Constitution and the ***Judiciary Act 1903*** (Cth). Under it, the court can consider constitutional matters, matters involving disputes between the states, and matters where the Commonwealth is a party. Its appellate jurisdiction is conferred by s 73 of the Constitution. Appealing to the High Court requires **special leave to appeal**, which is like special permission to have the case heard. In deciding whether to hear an appeal, the High Court will consider whether the matter is of public importance, whether it would resolve differences of opinion between state courts, or whether it is in the 'interests of the administration of justice'. These requirements are set out in s 35A of the ***Judiciary Act 1903*** (Cth).

Special leave to appeal: permission to have an appeal heard in the High Court

Once the High Court hears an appeal, there is no higher court to appeal to—even if a person disagrees with the outcome. It is the highest court in Australia, so its decisions are 'final and conclusive' (Constitution, s 73). Until 1975, the Privy Council in England could still hear some appeals from the High Court, and until 1986 it could hear appeals from state courts, but this is no longer possible.

2. WHERE CAN I FIND CASE LAW?

You can find case law in a similar way to legislation, as most of it is available online. AustLII allows you to search and browse case law across all Australian courts and jurisdictions. This will serve you well for most purposes. However, your university library will also have a subscription to a specialised legal database (usually **LexisNexis**). You can find LexisNexis by searching your university library website.

LexisNexis: database of case law accessible through university libraries

LexisNexis can be more difficult to navigate at first, but once you get the hang of it, you will be able to access the official law reports published by the courts (AustLII, by contrast, sets out the judgments in HTML). You can download these judgments as a PDF file and save them to your computer. Technically, these are the versions that you should be referencing in your assignments.

Increasingly, more judgments are available directly on court websites, but this can be patchy. Going directly to court websites can be a useful strategy if you are looking for a summary of a recent judgment issued by a particular court, as it might not yet be published elsewhere.

Using a general search engine to find case law is less reliable than using one to find legislation. It is usually too difficult to know from an internet search which judgment is the right one to read. There are similar case names and judgments from many different stages of proceedings.

For advice on using databases like LexisNexis, browse your university library website or contact your library staff to see what tutorials or other help may be available for students. University libraries offer a wide range of services for students, including help with searching databases, writing assignments, referencing sources, and more. Their staff are there to help students find sources in online databases and physical collections, but their services are frequently under-used. Library staff are a great source of help, particularly with legal sources, which can be hard to find!

3. HOW DO I READ CASE LAW?

Catchwords: collection of key words at the start of a judgment that summarise what the case is about

When you read a judgment, take note of its citation and the **catchwords** near the top of the judgment. You read the body of the judgment to find the material facts and *ratio*: the key facts of the case and the rule that should be applied in future cases.

A. Citation

First, take note of the case name, the year it was reported, and the law report citation. We refer to judgments like this:

The title of the case tells us the names of the two parties involved. In criminal cases, one of the parties is '*R*', meaning the Crown ('R' stands for Rex or Regina, which are Latin for 'king' and 'queen'). Next, in brackets, is the year the judgment was published.

The remainder of the citation tells us the judgment's location in law report volumes published by courts. The number before the letters is the volume and the one at the end is the first page number of the judgment. The letters in

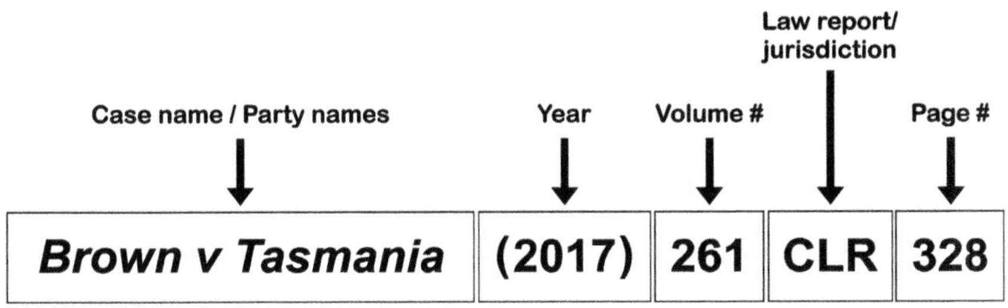

Figure 3.2 Citing case law

between the numbers indicate the **law reports** in which the judgment is published. Essentially, this tells you the jurisdiction (where the case was decided, and depending on the type of report, sometimes the area of law as well). There are too many law report abbreviations to list, as there are many different courts and tribunals across Australia. Some of the most common are:

Law reports: volumes of judgments

- Commonwealth Law Reports ('CLR').
- Federal Law Reports ('FLR').
- New South Wales Law Reports ('NSWLR').
- Queensland Law Reports ('QLR').
- Victorian Reports ('VR').

These letters do refer to physical volumes of judgments. Law reports are large books which look like old encyclopaedias. You can find them in university libraries, state libraries, court libraries, and smaller dedicated libraries in law firms and other places. Nowadays, though, most people find case law online; it would be rare for students to browse through the physical volumes. But you still can if you prefer, and regardless, the citation system is crucial to know which case is being referred to, which court decided it, and when it was decided.

Because of the move to online judgments, case law is increasingly referenced with medium-neutral citation: a simplified, less official citation that is commonly used for online sources. You can see this type of citation in Figure 3.3.

Medium-neutral citation: a simplified, less official citation that is often used for judgments found online

This citation tells us the title, year, court and page number but not the physical volume of law reports. The year is indicated with square brackets instead of rounded parentheses. This is still an acceptable way to reference case law in your

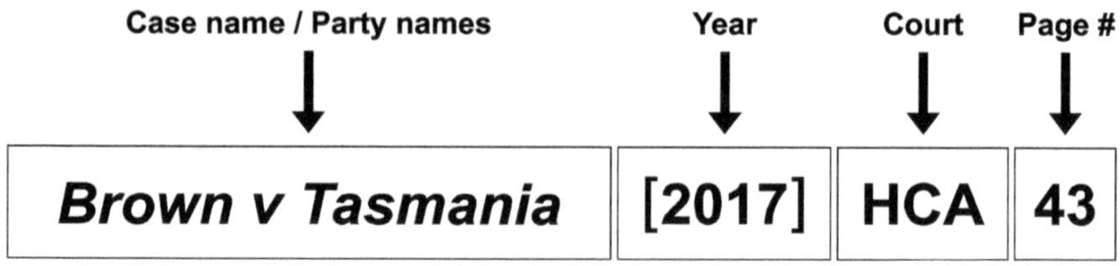

Figure 3.3 Medium-neutral citation

assignments. Sometimes it is the only citation available if an official report is yet to be published.

In an assignment, it is important to cite case law for the same reasons you would cite an academic book, book chapter or academic journal article. Instead of author names and academic journals, legal cases are cited by reference to their party names, law reports and volume numbers.

B. Catchwords

After looking at the citation, look at the top of the judgment for a series of catchwords. These are a short list of key words that give you an idea of what the case is about. This is particularly helpful if you are researching case law and need to know whether a case is relevant.

You can see the catchwords and other features of the Mabo judgment in Figure 3.4.

C. Material facts and *ratio*

There are two main things you read the body of a judgment for:

1. The important facts of the case (material facts).
2. The rule and reasoning that should be applied to future cases (*ratio*).

The facts and circumstances that gave rise to a case are important because they help us to determine if a future case, according to the doctrine of precedent, should lead to a similar result. Reading the facts of a case sounds easy but is often quite difficult. The facts can be long, complicated and spread throughout the

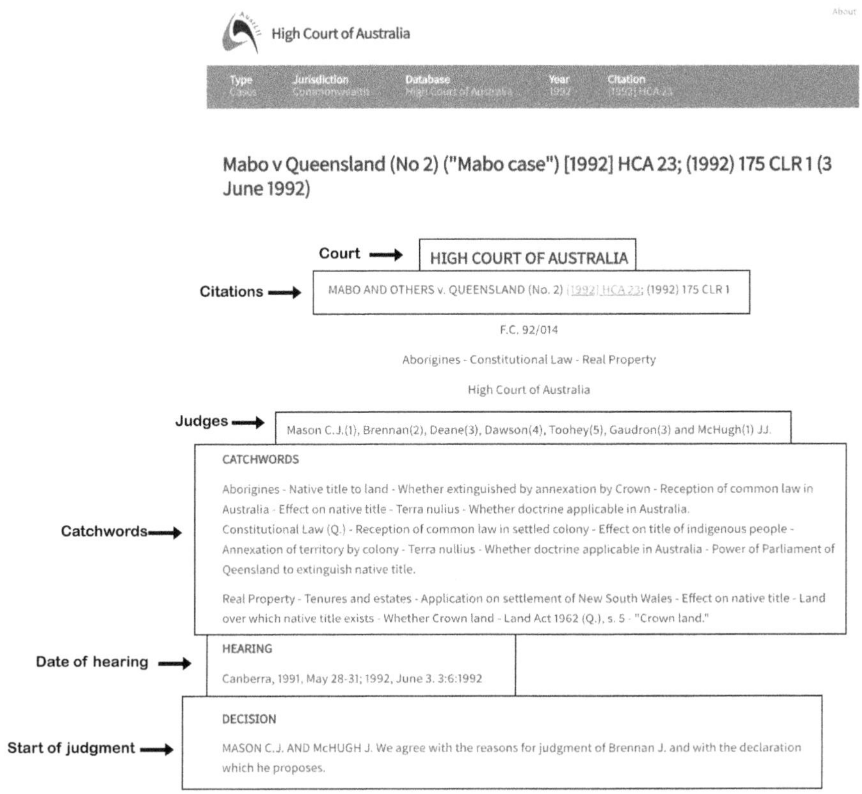

Figure 3.4 *Mabo* judgment from AustLII

judgment. On top of that, it can be difficult to work out which facts were important to the judge's reasoning and which were not. We refer to this as determining the **material facts**. In a robbery case, for example, the fact that the accused was 28 years old and owned a small business is not likely to be very important, but the circumstances surrounding the robbery (like whether they used a weapon) will be crucial.

Material facts: the most important facts from a judgment that are relevant to precedent

Your second major task—and the most difficult and important one—is to work out the rule and reasoning that should be applied in future cases. When reading case law, it is important to understand that judges are also setting out rules that are part of Australian law. However, the rules in case law are expressed in a long statement of reasons from a judge, rather than neat sections and subsections of legislation. In this respect, reading case law is harder than reading legislation.

You need to identify a legal rule from many pages of text, which are usually very difficult to read. It can be like finding a needle in a haystack.

The most common task while studying for a law degree is to understand the rules set out in case law, and condense them down to briefer statements that can be applied more easily to new cases. The most common exam type in a law school is a **problem question**, where students are given a hypothetical fact scenario. These are made-up stories that have uncertain outcomes or test the boundaries of the law in some way. To complete the exam, you apply rules from legislation and case law to determine the most likely outcomes. You work through the elements of the law, like you learnt about in the previous chapter, and apply rules from case law at each step.

Problem question: common exam type given in university law schools, where students determine likely outcomes in hypothetical cases

The rule from a judgment is known as the ***ratio decidendi*** (in Latin, this means 'the reason for the decision'). We usually shorten this to *ratio*. The *ratio* is the core rule and reasoning from a written judgment. Where multiple judges decided a case, the *ratio* is found in the principles that a majority of the judges decided.

Ratio decidendi: the key rule or reasoning from a judgment that must be applied as precedent (means 'the reason for the decision')

The *ratio* is technically the thing that lower courts from the same jurisdiction must apply in future cases, according to the doctrine of precedent. In a criminal law judgment, for example, the *ratio* might specify what it means for a person to 'consent' to sexual intercourse for the purposes of a sexual assault charge. If the case was decided in a state supreme court, that meaning of consent would need to be followed by all district and local courts in the state. If the matter was appealed from the supreme court, the High Court would not be required to follow that decision. If the High Court determined that consent meant something different to what the state supreme court decided, every court across the country would need to follow that meaning from then on.

A judgment will include many other statements from judges that were not essential to the decision. These are known as ***obiter dicta***, which is Latin for 'things said in passing' (or *obiter dictum*, for a single statement). We usually shorten this to *obiter*. *Obiter* are incidental remarks that are not binding as precedent but may be useful in future cases.

Obiter dicta: things a judge says which are not part of the *ratio decidendi* but may be relevant to a future case (means 'by the way')

A typical exercise in the early years of law school is to write up a **case note** that summarises the material facts and *ratio* of the case. These assignments often ask students to critically analyse the judge's decision (for example, by analysing whether the judge's logical reasoning is sound and whether the judgment is consistent with previous cases).

Case note: academic summary of a judgment, which often includes critical analysis

Academic journals publish case notes to update their readers on how case law is developing in different topic areas. You can find case notes in academic journals through your university library website. There are also online resources to help with writing case note assignments. Two good examples can be found on the Monash University library website and survivelaw.com, a blog and online community for Australian law students.

KEY POINTS

- Case law is the collection of judgments published by courts. When reading case law, your main tasks are to determine the material facts and *ratio decidendi* (the reason for the decision).
- Precedent means that courts must apply the decisions of higher courts in similar cases.
- Jurisdiction means not only the geographical area in which laws operate but also the power of courts to hear different types of cases.

DISCUSSION QUESTIONS

1. Can you find a copy of *NZYQ v Minister for Immigration, Citizenship, and Multicultural Affairs* [2023] HCA 37? After reading the key words, what do you think this case is about?
2. What are the levels in the court hierarchy? Can you redraw the diagram without looking?
3. What is the difference between binding and persuasive precedent?
4. What are two main things you should look for when reading a judgment?
5. What is jurisdiction and why is it important to case law?

Chapter 4
Politics

In this chapter, you will learn about:

- Politics and law reform
- The houses of parliament and how politicians are elected to them
- Political parties, independent candidates and ministers

It is one thing to say that legislation is enacted by parliaments, and another to realise that the people debating and approving those laws are politicians. Every single piece of legislation in Australia—whether it contains criminal offences, immigration powers, or public health responses—was enacted by politicians in a parliament. In this chapter, you will learn about politics and law reform, the houses of parliament, and how politicians are elected to them. You will learn about political parties, independent candidates, and ministers who introduce laws for debate and approval.

1. WHAT IS POLITICS ALL ABOUT?

You might see politicians on TV, wearing hard hats, waving at crowds, trying to sing or dance, bowling a cricket ball into their feet, screaming at each other in parliament, or nodding a lot and saying 'hear hear!'. You wonder what on earth they are all doing and how anyone could be interested in it. Or you might think politicians lie all the time, can't be trusted, and are in it only for the perks and power. You might be frustrated that governments never seem to solve the big issues, so you stop paying attention and do something fun instead because there is nothing you can do to change it.

DOI: 10.4324/9781003433408-5

If any of those thoughts sound familiar, you should know that people who are interested in politics often think exactly the same things. We feel frustrated because we elect politicians to act in the best interests of the Australian people. If we believe they are not living up to that role, or are taking advantage of it in some way, we are justified in wanting to hold them accountable. Ultimately, their job is to represent the Australian people, in parliament and on the global stage.

It is important not to let frustration at politics get in the way of issues that you care about. If you say you are not interested in politics, I guarantee there is an issue you care about that involves it. Do you care about local sport, or art and music having enough funding? There's politics in that. Does it take you hours to get to uni or work in the morning, because the freeway is a carpark, and there's not enough public transport? There's plenty of politics in that. Are you paying too much for groceries? Can you no longer find a doctor who bulk bills? Does your boss have too much power in the workplace? There's politics in all of those issues too.

Politics is about who we elect to address the issues we care about most, and what they are going to do about it. Browsing the daily news will show you how frequently politicians are involved in debates around different problems in society and how to fix them. Politics is about what some people in power want to do about an issue, why the other side disagrees, and what they would do instead.

And yes, politicians do want to get into a position of power, and stay there. For that, they need you to vote for them at the next election. This involves plans, pitches and promises, so you choose them at the ballot box and not the other side. It is easy to be cynical about this, but they are trying to achieve what they believe is the best path forward for Australian society. You might not feel like there is an ideal choice available to you at election time, but you can make the best choice available, based on the issues you care about most, for yourself, those close to you, and others in society.

Not everything that governments do once they are elected requires legislation. A lot of it is based in executive power (which you can read more about in Chapter 6). However, enacting new laws and changing existing ones is one concrete way they put their plans, pitches and promises into practice. As we learned in Chapter 2, the major workload of Australian parliaments is to debate and approve legislation on different topics. Law reform involves proposing, debating, approving and enacting legislation that will address some issue in society.

To understand law reform, it helps to understand more about the houses of parliament, how politicians are elected to them, the political parties they represent, and the role of Ministers. In fact, learning more about our parliaments and our elected representatives helps to understand the key role that ***all*** of us play in Australian law and government.

The sections below help you to understand the fundamentals of these topics. The content focuses on the federal parliament, but much of it also applies in the states and territories. The major differences are that the states have premiers instead of a Prime Minister and their two houses of parliament are usually called the Legislative Assembly and Legislative Council. Queensland, the ACT and the Northern Territory also have unicameral parliaments with only one chamber.

2. HOUSES OF PARLIAMENT

House of Representatives: lower house of the federal parliament

Senate: upper house of the federal parliament

Political party: an organisation with a set of beliefs, values and goals that puts forward members for election to parliament

There are two houses of the federal parliament: the **House of Representatives** (lower house) and the **Senate** (upper house). Each has seats that are occupied by members of political parties. A **political party** is an organisation with a set of beliefs, values and goals, which puts forward its members to be elected to parliament.

Any Australian citizen over the age of 18 can be elected to a house of parliament. A few exceptions are listed in section 44(i) of the Constitution, including dual citizens and anyone convicted of a crime punishable by a prison sentence of 12 months or more. The restriction on dual citizens entering parliament means that many diverse Australians reflecting a multicultural Australia cannot be elected. The rule also caused a crisis after the 2016 federal election. In ***Re Canavan*** [2017] HCA 45, the High Court found that five high-profile politicians, including the Deputy Prime Minister, were ineligible to sit in parliament. Several more resigned or faced scrutiny over citizenships they held in other countries.

A. House of Representatives

The House of Representatives has 151 seats. Elections for these seats happen every three years, when the whole chamber is replaced (though many candidates win their seats again). The party that wins the majority of seats (76) in the House of Representatives becomes the **government**. The leader of that party becomes the **Prime Minister**: the leader of the government and our nation. The political party with the second highest number of seats is known as the **opposition**. Each seat is literally a place to sit on the long benches in parliament, but it is also a metaphor for the people they represent, and the geographical area where those people live.

Government: political party with a majority of seats in the House of Representatives

Prime Minister: the leader of the government

Opposition: the political party with the second highest number of seats in the House of Representatives

It is important to recognise that these and many other core aspects of politics and government are not written into the Constitution. It might come as a surprise, but the Constitution does not even mention the Prime Minister. Rather, these sorts of practices are simply determined by convention. **Conventions** are the unwritten, traditional ways that things are done in a system of law and government—and we base most of ours on England's Westminster Parliament. Strictly speaking, there is no legal requirement that the Prime Minister steps down and hands power over to the other side when they lose an election. Thankfully, though, this is what happens each time, and the system runs as intended. When constitutional conventions are not followed or undermined, this creates unique challenges, as it is not clear whether conventions are legally forceable to the same extent as something written into the law.

Conventions: unwritten, traditional ways that things are done in a system of law and government

Members of the House of Representatives (Members of Parliament or **MPs**) are elected to their seats based on a **preferential voting** system. This is where candidates need a 50% majority vote from a defined geographical area known as an **electorate**. The physical size of electorates differs significantly across Australia: the smallest is 32 square kilometres and the largest is 1.3 million square kilometres! In urban areas, they usually cover several suburbs, and each has around 115,000 people voting.

MP: abbreviation for Member of Parliament

Preferential voting: voting system used in the House of Representatives which is based on candidates winning a 50% majority of the vote from an electorate

Electorate: a defined geographical area that elects one member to the House of Representatives

Electoral roll: register of all voters in Australia

Australian Electoral Commission: independent body responsible for running elections

According to section 93 of the *Commonwealth Electoral Act 1918* (Cth), all Australians above the age of 18 are entitled to be on the **electoral roll**: a register of all voters in Australia. The federal electoral roll is maintained by the **Australian Electoral Commission** (AEC). The AEC is responsible for running elections to ensure they are run fairly and in accordance with the law.

There are some exceptions to who can vote, including those of 'unsound mind' and those serving sentences of three years or more in prison. In 2006, John Howard's Liberal government enacted legislation to limit prisoner voting further (so that prisoners serving a sentence of one year or more were ineligible). That legislation was struck down by the High Court as unconstitutional. We do not have an explicit, absolute right to vote in Australia, but the High Court read an implied right into sections 7 and 24 of the Constitution. Those sections say that members of both houses of parliament must be 'directly chosen by the people'. The Howard government's legislation was said to disproportionately infringe that requirement, and so the three-year limit remains.

Compulsory voting: system that penalises people for not voting at elections

For everyone on the electoral roll, voting at elections is compulsory. Anyone who fails to vote at a federal election must pay a $20 penalty. That is not much, but the small penalty and the tradition of **compulsory voting** are enough to ensure that most Australians (more than 90 per cent) turn up to the polling booth. This is different from other systems of government where voting is optional and lower numbers of people turn up to cast their vote.

There is an argument that compulsory voting is anti-democratic because it forces people to make a choice. However, the High Court has ruled that compulsory voting only makes you turn up to the polling booth and have your name ticked off the register; it does not force you to choose a political party (*Faderson v Bridger* (1971) 126 CLR 271). Anyone who does not want to support a party can mark an invalid vote, so the vote will not be counted.

At election time, preferential voting requires voters to number the candidates for their electorate in order of preference. Voters put '1' in the box for their favoured candidate and continue numbering the candidates down to their last choice. You must fill in each and every box, or the vote is invalid. The final number reached depends on how many candidates are contesting the seat. An example of a House of Representatives ballot paper can be seen in Figure 4.1.

Often, candidates win a 50% majority based on the **primary vote** (everyone's #1 choices). If this does not happen, the remaining preferences are dealt out (beginning with the #2 preferences) until a candidate wins the seat.

Primary vote: the 'number 1' vote cast on a ballot paper

This voting system means that the two major political parties (the Labor and Liberal parties) dominate the lower house. This is because most voters number the Labor or Liberal parties as one of their higher preferences. A government that favours two political parties is known as a **majoritarian system** of government. Some of the core ideas and beliefs guiding these two parties are explained below.

Majoritarian system: a system of government dominated by two political parties

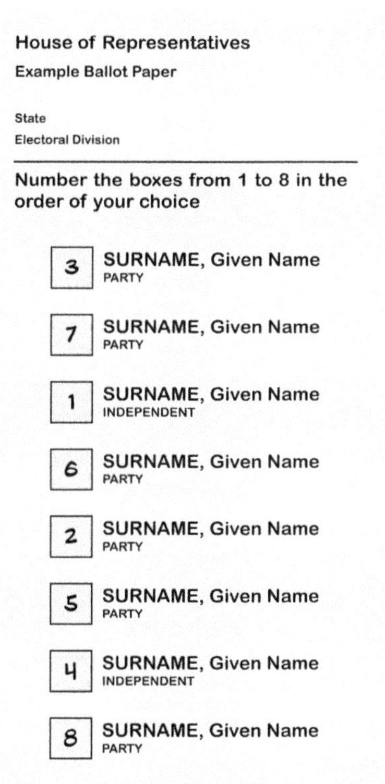
House of Representatives
Example Ballot Paper

State
Electoral Division

Number the boxes from 1 to 8 in the order of your choice

3 SURNAME, Given Name
PARTY

7 SURNAME, Given Name
PARTY

1 SURNAME, Given Name
INDEPENDENT

6 SURNAME, Given Name
PARTY

2 SURNAME, Given Name
PARTY

5 SURNAME, Given Name
PARTY

4 SURNAME, Given Name
INDEPENDENT

8 SURNAME, Given Name
PARTY

Figure 4.1 Example House of Representatives ballot paper

B. Senate

Senators: politicians elected to the Senate

The Senate has 76 members. Politicians elected to the Senate are known as **senators,** and there are twelve from each state and two from each territory.

Compared to voting for the House of Representatives, Senate voting is more complicated. You can see a summary of the major differences between the House of Representatives and Senate in Figure 4.2.

i. Staggered elections

At a federal election, only half the Senate is replaced. At the next federal election, the other half is replaced. This means that senators are elected for six-year terms. So, whereas the government and Prime Minister can change every three years, the Senate is a little more stable.

The exception to this is a double dissolution election. This process can be triggered when the Senate refuses more than once to pass a Bill that was

	House of Representatives	Senate
house	lower	upper
colour	green	red
number of seats	151	76
voting method	preferential	proportional
voting based on	majority	quota
members represent	electorates	states
composition	dominated by Labor and Liberal parties (majoritarian system)	balance of power often held by minor parties and independents

Figure 4.2 Comparing the House of Representatives and Senate

approved in the lower house. A **double dissolution** is a special procedure that helps to break a deadlock when legislation cannot pass through the federal parliament. This is needed because a government that cannot secure the passage of legislation through parliament cannot govern the Australian people effectively.

Double dissolution: special election in which both houses of parliament are dissolved

The procedure for a double dissolution is set out in section 57 of the Constitution. A double dissolution can be called if the Senate refuses to pass the same Bill twice and three months have passed in between. If this happens, the Prime Minister can ask the Governor-General to **dissolve** both houses of parliament. This means all members and senators are dismissed and every seat is contested again. This is the only time the whole Senate is replaced at a federal election.

Dissolve: to dismiss an entire house of parliament and re-elect its membership

Double dissolutions are rare: there have only been seven in Australia's history. The most recent was in 2016, when the Senate rejected two Bills relating to employment conditions and accountability in the construction industry. This was the first time the procedure had been used in nearly 30 years, since 1987. Very rarely, if there is still a deadlock after a double dissolution, the Governor-General can call for a joint sitting of both houses of parliament. This has happened only once, in 1974.

ii. Proportional voting

The Senate relies on a different voting system known as **proportional voting**. Candidates are elected if they reach a required quota (percentage or proportion) of the vote, rather than a 50% majority. The precise **quota** depends on the number of voters and senators to be elected, but it is normally around 14%.

Proportional voting: voting system used in the Senate that requires candidates to reach a quota

Quota: a defined percentage of a vote

Candidates are elected to the Senate on a smaller proportion of the vote because several candidates are elected for each state and territory. At each federal election, the people of Queensland vote in six people for their state, the people of New South Wales vote in six people for their state, and so on (remember, only half the Senate is elected each time). These seats are divided between the different political parties according to the proportion of votes they receive.

Voting for the Senate also requires voters to number candidates in order of preference. Candidates who reach the required quota based on the primary vote (everyone's #1 choices) are automatically elected. The remaining preferences are then dealt out until the right number of seats are filled. You can read more about how to vote on a Senate ballot form below.

This is similar to preferential voting, but the process for distributing Senate preferences becomes more complicated. Because candidates only need 14% to win a seat, any more votes they win on top of that are additional and not needed for that candidate. Those **surplus votes** should not be wasted, so they are transferred to other candidates. However, there is no good way to determine which votes made up the 14% and which did not. To solve this problem, all the votes are transferred to other candidates, but at a reduced value. This **transfer value** is worked out as a ratio of the surplus to total votes.

Surplus votes: votes for a candidate in excess of the quota required to win a senate seat

Transfer value: reduced value of surplus votes when redistributed to other candidates

You do not need to understand the technicalities of how preferences are allocated in Senate elections. The important thing to remember is that this system makes it much easier for minor parties (political parties other than Labor and Liberal) and independents (those not belonging to any political party) to win senate seats. This is because candidates with less of a following than the major parties need only reach a much smaller quota, not a 50% majority, and they benefit from surplus votes being transferred to them. It means that the Senate represents more diverse voting interests, and it acts as a check on the lower house of parliament, because it tends not to vote along the same party lines.

iii. Senate ballots

Voting in multiple candidates for each state and territory means that the Senate ballot paper is much larger and more complicated. To account for this, it has a dividing horizontal line: above the line is a list of political parties, and below the line is a much longer list of candidates. You can see a sample Senate ballot paper in Figures 4.3 and 4.4. To fill out the form, you vote either '**above the line**' or

Above the line: approach to Senate voting where voters indicate their preference of political parties

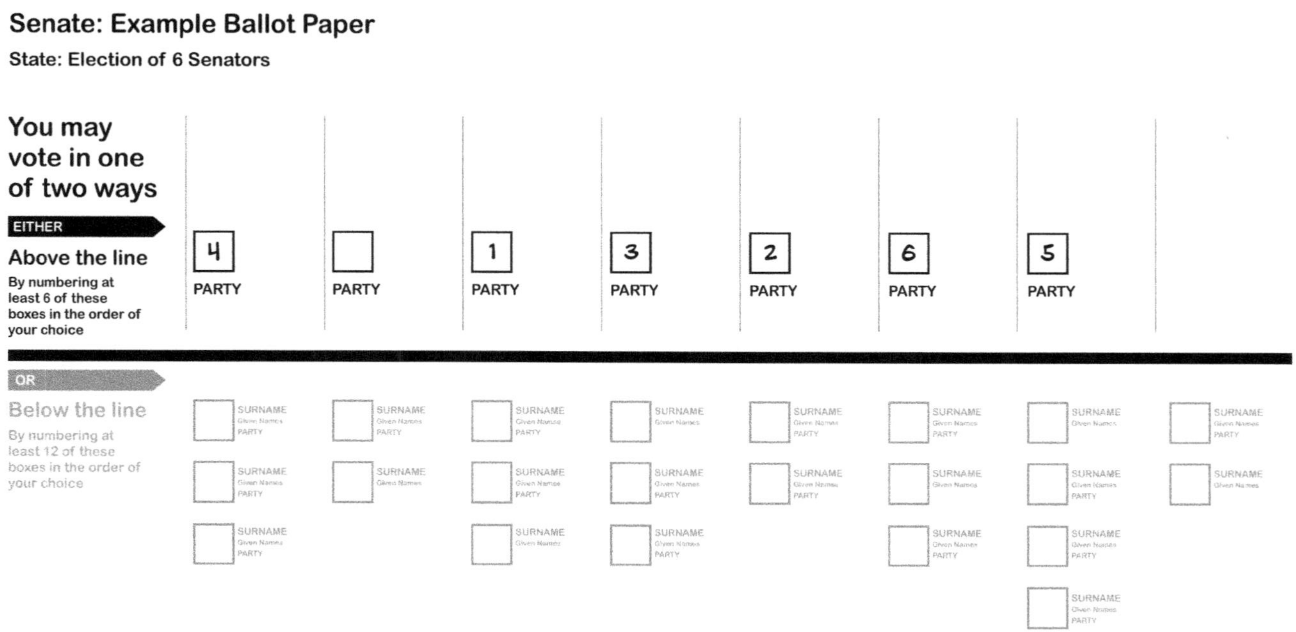

Figure 4.3 Example Sample Senate Ballot Paper: Voting Above the Line

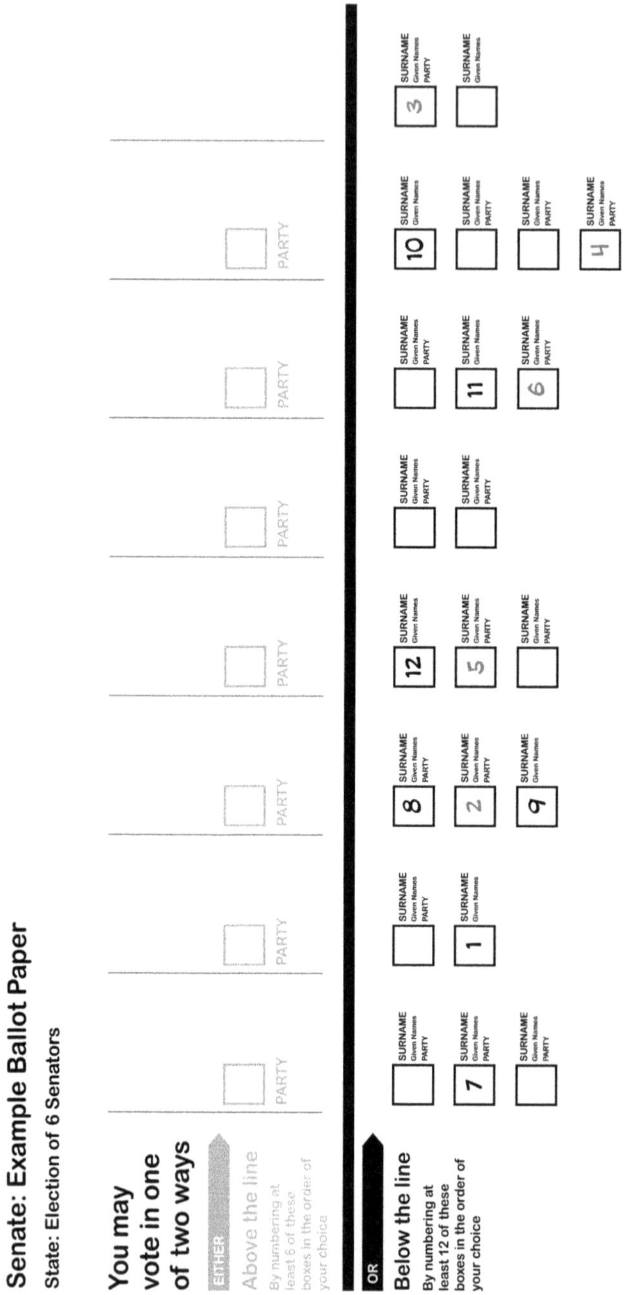

Figure 4.4 Example Sample Senate Ballot Paper: Voting Below the Line

'**below the line**' (not both). If you vote above the line, you must number at least six political parties in order of preference. If you vote below the line, you must number at least 12 candidates.

Below the line: approach to Senate voting where voters indicate their preference of candidates

This is fairer and simpler than how Senate voting worked before the 2016 federal election. Before then, you could vote above the line simply by placing a #1 next to your favoured political party. If you voted below the line, you were required to fill out preferences for every single candidate, or your vote was invalid. Given that Senate voting forms can be more than a metre long and have more than 100 candidates, this was an onerous task.

Voting above the line was much easier, but it had a hidden problem. By placing a #1 next to a single political party, voters were effectively filling out the rest of the form. However, this was done behind the scenes according to preference deals negotiated between the parties. A **preference deal** is where a party that receives a #1 vote agrees to allocate the rest of that voter's preferences to other parties. In other words, the parties get to determine how a voter's preferences are allocated. Determined voters could find out how each party had agreed to allocate their preferences, but this required trawling through complicated forms on the AEC website. Most voters were unaware of how their preferences were being allocated (or the fact that they were being allocated at all).

Preference deal: negotiated agreements between political parties to allocate their preferences other than the primary vote

These hidden preference deals meant that some candidates were elected to parliament with only a tiny proportion (as low as 0.5%) of the primary vote. In the 2013 federal election, several new senators were criticised for lacking relevant experience and failing to understand important issues facing the nation. The rules were changed in the lead-up to the 2016 election to stop that from happening again. The current system is not perfect; it still relies on preference deals, and senators can still be elected with a small percentage of the primary vote. But it is more transparent and reduces the risk of candidates being elected with very few primary votes.

iv. Accountability

Staggered elections and proportional voting make senate elections quite complicated. However, it all serves a very important function.

Because the Senate relies on a different election cycle and voting system, it is very uncommon for the same political party to have a majority of seats in both houses of parliament. This means the Senate acts as an important check on government power. Remember the lawmaking procedure from Chapter 1? A Bill needs to be approved by both houses of parliament according to a majority of votes in each. If a different political party has a majority of seats in the Senate, proposals for new legislation will not automatically be approved by the upper house. This is an important feature of our political system which helps to keep the government accountable.

On the rare occasion that a government does have a majority in both houses of parliament, it can approve any Bill it introduces without needing support from other parties. This happened with the Howard government between 2004 and 2007. During that time, several controversial laws were enacted, including the WorkChoices legislation, which made it easier for employers to dismiss their workers, and many new counter-terrorism laws (which you will read about in Chapter 14).

More commonly, approving legislation in the Senate depends on difficult negotiations between the government, opposition, minor parties, and independents. Typically, neither major party has a majority of seats in the Senate, so minor parties and independents hold the deciding votes, known as the **balance of power**. The group of minor parties and independents is also called the **cross-bench**, because they sit in between the two major parties and can vote to support either side, depending on the issue being debated. If one of the major parties wants to get something through the Senate, they often need to negotiate with the cross-bench. These negotiations are a common feature of media coverage and public discussion about politics.

Balance of power: the deciding votes in a house of parliament

Cross-bench: minor parties and independents who often hold the balance of power

When minor parties and independents hold the balance of power, more diverse voices influence the laws that are enacted. However, it can make law reform more about politics than the law itself, and it gives minor parties and independents a level of power that is disproportionate to the vote they receive from the population. If the votes are very close, it can be up to one independent senator, or a small number from a minor party, to decide whether a Bill becomes part of the law of Australia. They might agree to support the Bill for some unrelated reason. For example, the government might promise to provide funding or roll out a program that will benefit their electorate. That does not seem very fair, but it is a common feature of politics and law reform.

3. POLITICAL PARTIES

Nearly all members of parliament are members of a political party. Some members of parliament are independents, which means they sit as individuals and not as representatives of a political party.

In Australia, the two main political parties are the **Liberal Party** and the **Labor Party**. To understand these and other political parties, it helps to understand what it means to be 'left-wing' or 'right-wing'. **Left-wing** means that a person is more progressive and **right-wing** means that a person is more conservative. Being **progressive** or **conservative** refers to how much social or economic change a person is willing to accept. People with left-wing views are comfortable with more radical change to society's rules and structures, especially to achieve social justice. People with right-wing views are more conservative. They focus on managing the economy, protecting Australia's national identity, securing the country against external threats, and maintaining longstanding institutions, including religion, marriage and traditional family structures.

Liberal Party: a centre-right political party and one of two major political parties in Australia

Labor Party: a centre-left political party and one of two major political parties in Australia

Left-wing: to have political views which are more progressive

Right-wing: to have political views that are more conservative

Progressive: in favour of social or economic change

Conservative: reluctant to accept significant social or economic change

Left and right are crude distinctions, as people hold differing views on a range of issues, but you may know some friends, family members or politicians who fall into either of the descriptions above. The rights that should be afforded to refugees and asylum seekers is an area that tends to spark vigorous debate. Should we protect the rights of all refugees and welcome them into our country (left-wing), or should we protect our national security and identity by stopping those who arrive 'unlawfully' (right-wing)? This is an overly simplistic picture of a very complex issue, but it is an example of how governments can favour very different responses to same issue, depending on whether they adopt a more progressive or conservative approach.

Centrist: a person who falls between left- and right-wing political views

Being in the 'centre' (also known as being a **centrist**) means that a person favours a moderate middle ground. They might have left-wing views on some issues, right-wing views on others, or they will aim to compromise between the two.

The major political parties in Australia are explained below. Because these parties have different beliefs and values, parliaments and the laws they enact can look very different depending on who is voted in at election time.

A. Labor party

The Labor Party is one of two major political parties in Australia. It is typically considered centre-left, meaning its views are moderately left-wing. Some of its members are further to the left, and others are closer to the middle. There is also a 'right faction' which is more conservative.

Faction: semi-organised grouping in a political party that strategises and votes together

A **faction** is a semi-organised grouping within a political party whose members tend to strategise and vote together because they have a common view for how that party should advance its agenda. The presence of factions within the two major parties means it is too difficult to categorise them as simply 'left-wing' or 'right-wing'. Increasingly, the views of the major parties coincide on major issues like immigration and counter-terrorism, which makes the distinction even less helpful. However, those concepts can help us understand when the views of the two major parties do contrast, and the factions within them.

The Australian Labor Party is the oldest political party in Australia. It was founded during the first federal parliament in 1901, when several labour parties from the colonies joined to form a federal Labor Party. Those labour parties, which formed in the 1890s, campaigned for the rights of workers in early Australia (but they adopted the American spelling). That tradition continues today, as Labor maintains close ties to the trade union movement. In addition to supporting workers' rights, Labor often campaigns in elections by supporting increased funding for health and education.

Labor's longest-serving Prime Minister was Bob Hawke, who held the office from 1983 to 1991. One of its most famous leaders was Gough Whitlam, who served as Prime Minister from 1972 to 1975 and was famously dismissed by the Governor-General, Sir John Kerr.

In 2010, Labor Prime Minister Kevin Rudd was ousted from the prime ministership after a successful challenge to the party leadership by Julia Gillard. In 2013, Rudd contested Gillard's leadership and reclaimed the office, before losing the federal election to Tony Abbott's Liberal Party.

The 'Rudd–Gillard–Rudd' years served as a reminder that the Australian public votes in a political party at election time, not an individual candidate (as in a presidential election). The Prime Minister is simply the leader of the party that wins a majority in the lower house. The leader of that party can change, even while they are serving as Prime Minister.

Traditionally, a challenge to a party's leadership (called a **leadership spill**) was decided by a majority vote of elected party members. In recent years, both the Labor and Liberal parties have put in place additional hurdles to reduce the chance of leadership changes like this happening again.

Leadership spill: when a vote is held to contest the leadership of a political party

In the 2022 federal election, Labor's Anthony Albanese became the 31st Prime Minister of Australia. In that election, Labor won 77 seats in the lower house with around 32% of the primary vote (#1 choices on the ballot paper). This was only a very slim majority (76 seats are needed to form government) and an historically low primary vote. There was a swing away from both major parties towards the Greens and independents. In politics, a **swing** is where voter preferences shift from one election to the next—they can swing towards a party and away from another.

Swing: a shift in voter preferences, either towards or away from a party

B. Liberal Party

The Liberal Party is the other major political party in Australia. It was founded in 1944, though its roots go back to anti-Labor groups in the early Australian parliaments. The two longest-serving Liberal Prime Ministers were Sir Robert Menzies (1939–1941, 1949–1966) and John Howard (1996–2007).

The Liberal Party is typically considered centre-right (moderately right-wing). Some of its members are further to the right and some are closer to the centre. The party's philosophy is usually described as blending social conservatism and economic liberalism. This means that it favours traditional values and institutions and a free economic market.

Some Liberal politicians see themselves as being closely aligned with the classical liberal tradition, which supports freedom of speech and other individual rights (you will read more about liberalism in Chapter 4). Politicians who identify closely with liberalism are sometimes called 'small-l' liberals, to contrast the philosophy of liberalism with the Liberal Party. That makes dividing people into left-wing and right-wing even more confusing, because small-l liberals in the Liberal party can be more progressive. The classical liberal tradition has also created tensions within the Liberal Party as to whether it should market itself as more moderate or conservative.

Small government: idea that governments should interfere minimally in business and the lives of their citizens

The Liberal Party has a tradition of supporting business owners and, like other political parties in Australia, it has many major business donors. It favours **small government**, which is the idea that governments should interfere minimally in the lives of their citizens. Ideally, this means lower taxes, less bureaucratic 'red tape' and greater economic competition.

The Liberal Party supports strong approaches to national and border security. Most of Australia's controversial counter-terrorism laws were introduced by the Howard government between 2002 and 2007. The party's recent immigration policy was dominated by Operation Sovereign Borders, a security operation to stop people smuggling that was based on the slogan 'Stop the Boats'.

In 2018, Scott Morrison became Prime Minister after challenging Malcolm Turnbull in a leadership spill. This was yet another example of Australia's Prime Minister changing between elections. The Liberal Party won the 2019 federal election and Scott Morrison oversaw Australia's response to the COVID-19 pandemic.

After the 2022 federal election, when the Liberal Party lost its majority in the lower house, Morrison stood down as leader and Peter Dutton took on the role in opposition. In February 2024, Scott Morrison delivered his valedictory speech in parliament. A **valedictory speech** is a final, farewell speech given by a serving MP who has decided to resign or not contest their seat at the next election.

Valedictory speech: a final, farewell speech given by a serving member of parliament who has decided to resign or not contest their seat at the next election

C. National Party

When we refer to a 'Liberal government', we are usually referring to a **coalition** of the Liberal Party and National Party. A coalition is an alliance where two or more political parties decide to vote together in parliament. This means their seats can effectively be counted together at election time, boosting the numbers of both parties.

Coalition: agreement between political parties to vote together in parliament

The **National Party** began as the Australian Country Party in 1920 and it continues to campaign for the rights of rural and regional communities. It advocates for stronger regional economies, including support for Australian farmers and more jobs and growth outside metropolitan areas.

National Party: centre-right country party that forms a Coalition with the Liberal Party

The alliance between the Liberal and National parties is strong enough that we often say 'the Coalition', meaning both parties combined. When the Coalition has a majority of seats in the lower house, the leader of the Liberal Party is the Prime Minister and the leader of the National Party is the Deputy Prime Minister.

The Liberal and National parties vote together because they are both centre-right on the political spectrum, but they have different voter bases and different priorities when campaigning for elections. This can lead to tensions and disagreements, especially on matters that affect mining, farming, and other concerns for voters in seats held by National Party candidates.

D. The Greens

The Australian Greens (usually called the **Greens**) are considered a 'minor' party compared to the Labor Party and Liberal–National Coalition, as they have fewer members and win a much smaller number of seats. However, the Greens are an important player in Australian politics. In the 2016 federal election, they won one seat in the lower house and nine seats in the Senate. In the 2022 federal election, they won 11 Senate seats and 4 in the lower house, including 3 in Brisbane electorates. Those 3 seats were unexpected victories in a traditionally conservative state.

Greens: influential minor party that advocates for protecting the environment

Green politics: political views that typically support environmental conservation, renewable energy, animal rights, non-violence and social justice

The Greens party was founded in 1992 when many different 'green' groups joined together at the federal level. **Green politics** refers to groups that typically support environmental conservation, renewable energy, animal rights, non-violence and social justice. The first federal leader of the Australian Greens was Dr Bob Brown. Brown led one of Australia's most significant environmental campaigns against the building of a dam that would have flooded Tasmania's Franklin River. In February 2024, he was arrested during a protest against logging in Tasmania's Styx forest. He is still fighting to protect Australia's natural heritage.

E. Minor parties

Minor parties: smaller political parties other than the Labor, Liberal and National parties

In addition to the Labor and Liberal parties, the Nationals and the Greens, a long list of **minor parties** contest seats at federal elections. This contributes to a diversity of voices and voting interests in parliament. However, minor parties can have quite specific and sometimes controversial agendas. This can make negotiations to enact laws more complex if minor parties and independents hold the balance of power in the Senate.

Pauline Hanson's One Nation is a right-wing party strongly opposed to immigration. The party was founded in Ipswich, Queensland, in 1997. After a long break from politics, Hanson returned to win four Senate seats in the 2016 election. She revived her previous statement that Australia was being 'swamped by Asians' to say the country was now being 'swamped by Muslims' and that all immigration should be banned. In 2017, she caused significant controversy by wearing a burqa into the Senate chamber. In the 47th parliament (with Anthony Albanese as Prime Minister) Hanson and one other member of her party had seats in the federal senate.

The United Australia Party (UAP) has a short but colourful history. In the 2013 federal election, billionaire mining magnate Clive Palmer won a seat in the lower house and three Senate seats for the Palmer United Party (PUP). Two of the senators quickly resigned to become independents and the party disbanded. In the 2019 election, then rebranded as the UAP, the party ran candidates in the senate and every lower house seat around the country. Palmer spent more on advertising than both major parties combined, including bright yellow billboards, repeating TV ads, and a controversial SMS campaign—but the party did not win any seats. In 2021, Craig Kelly, a controversial former Liberal MP turned independent, took on the party's leadership. The party chose to deregister itself in 2022.

F. Independents

Independent candidates (usually just called **independents**) are elected representatives who do not belong to a political party. Some establish a political party in their name so they can sit in the senate, but they are still considered to be independent because they are not aligned or committed to vote with anyone else.

Independent: elected representative who is not a member of a political party

Some independents, like Andrew Wilkie, have had a long career in parliament without belonging to any party. Wilkie is a former intelligence officer and **whistleblower** who opposed the Iraq war. He has fought for increased hospital funding, same-sex marriage, and reforms to poker machines to address problem gambling. Other independents start out in a party before going out on their own. Some create a minor party but are still thought of as independent. Jacqui Lambie is a former army corporal who was first elected as one of the Palmer United Party senators. She soon resigned from the party to become independent. Now as leader of the Jacqui Lambie Network, she continues to advocate for veterans' rights, anti-corruption, and Australian manufacturing.

Whistleblower: someone working for an organisation or government department who exposes misconduct, corruption or criminal behaviour

The power that independents can hold was clear following the 2010 election. That election resulted in a **hung parliament**: neither of the major parties won a majority in the lower house (so the result was left 'hanging'). Julia Gillard secured agreement from 3 independents (including Wilkie) and one Greens MP to reach a majority, form government, and become Prime Minister. This is called a **minority government**, as Labor did not technically have a majority but they secured the additional seats needed. The Greens MP and independents did not agree to support Labor on

Hung parliament: when neither major party wins a majority in the lower house

Minority government: a government that achieves a majority in the lower house by securing support from the cross-bench

Supply: the passage of money Bills so the government can pay for its policies

every single vote, so a minority government is less stable than a true majority government. However, they guaranteed a minimum degree of support to achieve **supply** and maintain a functioning government. Those three independents (and others who sided with the Liberal Party) had enormous power: they could essentially choose the outcome of the federal election, for one side of politics or the other.

Since then, independents have become increasingly important to the make-up of the federal parliament at all times—not just in a hung parliament. In the 2022 federal election, six seats were won by so-called **teal independents**: candidates fighting for greater action on climate change, integrity in politics, and gender equality. They joined former winter Olympian Zali Steggall and another independent to form a loosely aligned group of eight centrist independents. They are all women who won seats once held safely by prominent male Liberal Party leaders, including former Prime Ministers Tony Abbott and Malcolm Turnbull and former treasurer Josh Frydenberg. The reference to teal is because many (but not all) of the candidates used teal as their campaign colour. Most of them sourced funding from Climate 200, a political donation company set up by Australian billionaire Simon Holmes à Court. Combined with the strong result for the Greens in the 2022 election, the rise of the teal independents shows that voters are increasingly dissatisfied with both major parties, and that the results of future elections may well be decided by the cross-bench.

Teal independents: group of independent candidates loosely aligned on issues relating to climate change, anti-corruption and gender equality

4. MINISTERS

Executive: branch of government which administers (uses) laws in practice

Minister: senior member of government with responsibility over a specific policy area

The group with the greatest influence in parliament is not a political party but rather part of a political party. The **executive** government refers to the senior members of the party that holds a majority of seats in the lower house. This includes the Prime Minister (the leader of that party), the Deputy Prime Minister, and other senior members of the government known as Ministers. **Ministers** are appointed by the Governor-General, on the advice of the Prime Minister, to take charge of government policy in different topic areas. These topic areas are known as **portfolios**.

Portfolio: an area of government policy that a minister is responsible for

Key ministers include the Attorney-General (who looks after law and justice), the Treasurer and Finance Minister (who look after Australia's budget and finances), the Minister for Foreign Affairs (who looks after Australia's relations with other countries), and the Ministers for Defence, Education, Health and the Environment.

These and other senior ministers are known as **Cabinet**. Cabinet is the lead decision-making body for the executive government. Essentially, it is a committee meeting of these senior Ministers to determine the government's position on issues affecting the nation. All Cabinet members are bound by the principle of **collective responsibility**, which says they must all publicly support decisions agreed by the group, even if they personally disagree with it. For this reason, Cabinet discussions are kept strictly confidential.

Cabinet: meeting of senior Ministers with responsibility over important portfolios like defence, finance and education

Collective responsibility: principle that says members of Cabinet must publicly support decisions reached by Cabinet as a whole

Cabinet ministers have a significant influence on the laws that are introduced in parliament. It is typically Cabinet ministers who introduce Bills in their respective policy areas, so it is essentially the political agenda of Cabinet that becomes the law of Australia (whether this be new criminal laws, improved rights for people with a disability, support for same-sex marriage, or laws on any other topic). This is the main reason why a change in government at a federal election is such a major event.

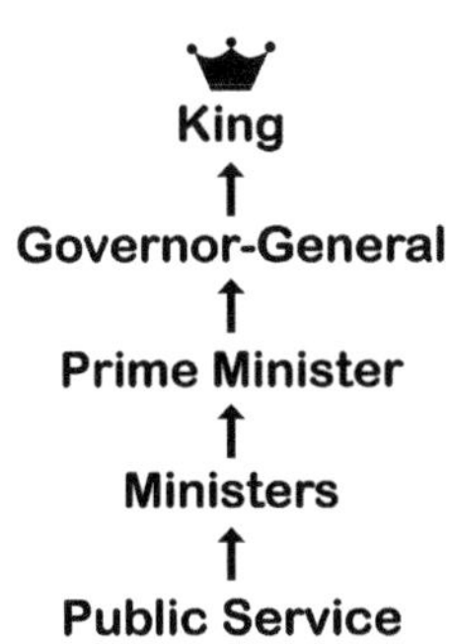

Figure 4.5 Executive branch of government

Administer: use laws in practice

The executive government is a much broader concept than just Ministers. It refers to the entire branch of government that '**administers**' (uses) legislation in practice (you will read more about this in Chapter 6). The executive branch of government extends up to the Governor-General and the King, and down to every employee working in a government department (i.e., the public service). You can see a list of who makes up the executive government in Figure 4.5.

In practice, though, it is Ministers (and Cabinet especially) that have the greatest say on which laws are enacted in Australia. The Governor-General as the King's representative essentially plays a symbolic role by signing off on legislation.

5. YOUR VOTE MATTERS

Voting for the houses of parliament is complex and the politics involved can be frustrating. But this should not get in the way of all Australians thinking about the issues they care about and exercising their democratic choice carefully. The choice we make at election time matters. It matters because the political party that is elected to government sets the agenda for which new laws will be enacted, which existing laws will be amended, and which laws will be repealed—for the next three years. It matters because a Senate with a different majority to the lower house acts as a critical check on government power.

Elections are not the only time you can influence lawmaking. You can write to your local member of parliament on any issue that affects you. You can also make submissions to a parliamentary committee inquiry. You do not need any qualification or special knowledge to do so: your qualification is that you are a citizen in our democracy. Much of the legislation created by the federal parliament might not impact you directly—but you can have your say when something does. For example, as you will read about in Chapter 14, Australia's metadata laws raise important questions about when government agencies should be able to access data about our phone calls and SMS messages from telecommunications providers. Do you think police and other agencies should be able to access this data without a warrant? This is just one example of the many ways that law impacts all our lives.

KEY POINTS

- The seats in both houses of parliament are occupied by members of political parties, who are voted in at election time. In the Senate, proportional voting gives a greater chance for minor parties and independents to be elected.
- Labor and Liberal are the two main political parties in Australia, but voters are increasingly turning to the Greens, minor parties, and independents.
- Ministers are senior members of the government who have responsibility over different policy areas, such as defence, health and education. Ministers are part of the executive branch of government, and they have a significant influence on which laws are enacted.

DISCUSSION QUESTIONS

1. What is a political issue that is important to you?
2. Would you describe yourself as having left-wing or right-wing views? What about your friends and family?
3. How does the Senate act as an important check on government power?
4. Do you think that minor parties and independents should be able to hold the balance of power in the Senate?
5. What is the executive branch of government, and why is it important to law-making in Australia?
6. Which Australian politicians can you find on social media? How many followers do they have and what have they been posting about recently?

Chapter 5
Media

In this chapter, you will learn about:

- Media ownership and bias
- The role that media plays in holding governments accountable
- Social media, misinformation and disinformation.

Media: broadcasting and publishing companies that communicate information to the public

Prejudice: discrimination towards groups in society, especially on the grounds of race, religion or ethnicity

We learn about most public events in Australia and around the world from the media. The **media** is the group of broadcasting and publishing companies that communicate information to the public. Media content comes to us through newspapers, radio, television and, of course, social media. In this chapter, you will learn about media ownership, the role that media plays in holding governments accountable, and risks of media bias and **prejudice**. Finally, you will learn about the dangers of misinformation and disinformation on social media.

1. MEDIA OWNERSHIP

Mass media: group of publishing and broadcasting companies that communicate to a very large audience

You have probably heard of the '**mass media**', meaning the group of publishing and broadcasting companies that communicate content to a large audience. In Australia, major media companies include the Australian Broadcasting Corporation (**ABC**), Special Broadcasting Service (**SBS**), Sky News and many different newspapers and radio stations. These outlets report continually on Australian politics, including

DOI: 10.4324/9781003433408-6

changes to the law. This is how we understand daily what the government is doing. In fact, we learn about most public events in Australia and around the world from these outlets and others based overseas.

ABC: the Australian Broadcasting Corporation, one of Australia's public broadcasters

SBS: the Special Broadcasting Service, one of Australia's public broadcasters

Of course, social media means that reaching a large audience is no longer something that only large media companies or governments can achieve. There is no longer a monopoly on mass communication. You can reach millions of people around the world just by uploading a quick post or video on your smartphone. There are countless bloggers, influencers, independent journalists and smaller media companies who report news about public events. They also critique and analyse content produced by the larger companies.

This makes defining 'the media'—and even who is a journalist—more complicated. A **journalist** is someone involved in the profession of reporting news. Usually, they operate under a media **code of ethics**, which includes rules and standards to ensure that journalists act fairly and with integrity. These include striving for objectivity, disclosing conflicts of interest, and protecting the identity of sources. Now, though, the lines between professional journalists and other content producers are often blurred.

Journalist: someone involved in the profession of reporting news

Code of ethics: for journalists, a document containing agreed rules and standards to maintain integrity in the profession

We should also avoid drawing a line between professional journalists and others on the grounds of quality. Many bloggers and independent journalists produce high-quality, impartial content—and professional journalists do not always follow their ethical guidelines. However, the distinction can be helpful to know where you source information about public events from and how likely it is to be fair and accurate. In this chapter, we focus on the large media companies in Australia, but it helps to be aware of the more complex online landscape, and we will return to consider the benefits and risks of social media.

A key distinction in the large outlets is between the public broadcasters and commercial media. A **public broadcaster** is a media company funded by taxpayers that has responsibilities to the entire community (in other words, all of us pay for them from our salaries as

Public broadcaster: taxpayer-funded media organisation with a legal duty to produce diverse, independent and educational content a public good). Their functions, prescribed in law, are to produce diverse, independent and educational content for the whole country.

Charter: in relation to public broadcasters, a section of legislation that sets out their functions and obligations to the community

ABC Charter: section of legislation setting out the ABC's legal functions to produce diverse, independent and educational content

Statutory functions: the purposes of an organisation and the tasks it performs, as set out in legislation

We have two public broadcasters: the ABC and SBS. Both have a **charter** which sets out their functions and legal obligations. The **ABC Charter**, which sets out the ABC's **statutory functions**, is found in section 6 of the *Australian Broadcasting Act 1983* (Cth). It says, among other things, that the ABC is responsible for providing a high standard of journalism that is independent of government, to broadcast programs of an educational nature that reflect our cultural diversity, and to encourage musical, dramatic and other performing arts. The ABC also plays a critical role keeping the public informed during natural disasters and emergencies (such as floods, bushfires, and the COVID-19 pandemic). It does this through local radio stations around the country as well as its national TV programs and 24-hour news channel. All media keep people informed about emergencies, but this role is especially important for the ABC.

The SBS is also a public broadcaster, though it is partly funded by advertising. It began in the 1970s as a radio service to keep migrants informed in different languages about how to access medical care. Now, it has multiple TV channels, streaming services with foreign language content, and radio stations in over 60 languages. It provides an online 'settlement guide' for migrants who have recently arrived in Australia. Under the SBS Charter, found in section 6 of the *Special Broadcasting Act 1991* (Cth), its main function is to 'provide multilingual and multicultural broadcasting and digital media services that inform, educate and entertain all Australians, and, in doing so, reflect Australia's multicultural society'.

In contrast to the public broadcasters, commercial media companies are privately owned corporations. They are accountable to their shareholders, based on the profits they raise and return to them—not to the Australian people. The largest is **News Corp**, a massive **multinational** founded by the Murdoch family. News Corp owns a long list of newspapers, magazines and TV stations, including Fox News in the United States and **tabloid** newspapers in the United

News Corp: international media organisation owned by the Murdoch family, which is widely recognised as favouring right-wing viewpoints

Kingdom. It owns more than half of Australia's print media market by readership.[1] This includes ***The Australian***, ***The Daily Telegraph***, ***The Courier Mail***, ***The Advertiser*** and many other widely read newspapers around the country. It owns the Sky News TV channels, news.com.au, realestate.com.au, horse racing and gambling websites, Vogue magazine, and even a two-thirds share of the Brisbane Broncos rugby league team. In addition to News Corp, the other major commercial media companies in Australia are those associated with the commercial, free-to-air TV networks (Channels 7, 9 and 10). These familiar TV channels are, however, just one part of more complex business structures which can extend globally. For example, Channel 10 (officially Network 10) is owned by Ten Network Holdings, which is owned by a **subsidiary** of Paramount Global, which also runs the Paramount Plus streaming service.

Tabloid: a newspaper associated with sensationalist content and celebrity news

Subsidiary: a company owned by a parent company

It is important to keep the public/commercial distinction in mind when sourcing news content. Both public broadcasters and commercial media can produce high-quality, fair and unbiased journalism. But it is worth thinking about the primary goals of an organisation when they report news to you. Especially in the age of social media, whether news content is considered successful by those producing it can have less to do with how objective or educational it is, and more to do with how many people view, click on or share it. The need to entertain and engage audiences for profit is a very different goal to producing high-quality, **investigative journalism**.

Investigative journalism: news reporting that involves deeper inquiries into matters of public importance, typically presented in longer articles and documentary-style TV programs

Those goals can overlap—they are not mutually exclusive—but they can also clash. In 2018, for example, Fairfax Media, a news company that previously owned and ran newspapers like ***The Sydney Morning Herald*** and ***The Age***, merged with the Nine Entertainment Network. This was seen as a loss to investigative journalism because it meant those newspapers are now owned by a company primarily in the business of entertainment, not news reporting. This was possible because Malcolm Turnbull's Liberal government changed media ownership laws the previous year. They removed legal rules that prevented companies from reaching an audience larger than 75% of the population, or more than two out of three media types (newspaper, television and radio) in the same market.

Those changes to media ownership laws reinforced the power of the largest companies. The dangers of this are explained well in a report by two researchers from the University of Sydney.[2] Brevini and Ward found that News Corp and Nine Entertainment own 82% of the print media market. They found that News Corp, Nine, and Seven Media Holdings (which owns Channel 7) collect 80% of free-to-air and subscription TV revenues. In theory, **deregulating** the media industry was meant to generate competition between companies, which would lead to more diverse platforms and content. In reality, the opposite was true, and Australian media became far more concentrated. This was unsurprising, as Brevini and Ward explain, given that the large commercial media companies **lobbied** the government for the changes to be made.

Deregulate: change or remove rules to make something legal

This is a common story when government policies are based in neoliberalism. **Neoliberalism** is a theory of government which favours minimal intervention in economic markets. It favours **privatisation**, meaning the selling of public assets, industries and services so they are owned by profit-making corporations. This is meant to generate higher-quality services, but it tends to benefit corporations and shareholders at the expense of public goods. As Brevini and Ward write, the influence of neoliberalism on Australian media has created a highly concentrated market where a small number of very large companies offer most of the available content. This has impacted the health of our democracy because it reduces the chance that diverse voices will be heard:

Neoliberalism: a theory of government which favours free economic markets and the privatisation of public services

Privatisation: the selling of publicly owned assets, industries and services to private corporations

> Excessive concentration of media ownership threatens media plurality—a vital pillar of a healthy democracy—by limiting opportunities for diverse views and perspectives, and concentrating power in the hands of a few.[3]

Public broadcasters offset this highly concentrated commercial market. Their charters contain legal obligations to provide diverse, independent, and educational content that celebrates multicultural Australia. But they have faced ongoing funding cuts over recent years: between 2014 and 2020, under the Coalition government, the ABC lost $783m in funding—despite Tony Abbott promising in the lead-up to the 2013 election that the ABC's budget would not be reduced.[4] As a result of the cuts, key programs have been dropped and the ABC has closed many smaller radio stations, which provided locally relevant content to regional communities, especially during emergencies.[5]

Valuing and protecting public broadcasters is not about favouring their views over commercial media. It is about making sure that some media organisations have legal responsibilities to the Australian people as a whole, and are not influenced by a desire to make profits. It is about having diverse, independent views represented across the media landscape and the country, so that all members of society can seek information from a variety of sources. This is required by article 19 of the *International Covenant on Civil and Political Rights* (ICCPR), an international human rights treaty that you will read about in Chapter 9. Article 19(2) of the ICCPR protects freedom of expression and says:

> Everyone shall have the right to freedom of expression; this right shall include freedom to seek, receive and impart information and ideas of all kinds, regardless of frontiers, either orally, in writing or in print, in the form of art, or through any other media of his choice.

The more that media ownership becomes concentrated in Australia, the greater the risks to freedom of expression. We are all less able to seek diverse, high-quality content about politics and other issues from diverse sources.

2. THE MEDIA AS 'FOURTH ESTATE'

All media companies, but especially the ABC as our main public broadcaster, play a critical role in holding politicians and governments accountable. For this reason, the media is sometimes called the '**fourth estate**'. This is an old term referring to the clergy, nobility and commoners as the three estates of the realm. Today, it is similar to saying that the media is a fourth arm or branch of government, which keeps the others in check. (You will read more about the three arms of government—parliament, courts and the executive—in the next chapter.)

Fourth estate: phrase used to describe the media because of the important role it plays in holding governments accountable

This creates a close relationship with some mutual interests and some competing ones. The government needs media to tell the public about its plans and priorities. There is a **press gallery** of around 250

Press gallery: group of around 250 journalists and other media staff who work in Parliament House

journalists, editors, camera operators and other media staff who work in Parliament House for this purpose. But governments speaking to the media does not simply mean outlining proposals and policies. Communicating with journalists, and via them to the Australian population, is an exercise in public relations. Political parties employ media advisors, public relations experts and advertising consultants to ensure their image is carefully managed. This can mean that positive changes for society are communicated in the best possible way for maximum impact—but it can also aim to benefit the party more than the public.

Damage control: public relations strategies designed to minimise the impact of mistakes and controversies

Taking out the trash: when governments release information that makes them look bad at a time when fewer people are likely to see it

Transparency: when governments communicate information openly with their citizens

It can also involve **damage control** to protect their image. For example, a government might delay the release of an important report that criticises them until the Friday afternoon before a holiday, when fewer people are likely to notice it (this is known as '**taking out the trash**'). Or they might downplay conflicts between party members to create an image of unity in the party and prevent the other side from gaining an advantage in public opinion. These sorts of strategies are common, and they can come at the expense of **transparency**, as the public is receiving a curated image and not the full picture. It is also no secret that politicians sometimes leak information strategically to journalists to harm the other side politically. Ultimately, it is important to remember that governments depend on public opinion to win their seats again at the election, and to win a majority of those seats in the lower house.

Public relations efforts by political parties can be as detailed as the colours they wear in public. Next time you see a politician on TV, especially at election time, see if you can notice them wearing red for Labor or blue for the Liberal Party (or green, orange or teal for other parties and independents). This does not necessarily happen every day, but for key announcements, formal events and election campaigns, it becomes much more likely. You might see their party colour in a jacket, dress, or an accessory like a tie. That might sound extreme, but think of press conferences for the rugby league at State of Origin time. You would never see the NSW coach fronting up to the media wearing a maroon shirt or tie! Imagine the backlash and ridicule if they were seen to be wearing the other team's colours. In all sorts of professions, brands are very carefully managed.

In turn, the media needs the government so it can inform people about current affairs. A large portion of their content would not exist if not for the information they receive from and report about governments. The media generates clicks, likes, shares, comments, and other engagements based on their political reporting. This is true of the public broadcasters, who need to maintain a large audience to remain viable, but especially so for the commercial media companies, which generate profits through advertising. The more people view their TV channels or webpages, the more other companies will pay them to advertise their products and services to reach the widest possible audience. There is no point paying for advertising during the nightly news on TV, or in the space next to online news stories, if no one is watching that news.

Unfortunately, the need to engage audiences means that media content about politics tends toward the dramatic and sensational, covering arguments between politicians, scandals, affairs, and other happenings in parliament that do not have much to do with policies and changes that affect society. This is understandable, as the content is more entertaining than the technicalities of changing legislation—but it does mean that the public's knowledge about substantive issues is often reduced in favour of more trivial tidbits. You are more likely to hear about it if our Prime Minister does an embarrassing dance at a ceremony overseas, than if a technical change to the law would improve outcomes for victims of crime.

Because of its reach, the media also has enormous power to shape public opinion on politics and government—not simply to report on it. This is particularly important around election time, when public opinion can directly influence who is elected to parliament. Media reporting might even sway the outcome of a closely fought election.

Influencing public opinion can be a good thing, if it helps the population understand what different political parties stand for and to make informed choices. But there are downsides, if the reporting aims to generate fear and anger, or it unfairly favours one side of politics over the other. At its worst, media coverage of politics can be designed quite directly to undermine a sitting government in favour of the opposition. You can read more in the next section about the risks of media bias and prejudice.

At its best, though, media can hold governments accountable in a way that few others in society are capable of doing. Media organisations rely on governments feeding them information for content, but they are independent and not simply a mouthpiece for those in power. Indeed, it is critical for our society, democracy, and fundamental freedoms that they are not. A hallmark of **authoritarian systems** and **dictatorships** is that their governments tightly control what the media reports. If they can control what people think, they can control the people. An

Authoritarian system: system of government where power is highly centralised and populations are often controlled by fear and coercion

Dictatorship: system of government ruled by a leader with absolute power

independent press, free from the influence of government, is recognised by the United Nations as 'one of the cornerstones of a democratic society'.[6] This means that journalists and their editors—not politicians—must have the final say on what is reported to the public, and how it is reported.

Across all platforms, public and commercial, media outlets hold government accountable by interviewing politicians about their plans and priorities, as well as mistakes they may have made, scandals, corruption, and many other things. Politicians are practised at avoiding questions put to them by journalists, but this kind of questioning helps to expose wrongdoing, and it gives us a more accurate picture of who we are voting for. Even if a politician keeps dodging a question put to them by a journalist, this still tells us something. You can see this play out especially in dedicated political slots like the ABC's Q&A program: a weekly, televised forum where members of the public ask questions to politicians sitting on a panel. In a way, Q&A is like a 'people's parliament'.

Beyond these regular interactions, longer-form, investigative journalism can produce news reports with major impacts. A key example was a 2016 report by ABC TV's Four Corners program on youth detention in the Northern Territory. Four Corners combines investigative journalism with documentary filmmaking techniques to produce impactful news reports on topics of public interest. It first aired in 1961 and is still producing weekly episodes, more than half a century later. In its report on youth detention,[7] it exposed the shocking treatment of Australian children in the Northern Territory's Don Dale Youth Detention Centre. Among other incidents, children being detained in the centre were shackled to restraint chairs and their heads covered with 'spit hoods' (full-head masks). They were tear-gassed while prison officers laughed at them. They were taken outside and hosed on the ground with their hands tied behind their backs. They told the officers multiple times they could not breathe.

Chief Minister: the equivalent of a state premier in the territories

Royal commission: the highest level of public inquiry in Australia, usually chaired by a former judge

The footage was so shocking and the public uproar so significant that the **Chief Minister** for the NT stood down the Corrections Minister the morning after the show aired. Soon after, Prime Minister Malcolm Turnbull announced a royal commission. A **royal commission** is the highest level of independent public inquiry in Australia. Royal commissions are established only for matters of public importance. They are usually chaired by a former judge. They involve public and private hearings, written submissions from members of public, and large volumes of evidence. The chair has significant powers to gather this information: they can compel (require) people to appear before the inquiry, answer questions, and produce documents.

Following an inquiry, a Royal Commission publishes a report containing findings on what happened and recommendations on how laws, policies and procedures should change to prevent harm and misconduct from happening again. A royal commission report does not have legal consequences, but it can lead to criminal prosecutions and civil court proceedings for damages (compensation).

The Royal Commission into the Protection and Detention of Children in the Northern Territory ran more than 50 days of public hearings, interviewed more than 200 witnesses, and generated more than 6,000 pages of transcripts.[8] It found, among many other things, that youth detention centres in the Northern Territory were 'not fit for accommodating, let alone rehabilitating children'.[9] It found that children were subject to verbal abuse and physical control. They were denied access to basic needs including food, water, and the use of toilets. Keeping them in **solitary confinement**, separate to the other children, was very likely in some cases to cause 'lasting psychological damage'. The commission made more than 200 recommendations, including to close Don Dale, raise the age of criminal responsibility, and develop a 10-year strategy for child protection.

Solitary confinement: when prisoners are detained separately to other detainees under stricter conditions

These were important recommendations, though the Northern Territory government has been criticised for failing to implement them. More young people were detained in Don Dale five years after the Four Corners report than when it aired.[10] Still, progress has been made: spit hoods and restraint chairs are now banned, and the age of criminal responsibility in the NT has been raised from 10 to 12. In late 2023, the NT Supreme Court ruled that 4 of the children would be paid nearly $1 million total compensation.[11] The NT government earlier reached a $35 million settlement for all children detained there between 2006 and 2017.[12] That agreement was triggered by a **class action**: a legal claim where at least seven people are affected by the same circumstances, and one or more people pursue the claim on behalf of a larger group. Class actions are much more efficient than tens, hundreds or even thousands of people making similar claims in court.

Class action: legal claim where at least seven people are affected by the same circumstances, and one or more people pursue the claim on behalf of a larger group

The Four Corners episode was not the first time that terrible conditions in youth detention, in the NT and elsewhere, had been reported on by journalists. But it was the first time that such shocking footage was broadcast publicly. The reporting and response showed that investigative journalism and strong visuals have 'the power to move people and force governments to act'.[13] Progressing the Royal Commission recommendations further will likely take many years. But it is fair to say that, without the Four Corners reporting, the recommendations, reforms and **reparations** made so far might not have been achieved for much longer, or even at all.

Reparations: compensation payments

Unfortunately, for multiple reasons, investigative journalism is at risk in Australia. Commercial outlets dominate the media landscape, and they can generate clicks, likes, shares and profits without needing to invest in longer-form journalism. Quality investigative journalism takes time and is expensive to produce, and unless a story provokes a major public reaction, other content that is more immediately entertaining can attract a larger audience. Funding cuts to the public broadcasters have also meant that many journalists dedicated to investigative journalism have fewer staff and resources available to produce it.

Even more concerning is that journalists and **whistleblowers** in Australia have recently been investigated for reporting stories in the public interest. For example, in 2019, the Australian Federal Police (**AFP**) raided the Sydney offices of the ABC to gather evidence for a criminal investigation. This was criticised around the world as an attack on press freedom. The New York Times claimed Australia 'may well be the world's most secretive democracy'.[14] The raid happened because a defence force lawyer, David McBride, gave confidential documents to ABC reporters. The documents, known after the ABC reporting as ***The Afghan Files***, contained information about possible war crimes committed by Australian soldiers in Afghanistan. An independent inquiry by the Inspector-General of the Australian Defence Force later found there was 'credible information' that Australian special forces soldiers committed war crimes by murdering 39 non-combatants and cruelly treating 2 more.[15] And yet, the only person to be prosecuted so far in relation to those war crimes is McBride. He pleaded guilty to three charges for stealing and communicating confidential information, after the ACT Supreme Court ruled he could not put key evidence before the court on national security grounds.[16]

Whistleblower: someone working for an organisation or government department who exposes misconduct, corruption or criminal behaviour

AFP: Australian Federal Police

Following the AFP raids and the McBride trial, investigative journalism can be risky business. Even if there is good reason for the public to know about a story, there are very few legal protections available if it exposes confidential or classified information. Of course, there are very good reasons for government, intelligence agencies and the defence force to keep information secret. But something is fundamentally wrong if whistleblowers and journalists are investigated for exposing possible war crimes, and not those who allegedly committed them. The risks are compounded by a series of offences relating to terrorism, espionage and foreign interference, which define national security very broadly and have a 'chilling effect' on journalists who report in the public interest.[17] You will read more about the risks that Australia's counter-terrorism laws pose to journalists in the final chapter of this book.

3. MEDIA BIAS

Media content informs us about politics and current affairs, but we should not treat it as objective fact. All events are subject to interpretation, and so accounts of politics and public events will differ naturally depending on who is producing the content. But media content can also reveal more concerning levels of bias. **Bias** means the tendency to favour one side or viewpoint unfairly. Bias can be conscious, with no attempts to hide it: media content can be designed intentionally to stir up feelings against a group in society or an opposing argument. It can also be unconscious and unintentional, resulting from assumptions that are false or inaccurate. This is not just about journalists; it is true of all content and everything we write and say. **Confirmation bias**—our tendency to seek out content that confirms what we already think or feel—is another powerful force.

Bias: tendency to produce content that favours one side or viewpoint unfairly

Confirmation bias: tendency to seek out information that confirms what you already think or feel

The ABC has long been accused of left-wing bias against the government generally, and the Liberal Party in particular. Former Prime Minister Tony Abbott famously called Q&A a 'lefty lynch mob'.[18] He believed the show aimed to grill Liberal Party politicians and embarrass them on air. This perception is changing, though, after the Liberal government substantially reduced the ABC's budget and appointed former News Corp editors and executives to the ABC's board of directors (including as its chair). Kerry O'Brien, founding host of the ABC's 7:30 program and one of Australia's most experienced and respected journalists, has warned that the ABC is drifting closer to a commercial model and away from its 'fundamental role' as a public broadcaster.[19] Former Prime Minister Kevin Rudd believes the ABC's political commentary has been 'tamed' by the cuts and continual attacks by right-wing commentators, because its journalists fear reinforcing the left-wing stereotype.[20]

At the other end of the political spectrum, News Corp is often accused of right-wing bias in favour of the Liberal Party. The clearest example was in the lead-up to the 2013 federal election, when News Corp urged Australians to vote against Labor. It ran large headlines with slogans including 'Kick This Mob Out!'.[21] This was a direct attempt to influence the outcome of a federal election, not by offering facts and critical analysis, but instead by fuelling emotions (anger, fear and resentment) in the community. There is certainly an argument for free speech and that media companies should be able to say whatever they like. This includes criticising government. Indeed, if media companies were punished for that, we would be living in an authoritarian state and not a democracy. But is concerning that a company with the largest share of the media market in Australia can be so obviously biased to one side of politics. They do not even try to hide it. Criticising governments and their policies is one thing, but stirring up anger towards a sitting government is much more serious.

That example is blatant, but even if media reporting in an individual story is fair and objective, there is often hidden bias in a choice to run one story over others. For example, media outlets have been criticised for reporting on missing or murdered persons when they are photogenic, white females, but not when the victims of similar crimes are Indigenous women. Media reporting will even favour stories of white, photogenic people missing in other countries over Indigenous women missing or murdered in Australia. You might remember media reporting on Gabby Petito, a young, attractive American girl who was murdered by her fiancé on their travels across the United States. Their 'van life' road trip was documented on social media and audiences followed the investigation like a murder mystery. Xanthe Mallett, a forensic criminologist at the University of Newcastle, called this yet another case of 'missing white woman syndrome'.[22] Nowhere near the same level of coverage is given to stories of Indigenous women murdered in Australia, even though the rates are 8 times higher than for non-Indigenous women.[23] Violence (including domestic and family violence) against Indigenous women is significantly under-reported.

Media coverage often reveals conscious or unconscious bias. It can be seen in 'tough on crime' reporting, which sensationalises perceived threats to society. Reporting on 'African gangs' in Victoria demonises African-Australians and generates fear, anger and further discrimination against those communities.[24]

In fact, one study found half of race-related opinion pieces in Australian media were likely to breach the media code of conduct for including racist content.[25] Reporting on the 'youth crime' epidemic (recently in Queensland, but elsewhere over time) is another example. That reporting fuels fears about young people being out in public when the story is far more complex, and youth crime overall has trended downwards over the last decade.[26] And there is a longer history of media closely linking terrorism with Islam and Muslim communities.[27] It is fair to say that the commercial media, and News Corp especially, are most responsible for this problematic reporting. In that study of racist content, ***The Australian***, ***The Daily Telegraph*** and the ***Herald Sun*** (all owned by News Corp) were the most responsible newspapers, and Channel 9's ***A Current Affair*** program was the biggest culprit on TV.[28]

It is easy to be cynical about media's capacity for bias, but it is important to remember that media organisations publish what we are more likely to click on, and show what we are more likely to watch. In part, media companies determine what we choose to focus on, but they are also responding to our previous choices in selecting content, commenting on and sharing it. Journalists, content producers and other people working in media organisations are not especially biased compared to anyone else in society. Their bias is our bias. Media is a mirror, showing us parts of ourselves that we might not comfortably admit. Unlike individuals, though, media outlets have the power to reach a mass audience easily, influencing and reinforcing their views. We can all help to encourage fair, unbiased reporting by learning more about the different news sources available to us and making informed choices about the content we consume.

4. SOCIAL MEDIA AND MISINFORMATION

Dangers of biased and inaccurate information are amplified on social media. Social media has become a core part of all our lives, and it is the same for journalists and politicians. Journalists rely on it to source their stories and share them with a larger audience than was previously possible. Outside the large media organisations, bloggers, influencers, independent journalists and the general public use it to research and report on public events, and also to critique governments and their policies.

Politicians, too, rely on social media like everyone else. It would be rare for a politician not to have a Facebook page or other social media profile. The platforms can be used to great effect, especially to communicate with younger audiences. Some politicians, like Barack Obama and Kevin Rudd, were pioneers in this space. Over time, different platforms become more and less popular, but social media is now a permanent feature of the political landscape, especially during election campaigns.

Politicians might not be up with the latest trends or make the best content, but their efforts benefit our democracy. Even if a post or video fails to hit the mark with young people, politicians can at least get their key messages out to different audiences. The more audiences they reach, the more likely it is that all Australians will make informed choices at election time, and that election outcomes will reflect diverse views. Voters who flick through TikTok will be different to voters who watch Sky News, who will be different again to those who listen to SBS radio. It is important in a democracy that everyone can access information that speaks to them about public affairs.

Social media can be especially effective for minor parties and independents, who have far less funding for political advertising and campaigning compared to the major parties. It can boost **grassroots campaigns**, where community members volunteer and mobilise around a cause. This can give new and relatively unknown candidates a greater chance of winning a seat against more experienced politicians. It helps to ensure a greater diversity of voices in Parliament, by allowing us access to candidates beyond the major parties.

Grassroots campaigns: where community members volunteer and mobilise around a political cause

At the same time, social media clearly comes with dangers and downsides. Content is less regulated on social media compared to traditional media: we can all say almost anything we like. Increasingly, **misinformation**—false or inaccurate content that intentionally misleads an audience—will be taken down or an account suspended if a social media company is notified about it and decides to take action. This happened to Craig Kelly (leader of the United Australia Party) and Sky News, when Facebook and YouTube found they published misinformation about COVID-19 vaccines.[29] But these are standout examples, and misinformation abounds on those and other platforms.

Misinformation: false or inaccurate content that unintentionally misleads an audience

At its worst, social media can be exploited by foreign governments who seek to influence political outcomes in other countries. **Disinformation** is false or inaccurate information that is spread intentionally to

Disinformation: false or inaccurate content spread intentionally to deceive or manipulate an audience

deceive or manipulate an audience. It is one aspect of **foreign interference**, which is a major national security threat in Australia and around the world. For example, it is widely recognised that Russia exploited social media to influence the outcome of the 2016 US presidential election, by targeting Hillary Clinton and making it more likely that Donald Trump would be elected. Russian-backed propaganda on Facebook reached up to 126 million Americans during the election campaign.[30]

Foreign interference: when one country seeks to manipulate political events and outcomes in another

Social media companies also play a significant role. When it comes to misinformation and disinformation, they are not simply passive actors. In that same election campaign, for example, Facebook not only failed to address Russian interference; it also failed to alert its users that Cambridge Analytica, a British company, had harvested data unlawfully from millions of their profiles.[31] That data was used by Trump's campaign team to target different voter groups. For example, Black American communities were targeted with negative ads about Hilary Clinton, to discourage them from turning out to vote.[32] As America does not have compulsory voting like Australia, voter turnout can have a significant impact on election outcomes.

Social media companies can be reluctant to counter misinformation on their platforms because their business models run on engagement. Similar to commercial media, social media companies gauge success by how many views, likes, shares and comments a post receives—not on whether the content is fair and accurate. The more engaging the content, the more other companies will pay to advertise next to it. If content is fair and accurate but less engaging, social media companies and their advertisers will make fewer profits. This is true not just for Facebook (and its parent company Meta) but also X (formerly Twitter), YouTube, TikTok and any other social media platform that generates revenue from advertising. It is no secret, but it remains an ongoing obstacle to achieving safer online spaces. Increasingly, social media companies are doing more so their users do not lose trust in them, and so governments do not regulate them with stronger laws and penalties. But getting them to trade profits for more objective content will always be a challenge.

In the meantime, we should all seek information from diverse, independent sources. If you often read news articles that come up in your social media feeds, try seeking out the same story directly from a few different outlets. This could include online media, radio and TV. Can you spot any differences in how the issue is reported? Are they making different arguments, or even reporting different facts? It would take too much work to do this for every single news story, but the more you practise it, the better you will be at spotting or false or inaccurate information, and knowing which outlets publish fair, unbiased content..

Fact-checking: where journalists or a dedicated organisation verify the accuracy of claims made in public content

Another thing you can do, if you are not sure about a claim made in news reporting, is to consult a fact-checking service. **Fact-checking** is where journalists or a dedicated organisation verify claims made in media and other public content. It usually involves journalists asking academics, scientists or other professionals whether the claims are accurate, based on the available evidence. Snopes.com is a leading example with international reach. Australian examples include the FactCheck websites published by the AAP (Australian Associated Press) and The Conversation. The Conversation is a news platform that publishes articles written by academics, based on their research. These sorts of organisations are playing an important role by helping us to identify false, inaccurate and misleading content reported in the media. This helps us develop a keener sense over time for which outlets produce fair reporting with minimal bias.

KEY POINTS

- Social and traditional media help us to understand politics and political parties, but there are risks of bias and misinformation.
- Public broadcasters have legal obligations to produce diverse, educational content, so they offset a highly concentrated commercial media market.
- Consulting fact-checking websites can help us to spot false and misleading content, and learn which outlets produce fair, unbiased content.

DISCUSSION QUESTIONS

1. What are the goals of public broadcasters compared to commercial ones?
2. Is it useful or possible to divide media organisations on a spectrum of left-wing to right-wing views?
3. On balance, do you think social media is good or bad for politics?
4. When you read news articles, where do you source them from?
5. How can members of the public best identify misinformation and disinformation?

NOTES

1 Brevini, B., & Ward, M., (2021). ***Who controls our media? Exposing the impact of media concentration on our democracy*** (GetUp!) 4.
2 Ibid.
3 Ibid. 23.
4 Dawson, E. (2020). ***It's our ABC*** (GetUp!) 10.
5 Ibid.
6 United Nations Human Rights Committee, ***General Comment No. 34, Article 19: Freedom of opinion and expression***, 12 September 2011 (CCPR/C/GC/34) 3.
7 See ABC News, ***Four Corners – video: Australia's shame*** (2016). Retrieved from: https://www.abc.net.au/news/2016-07-25/australias-shame-promo/7649462.
8 Royal Commission into the Protection and Detention of Children in the Northern Territory (2017). ***Report overview***. Retrieved from https://www.royalcommission.gov.au/system/files/2020-09/report-overview.pdf.
9 Ibid.
10 Breen, J., & Barwick, A. (2022). Five years since the NT royal commission into youth detention and child protection, there is hope, disappointment and fear. ***ABC News***, 17 November.
11 Brennan, D. (2023). NT Supreme Court awards nearly $1 million to Indigenous former Don Dale inmates tear-gassed in 2014. ***National Indigenous Times***, 7 September.
12 Gooley, C. (2021). Former Don Dale child inmates to share in record $35 million settlement. ***The Sydney Morning Herald***, 28 July.
13 Meade, A. (2016). Abuse of teenage prisoners in NT detention: how Four Corners got the story. ***The Guardian***, 26 July.
14 Cave, D. (2019). Australia may well be the world's most secretive democracy. ***The New York Times***, 5 June.
15 Inspector-General of the Australian Defence Force. (2020). ***Afghanistan inquiry report***. Commonwealth Government.
16 Canales, S.B., & Knaus, C. (2023). Whistleblower David McBride pleads guilty after court rules to withhold evidence over 'security' risk. ***The Guardian***, 17 November.
17 Ananian-Welsh, R., Kendall, S., & Murray, R. (2021). Risk and uncertainty in public interest journalism: the impact of espionage law on press freedom. ***Melbourne University Law Review***, ***44***(3), 764-811.
18 Kerin, J. (2015). PM brands Q&A a 'lefty lynch mob' over terror gaffe. ***Financial Review***, 23 June.
19 Meade, A. (2024). Kerry O'Brien criticises ABC, saying management needs 'clarity of thought' as Ita Buttrose departs. ***The Guardian***, 5 March.

20 Rudd, K. (2022). Far from having a leftwing bias, the ABC has been tamed by cuts and incessant attacks. ***The Guardian***, 10 May 2022.

21 Hobbs, M., & McKnight, D. (2022). 'Kick this mob out': The Murdoch media and the Australian Labor government (2007 to 2013). ***Global Media Journal***, ***16***(1).

22 Mallett, X. (2021). The Gabby Petito case has been exploited by the media. We need to stop treating human tragedy as entertainment. ***The Conversation***, 29 September.

23 Cripps, K. (2023). New research reveals harrowing stories of murdered Indigenous women and the failure of police to act. ***The Conversation***, 31 May.

24 Vedelago, C., Millar, R. (2021). One election later, the lessons from Melbourne's 'African gang' panic. ***The Age***, 23 November.

25 Ho, C. (2017). Racist reporting still rife in Australian media. ***The Conversation***, 15 December.

26 Goldsworthy, T., Brotto, G., & Cawthray, T. (2023). Is Australia in the grips of a youth crime crisis? This is what the data says. ***The Conversation***, 30 October.

27 Rane, H., Ewart, J., & Martinkus, J. (2014). ***Media framing of the Muslim world***. Palgrave Macmillan.

28 Ho, n 21.

29 Visentin, L. (2021). Craig Kelly permanently booted from Facebook for COVID-19 misinformation. ***The Sydney Morning Herald***, 26 April; Glover, R. (2021). Is the country that gave us Rupert Murdoch finally ready to tackle misinformation? ***The Washington Post***, 6 August.

30 Solon, O., & Siddiqui, S. (2017). Russia-backed Facebook posts 'reached 126m Americans' during US election. ***The Guardian***, 31 October.

31 Confessore, N. (2018). Cambridge Analytica and Facebook: the scandal and the fallout so far. ***The New York*** Times, 4 April.

32 Stracqualursi, V. (2020). Trump campaign microtargeted Black Americans disproportionally 'to deter' them from voting in 2016 election, Channel 4 reports. ***CNN***, 29 September.

Part 2

Rights and justice

Chapter 6

Founding principles

In this chapter, you will learn about:

- Liberalism and democracy
- Federalism and shared lawmaking powers
- The separation of powers and the rule of law

Australia's system of law and government is built on many important principles. In this chapter, we examine five of these: liberalism, democracy, federalism, the separation of powers, and the rule of law. Together, these concepts determined how our legal system was designed.

This does not mean that Australia always upholds these ideals. One way to think critically about law and government is to ask whether the systems live up to these founding principles in practice.

1. LIBERALISM

Australia is a **liberal democracy**. As the name suggests, this means our system of government combines ideas from both liberalism and democracy.

Liberal democracy: a system of government that combines principles of liberalism and democracy

DOI: 10.4324/9781003433408-8

Liberalism: political philosophy that emphasises individual freedom from government

Enlightenment: historical period following the Middle Ages and Renaissance which saw a move away from religion towards scientific and rational thinking

Liberalism is a political philosophy that values individual freedom from governments. It has its roots in seventeenth-century English and French philosophy, during a historical period known as The **Enlightenment**. This was the period following the Middle Ages and Renaissance which saw a move away from religious thinking towards reason and science. It was when ideas developed around liberty, constitutional government, and the separation of church and state.

The British philosopher John Locke, who wrote ***Two Treatises on Government*** in 1689, is considered a founding father of liberalism. Other famous liberal philosophers include Jean-Jacques Rousseau (who published ***The Social Contract*** in 1762) and John Stuart Mill (who published ***On Liberty*** in 1859).

State: term used in political philosophy to refer to the national government of a country

Harm principle: principle attributed to the British philosopher John Stuart Mill, who said the law should only prohibit conduct if it is harmful

Social contract: the hypothetical agreement we enter into as citizens living under a government, which grants us civil liberties

State of nature: term used by the philosopher Jean-Jacques Rousseau to describe a state of anarchy before we lived under governments

These philosophers believed that individuals have important rights and freedoms—like those to private property, liberty and free speech—which the **state** should not interfere with (in political philosophy, the 'state' refers to the government). They believed states should be limited by law, rather than having unrestrained power, and that people should be free to act however they like—unless they harm others. This is known as the **harm principle**. It is a key idea underlying the criminal law. Criminal laws say what we cannot do, but we are otherwise free to do as we please.

Rousseau explained this through a theory called the **social contract**. This is a hypothetical agreement we all enter into as citizens living under a government. Rather than living in **anarchy** (a state of disordered conflict he called the **state of nature**) we agree to live together under a sovereign. In his theory, a sovereign is essentially a government that has power over citizens. (You might have heard the term **sovereign state**, meaning an internationally recognised government that has legal and political power over its citizens within a defined territory. This is similar. We will return to ideas about sovereignty in Chapters 8 and 9.)

The social contract involves a trade-off. We lose the power to do absolutely anything we like. We are no longer free, for example, to hurt other people or steal their things. But in return, other people cannot do these things to us. The state can intervene only if we harm each other, and we are otherwise left free. The protected sphere of freedom we gain under this social contract is our **civil liberty**. This is why fundamental rights and freedoms, like those to privacy and free speech, are called **civil liberties**.

Sovereign state: an internationally recognised government that has legal and political power over its citizens within a defined territory

Civil liberty: the sphere of protected freedom we gain under the social contract

Civil liberties: individual rights we gain as citizens living under a government, including privacy and freedom of speech

Simply put, the social contract is a pact, in which we all agree to live with each other in relative peace under a common government. (Of course, things do not always turn out this way, but this is the theory.)

These liberal ideals are enshrined in historical documents. The *Declaration of the Rights of Man and of the Citizen* was published in 1789 during the French Revolution. It refers to the natural and 'sacred rights of men and of citizens', including 'liberty, property, security and resistance to oppression'.[1] It invokes the harm principle, explaining that liberty 'consists in the freedom to do everything which injures no one else'. It advocates for free speech, claiming that the 'free communication of ideas and opinions is one of the most precious of the rights of man'.

In most modern democracies, these and other fundamental rights are formally protected in a constitution. However, the Australian **Constitution** does not mention them. Still, there are often debates about whether new laws impact our fundamental freedoms. When anyone says, 'that law infringes my right to … ', those arguments are all based in the seventeenth-century philosophy of liberalism.

2. DEMOCRACY

In a **democracy**, the government is elected by the people. Democracy has its roots in the ancient world, especially in Athens around the fifth century BC. It is a combination of two Greek words: *demos*, meaning the people, and *kratos*, meaning 'power' or 'rule'.[2] In other words, democracy means 'rule by the people'.

Democracy: political system where governments are elected by the people

This matches well with ideas about liberalism and the social contract. In ***The Social Contract***, Rousseau says the power to govern is inherent within all of us. It is this power (the 'will of the people') that we pass up to the sovereign. The sovereign does not have any inherent power; it gains its powers from us.

When we vote at elections, we are choosing who to give our inherent power to, and who will govern on our behalf. We can therefore expect that the government will act in our best interests, and hold it accountable when it does not. This is why Abraham Lincoln famously said in the Gettysburg Address that democracy is government 'of the people, by the people, for the people'.

Democracies have two core features. First is a system of elections, where we choose our representatives. This is enshrined in our Constitution. Sections 7 and 24 say that both houses of the federal parliament must be 'directly chosen by the people'. Second is a parliament. Parliaments are where our elected representatives debate new laws and make decisions that affect us.

Representative government: a system of government where politicians are elected by the people and make decisions on their behalf

Direct democracy: hypothetical system of government in which people contribute to every decision

In other words, democracy is a system of **representative government**. We do not have the time or expertise to debate every single issue that affects us, and it would not be possible for 27 million Australians to decide on anything. (A **direct democracy** would be where every citizen has a say on every single decision, but this is not realistic in practice.) So we elect a smaller number of people—politicians who put themselves up for the job—to sit in Parliament and do it for us.

Representative government is a very good way to run a country, but it is not perfect. Winston Churchill, British Prime Minister during World War II, is often quoted as saying: 'Democracy is the worst form of government, except for all those other forms that have been tried from time to time'. People laugh at the comment, but it should also be taken seriously.

Populism: decisions that favour the interests and values of most people

One problem is that democracies, by definition, favour majorities over minorities. Majority decision-making is a fair system in the absence of anything better (hence Churchill's comment), but it can mean that the needs of those most disadvantaged in society are not given sufficient weight, or even ignored altogether. In other words, democracies can tend towards **populism**. Strictly speaking, populism involves decisions that favour the beliefs and interests of most people. However, the term is often used negatively to describe politicians (or media outlets) who play to and exploit the masses. For example, political leaders can stir up discontent and discrimination against minority groups, including migrants and people of colour, to win votes from larger sections of the population.

A second problem is that politicians are less accountable once they are elected. Members of the lower house are elected for three years, and senators for six. Our votes determine who wins those seats, but once we put the paper in the ballot box, there is not as much we can do to influence their decisions. This is why politicians are often criticised for 'broken promises': they campaign to win our votes on the basis that they will do one thing, but once they are in power, they do another. It is not until several years later that we can vote a politician or government out of power if we did not like what they did. In the meantime, we can disagree with a new law or policy, advocate for change, or protest in the streets, but there is less we can do to influence politicians directly.

A third problem is that some people in a democracy have more power than others. Formally speaking, we all have one vote at the ballot box. You do not get ten votes if you are rich, or a celebrity, or the Prime Minister. This is **equal suffrage**: every person's vote is worth the same value. Still, in reality, many people and groups in society have far more influence than you or me. A billionaire mining magnate, the owner of a TV network, or the CEO of a large company will all have easier, more frequent access to politicians and a greater chance of influencing their decisions. It is common practice for businesses, **trade unions** (who represent workers) and other groups to **lobby** government for changes they want to be made. This can lead to better policies, but it also means that some interests can be given more weight in decision-making than others.

Equal suffrage: principle that says every person's vote should be worth the same value

Trade unions: organisations that represent workers' rights

Lobby: when an individual or group petitions a political party to change law or policy

It does not sit well with the ideals of democracy, but simply having more wealth can lead to greater influence. Political parties rely on large donations to run expensive election campaigns, including advertising on radio and TV. In the year leading up to the 2022 federal election, the Liberal Party spent $132 million convincing us to vote for them, and the Labor Party spent $116 million.[3] Most donations to Labor were from trade unions, and to the Liberal and National parties, from wealthy individuals and businesses. It is understandable that those individuals, companies and unions might expect some benefit in return for their support. As the Grattan Institute has written, political parties do not promise formally to do something in return for their donors, but the informal understanding is that money buys greater access and influence:

> [P]olitical donations buy access and sometimes influence over public policy. While explicit quid pro quo is probably rare in Australia, the risk is in more subtle influences – that donors get more access to policymakers and their views are given more weight. These risks are exacerbated by a lack of transparency in dealings between policymakers and special interests.[4]

By a lack of transparency, they are referring to a rule that says that political parties do not need to identify who donated the money if the payment is under about $15,000. One donor can also make multiple payments under that threshold and remain anonymous. In addition, donations registers are not made public until 9 months after an election, so we do not know who is funding the campaigns while they are happening. Political donations reform is a much larger topic that we cannot cover here, but more work needs to be done to ensure that election campaigns are transparent, and to reduce the risks that wealth buys political influence. In theory, money should not determine in a democracy how much influence someone has over political decision-making, but in practice this is quite common.

3. FEDERALISM

Federal system: system of government that shares lawmaking powers between a national government and several state or regional governments

Federalism: ideas and theories relating to federal systems of government

Australia has a federal system of government. A **federal system** is one that divides legal and political power between a central government and several regional or state governments. **Federalism** refers to the ideas and theories behind this two-tiered system.

In Australia, the national government in Canberra (also called the federal or Commonwealth government) shares power with six state governments (New South Wales, Queensland, Victoria, South Australia, Western Australia and Tasmania). Broadly speaking, the Commonwealth government looks after issues that are nationally relevant, including immigration, defence and foreign affairs. The states look after the major services needed day-to-day by their residents, including schools, roads, and hospitals.

Of course, we also have two territory governments on the same 'level' as the states (the Northern Territory and the Australian Capital Territory). However, when we speak about federalism in Australia, we usually mean the division of powers between the Commonwealth government and the states.

This relates to **Federation**: the moment on 1 January 1901 when the Constitution came into force and six British colonies joined together as states to form the Commonwealth of Australia. The Constitution was drafted in a series of conventions in the 1890s, leading up to Federation. It is the founding document of our nation. It created the federal Parliament, the High Court, and it shapes our system of law and government.

Federation: the moment on 1 January 1901 when the Constitution came into force and the colonies joined together as states to form the Commonwealth of Australia

Because of their role in Federation, the states have a special place in Australia's constitutional system. Sections 106–108 of the Constitution preserve the laws, constitutions and lawmaking powers of the state governments from the moment of Federation. By contrast, the territories did not exist at that time: they were created later by statute. They also have fewer lawmaking powers.

A. Shared lawmaking powers

The Constitution grants specific lawmaking powers to the federal Parliament and leaves everything else to the states. Section 51 of the Constitution says that the federal Parliament can make laws only on specific topics, such as immigration and foreign affairs. These are known as the **heads of power**. Every single piece of legislation passed by the federal Parliament must fall under one of these topic areas. If not, the law is invalid and will be struck down by the High Court. The High Court's power to strike down legislation is known as **judicial review**.

Heads of power: sub-sections in section 51 of the Constitution which list the federal Parliament's lawmaking powers

Judicial review: power of the High Court to strike down legislation that is incompatible with the Constitution

The heads of power are quite extensive: you can see a selection of them in Figure 6.1. However, the idea behind them was that the Commonwealth would have less lawmaking power than the states. This is also clear because the powers in s 51 are **concurrent powers**, meaning the states can also make laws on those topics. In

Concurrent powers: lawmaking powers belonging to the federal and State governments

Commonwealth of Australia Constitution Act 1900 (Imp)

Section 51: Legislative powers of the Parliament

The Parliament shall, subject to this Constitution, have power to make laws for the peace, order and good government of the Commonwealth with respect to:
(i) trade and commerce with other countries, and among the States;
(ii) taxation; but so as not to discriminate between States or parts of States;
...
(v) postal, telegraphic, telephonic, and other like services;
(vi) the naval and military defence of the Commonwealth and of the several States, and the control of the forces to execute and maintain the laws of the Commonwealth;
(vii) lighthouses, lightships, beacons and buoys;
(viii) astronomical and meteorological observations;
(ix) quarantine;
(x) fisheries in Australian waters beyond territorial limits;
(xi) census and statistics;
(xii) currency, coinage, and legal tender;
...
(xx) foreign corporations, and trading or financial corporations formed within the limits of the Commonwealth;
(xxi) marriage;
(xxii) divorce and matrimonial causes; and in relation thereto, parental rights, and the custody and guardianship of infants;
(xxiii) invalid and old-age pensions;
...
(xxvi) the people of any race for whom it is deemed necessary to make special laws;
(xxvii) immigration and emigration;
(xxviii) the influx of criminals;
(xxix) external affairs;
...
(xxxi) the acquisition of property on just terms from any State or person for any purpose in respect of which the Parliament has power to make laws;
(xxxii) the control of railways with respect to transport for the naval and military purposes of the Commonwealth

Figure 6.1 Section 51 of the Constitution

practice, however, the Commonwealth government makes laws in these areas. This happens in part because section 109 of the Constitution says that Commonwealth laws will override any state laws that address the same topic, to the extent of any inconsistency between them. There are only a couple of **exclusive powers** held by the Commonwealth in section 52. These relate to the seat of government in Canberra and the Commonwealth public service.

Exclusive powers: lawmaking powers belonging only to one level of government

To understand how section 51 compares to state lawmaking powers, it is first important to realise that the states also have constitutions. However, the state constitutions are just ordinary Acts of Parliament, and they do not list specific powers. Instead, they contain a more general phrase. For example, section 5 of the ***Constitution Act 1902*** (NSW) says that the NSW Parliament shall 'have power to make laws for the peace, welfare and good government of New South Wales in all cases whatsoever'. This (and essentially the same phrase in other state constitutions) grants state Parliaments **plenary power**. Having plenary power means the states can enact laws on any topic they like. The laws do not have to be for the peace, welfare and good government of the state, literally speaking; instead, the phrase is just a 'term of art'. This was debated and confirmed in a series of early English judgments. There are essentially no restrictions on the types of laws that a state Parliament can enact.

Plenary power: unrestrained lawmaking power

This importance of this distinction—between the specific powers granted to the federal Parliament, and the plenary power granted to the states—was crucial at the start of the COVID-19 pandemic. Many Australians might have expected, given the significance of the situation, that the Commonwealth government would have decided health responses for the whole country. However, health is not listed as a head of power under section 51. The States therefore had the power to determine their own responses. This is how we ended up with a patchwork of rules and border closures across the country. Many people were surprised at how much power the State Premiers had compared to the Prime Minister, but it was simply a by-product of how the Constitution was designed before Federation.

B. Local government

A third level of government in Australia—**local government**—sits below the states. Traditionally, federalism refers to the national and state governments, but local governments play an important, additional role.

Local governments: the lowest level of government in Australia

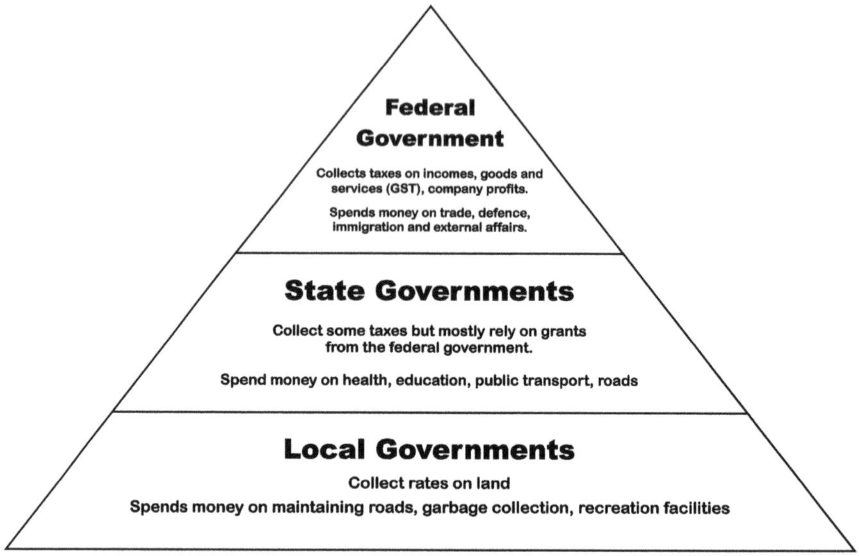

Figure 6.2 Levels of government in Australia

Councillors: elected representatives to local governments

Councils: another name for local governments, and the chambers where councillors meet

Mayor: head of a local government

Local governments also have elected members, called **councillors**, who sit in **councils**, which are like a local parliament. Councils have power to make by-laws on a range of topics. They are responsible for parks and recreation facilities, rubbish collection, town planning, some roads, and other local matters. The head of a local council is called a **mayor** or president. These local governments are not mentioned in the Constitution, though there have been proposals at different times for a referendum that would recognise them.

The three levels of government in Australia, their revenue sources and their main responsibilities are outlined in Figure 6.2.

C. Advantages and challenges

Federate: join together in a federal system of government

There are many reasons why Australia was designed as a federal system.[5] By **federating** as states, the colonies pooled their resources and increased their overall security (for example, by having a national military). They improved transport and no longer paid taxes to import goods from each other.

The system also promotes healthy competition: if one state creates an innovative law or policy, other states can follow. This gives us greater choice: if we don't like living in one state, we can move easily to another. We also gain a 'double democracy' because we elect representatives at both levels of government (or a triple democracy in our case, because we also vote at local council elections).[6]

However, our federal system also has many challenges. One, with the pandemic as the key exception, is that the Commonwealth government has gained greater lawmaking powers over time. This is known as **centralisation**, as power concentrates in the centre of the country, with less available to the states on the edges. Originally, the High Court interpreted the Constitution in favour of the states. It supported the **reserved powers doctrine**: the founding idea that the Commonwealth had limited, specific powers and anything residual (left over) was up to the states. Over time, however, this idea was left behind and the High Court interpreted the Constitution in favour of the Commonwealth. This was especially true with taxation powers during the Second World War, when more national resources were needed.

Centralisation: when a national government acquires greater lawmaking powers, at the expense of those held by state or regional governments

Reserved powers doctrine: principle that the federal Parliament has specific lawmaking powers, while the rest are left to the states

As a result, the Commonwealth now collects most of the money, but the states have most of the responsibility to deliver core, expensive services like schools, roads and hospitals. The technical term for this is **vertical fiscal imbalance** (VFI). VFI means that the national government (which sits 'above' the state governments) has more money than it needs, and the state governments cannot afford to pay for the services they need to deliver. Under section 96 of the Constitution, the federal government redistributes the revenue it gains from taxation by making grants to the states, but it can attach conditions to those grants saying how the money must be used. This leads to tensions and disagreements, especially when something goes wrong with a core service. For example, if there are not enough hospital beds or ambulances, the federal government might blame

Vertical fiscal imbalance: an imbalance in public revenue, where the federal government has most of the money and the States do not collect enough to deliver their key services

the states for not running the health system properly. In return, the states will say the federal government has not given them enough money to run it effectively.

Ultimately, like all relationships, the federal and state governments work well together at some times, and not so well at others. When there are clearly defined responsibilities between the two levels, this is known as **coordinative federalism**, as there are high levels of coordination.[7] When they are working well together on an equal basis, this is known as **cooperative federalism**. When the federal government dominates the states and determines their agenda, this is known as **coercive federalism**.

Coordinative federalism: when the federal and state governments have clearly defined responsibilities

Cooperative federalism: when the federal and state governments work well together

Coercive federalism: when the federal government dominates or unfairly influences the state governments

National Cabinet: meeting of the Prime Minister, Premiers and Chief Ministers

COAG: forum of leaders from the three levels of government (now replaced by National Cabinet)

It has long been said that centralisation and coercion characterise Australian federalism, but Australia's pandemic experience suggests the picture is more complicated. Because the states have primary responsibility for health, it was almost like returning to the reserved powers doctrine, which had otherwise been left behind. **National Cabinet**—a meeting of the Prime Minister, Premiers and Chief Ministers that began in March 2020—symbolised cooperation in trying times, but also disagreements between Premiers and the Prime Minister over border closures and other restrictions.

National Cabinet replaced **COAG** (the Council of Australian Governments) as the main forum where Australia's political leaders meet to discuss issues facing the nation. But it does not include the President of the Local Government Association, who previously attended COAG, which excludes our third level of government. National Cabinet has also faced ongoing criticism for its high levels of secrecy, and the Commonwealth, as it did in COAG, determines much of the agenda from the most powerful bargaining position.[8] How Australia's federal system will fare in the next major crisis remains to be seen.

4. SEPARATION OF POWERS

Both levels of government in Australia—national and state—are designed according to the **separation of powers**. This means that power is divided between three branches or arms of government. This is enshrined in the Constitution, which has separate chapters for parliament (Chapter 1), the executive government (Chapter 2) and the courts (Chapter 3).

Separation of powers: principle that says power should be divided between the legislature, executive, and judiciary

It is important to understand the difference between the separation of powers and federalism. Federalism refers to a vertical division of power between the national and state governments. At each of those levels, power is separated horizontally between parliament, the executive, and the courts.

The first branch of government is the **legislature**. This is a technical term for parliament because it enacts new legislation.

Legislature: a technical term for Parliament used when discussing the separation of powers

The second branch is the **executive**, which **administers** (uses) legislation in practice. The executive is the most difficult branch to understand. Often, if someone says 'the executive government', they are referring to Ministers: senior politicians, including the Prime Minister, who have responsibility for different policy areas. However, the executive is a broader concept, and it includes employees in all the agencies and departments that make up the **public service**. Government employees use legislation daily to make decisions that affect people. For example, employees in the immigration department make decisions under the *Migration Act 1958* (Cth) on whether temporary visas should be cancelled or renewed. Government employees in Centrelink, the Australian Taxation Office (ATO), the police services and intelligence agencies are all members of the executive branch of government.

Executive: branch of government that administers (uses) laws in practice

Administer: use laws in practice

Public service: government departments and agencies

In fact, the executive extends all the way up to the Governor-General and the King of England. It might seem strange that a graduate public service employee is in the same branch of government as King Charles (if you end up working in a government department, this can be your claim to fame). For this reason, some commentators have suggested that the executive should be split into a senior 'executive' branch (including the King, Governor-General and Ministers) and an administrative branch (the public service). This would be easier to understand, and it might still help you to think in this way. But there is a long history of the executive as one of the three branches of government, alongside courts and parliaments, and this is enshrined in the structure of our Constitution, so the meaning of the word is not likely to change.

Judiciary: technical term for the court system

The third branch is the **judiciary** (courts) which interpret laws and apply them to resolve disputes in individual cases. In Australia, the separation of judicial power from the other two branches of government is interpreted strictly by the High Court. This means courts are the only institution that can hear and decide legal cases.

These three branches of government and their different responsibilities are set out in Figure 6.3. This image captures the blurring between the executive and legislative branches in Australia, which we inherited from England. This blurring is explained below. In theory, an ideal separation of powers would have a clear distinction between each branch. A strict separation of powers is true of some countries, like the United States, where members of the executive branch of government (such as the Secretaries of State and Defence) do not also make laws in parliament.

It might seem obvious that parliament, government agencies and the courts perform these different tasks. But there is an important reason for this: we do not want too much power concentrated in too few hands. Imagine if our politicians determined what the laws were, then arrested you, then determined if you were guilty! The separation of powers aims to restrain government power, and it relies on a system of 'checks and balances' so the different arms can hold each other accountable. This idea is usually attributed to Baron de Montesquieu, a French Enlightenment philosopher who in 1748 wrote about the three branches of government in *The Spirit of the Laws*.

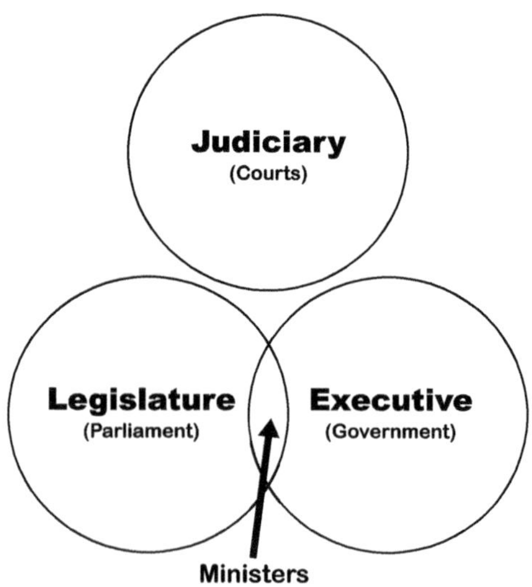

Figure 6.3 Separation of powers

Having courts that are independent of government is the most important part of this system. We need a court system for resolving disputes that is free from government interference. In other countries, courts are not fully independent and political influence on judges can be a major source of corruption.

Thankfully, this is not the case in Australia and other democratic nations. Our governments do, however, play an important role in appointing judges to the bench. This can be a very political exercise, particularly in the United States where the President is responsible for appointing judges to the Supreme Court. It is less of an issue in Australia, though the executive government can still appoint judges who are more likely to support Commonwealth interests over those of the states.[9]

In Australia, the separation of the judiciary is strict, but the line between executive and legislative power is blurred. Ministers are part of the executive branch because they are responsible for government departments in the public service. For example, the Home Affairs Minister is responsible for the Australian Federal Police, Australian Border Force, and the Australian Security Intelligence Organisation (ASIO). But Ministers are also part of the legislature because they are elected politicians who make laws in parliament. In fact, this is required by section 64 of the Constitution. Section 64 says that Ministers must sit in parliament within three months of being appointed.

This blurring of powers means that Ministers frequently introduce Bills that expand the powers of their own agencies. For example, the Attorney-General and Home Affairs Minister have been responsible for most of the counter-terrorism laws that have expanded the powers of federal police and Australia's domestic spy agency.

Why would our system of government blur the branches in this way, when the goal should be to separate power? It might sound like a problem, but it is intentional and designed to enhance **responsible government**. Responsible government is different from representative government. Representative government means a system of democratic elections, and responsible government means a political system where ministers sit in parliament. This makes ministers more accountable to the Australian people, as they are more visible and need to front up and answer questions. We inherited this system from the Westminster parliament in Britain.

Responsible government: a system of government where Ministers sit in Parliament, which blurs the legislative and executive branches

Question time: a regular, dedicated time in Parliament when ministers must answer questions without notice

Questions without notice: questions in parliament that ministers are not told about in advance, so they cannot prepare an answer

A core aspect of responsible government is **question time**, where ministers must respond to **questions without notice**. These are questions that ministers are not told about in advance, so they cannot prepare an answer (they can provide a written answer later, but they are expected to answer the questions immediately in person). Question time usually involves very heated debates between the two major political parties. It is used to 'catch out' the other side of politics, criticise them, or point out something they have done wrong. If you see politicians on the nightly news arguing loudly in parliament, it is often question time being shown.

You might not have heard about responsible government until now, but you might have heard about a controversy when Prime Minister Scott Morrison secretly took on multiple ministries during the pandemic. Throughout 2020 and 2021, he asked the Governor-General to appoint him as five extra ministers: for Health, Finance, Treasury, Home Affairs, Industry and Science. He did not tell the Australian people, or even most of the ministers who were already in those roles! It was not technically unlawful to do this, but the secrecy involved was a major problem for responsible government. How can we hold ministers responsible for something that goes wrong, if we do not know who the responsible minister is, and the rest of the government doesn't even know?

Solicitor-General: lawyer for the Commonwealth and second highest law officer in Australia after the Attorney-General

Once the story came out, Morrison said the extraordinary circumstances of the pandemic justified the appointments, as he might have needed to take over from someone who fell ill. But the secrecy of his plan was heavily criticised, including by the **Solicitor-General** and a former High Court Justice Virginia Bell, who ran an inquiry into the appointments. Justice Bell found that the levels of secrecy involved were 'corrosive of trust in government',[10] The Solicitor-General found that Morrison's actions 'fundamentally undermined' responsible government.[11]

5. RULE OF LAW

Overarching all these concepts is an idea that is crucial to our legal system but difficult to pin down to a single definition. The **rule of law** is an ideal that all countries should aim to achieve. Having the rule of law means that people are treated equally under the law, and the country's legal and political systems are free from corruption. In *Australian Communist Party v Commonwealth* (1951) 83 CLR 1, a famous High Court case about legislation that sought to ban Communist Party membership in Australia, Dixon J said that the rule of law 'forms an assumption' of the Australian Constitution.

Rule of law: a principle that says laws should be publicly accessible and clearly written, and that everyone should be treated equally under the law

A traditional definition of the rule of law comes from A V Dicey, a British legal theorist. In 1897, Dicey wrote that the rule of law will be present when three things are true. First, the country should be ruled by regular law rather than arbitrary power. Instead of kings and queens making decisions on a whim, through pure executive power, the government should be ruled by a parliament that enacts legislation. Second, everyone should be treated equally under the law. If the Prime Minister, a billionaire, or some other powerful person in society committed murder, they would be guilty like anyone else. There is no special treatment under the law. Third, Dicey believed that the courts, rather than a constitution, are the most effective way to protect individual rights.

This is a good definition of the rule of law, but it has some issues. We could have a society where everyone is treated equally under the law, but the laws are still terrible. Imagine, for example, that Australia had a criminal law that said a person will lose a hand for stealing a loaf of bread. This could be written down clearly in legislation and the law could apply equally to everyone. That would satisfy Dicey's definition of regular law, but it is not a society we would want to live in.

Put another way, there are formal requirements of the rule of law, but these are not enough to achieve an ideal legal system. A classic statement of these formal requirements comes from Lon Fuller. Writing in 1969, in a book called *The Morality of Law*, Fuller told a story about an unhappy king named Rex. He used this story to explain eight 'principles of legality'. These principles are eight failures that parliaments must avoid if they are to establish a valid system of law:

- a failure to achieve rules at all;
- a failure to publicise rules;
- the abuse of retrospective legislation;
- a failure to make rules understandable;
- the enactment of contradictory rules;
- the enactment of rules that require conduct beyond the powers of the affected party;

- introducing such frequent changes in the rules that subjects cannot adjust their conduct accordingly;
- inconsistency between the rules as announced and their application.

In other words, Fuller believed that laws should be publicly accessible, clearly written, applied consistently, and not contradictory or impossible to obey. The prohibition on **retrospective legislation** means parliaments should not make new laws that punish a person for something they did in the past. It would be unfair if somebody did something that was not a crime at the time but was later punished for it.

Retrospective legislation: laws that apply from a prior date so that a person can be punished for something that was not a crime when they did it

These formal requirements get us most of the way to a good legal system. However, some scholars argue that the rule of law will only be present where other, more substantive values relating to democracy, fairness, justice and equality are also upheld.[12] This gets into difficult philosophical questions about what makes a 'good' law, but it generally requires fair treatment and a minimum degree of protection for individual rights. The example of the stealing offence above would be clearly unfair according to our moral standards, and so would not uphold the rule of law.

The rule of law also requires that governments are accountable and not corrupt. Countries are often ranked on these measures according to a Rule of Law Index. In 2023, Australia was ranked 13th in the world according to the World Justice Project's Rule of Law Index.[13] That ranking acknowledges that there is very strong adherence to the rule of law in Australia, although we also had dropped several places from the rankings given five years earlier.

Substantive versions of the rule of law relate closely to human rights. The United Nations refers to them as 'two sides of the same principle'.[14] However, human rights are generally considered a separate concept.

In short, the rule of law is an ideal that governments should aspire to achieve. It means that laws should be publicly accessible and clearly written, and that everyone should be treated equally under the law. More substantive requirements—including ideas about justice and protecting individual rights—get us much closer to an ideal legal system. For more information on the rule of law, you can visit the website of the Rule of Law Institute (www.ruleoflaw.org.au), a not-for-profit organisation that aims to promote the rule of law in Australia.

KEY POINTS

- Australia is a liberal democracy with a federal system of government. Federalism means lawmaking powers are shared between the Commonwealth and state governments. This works well when governments cooperate, but it also creates tensions and disagreements.
- The separation of powers says that power should be shared between the legislature (parliament), the executive (government) and the judiciary (courts). This provides checks and balances and helps to ensure that too much power is not concentrated in too few hands.
- The rule of law is an ideal that all countries should aim to achieve. It means that laws should be clearly written and publicly accessible, that everyone should be treated equally under the law, and that governments should uphold notions of fairness, justice and equality.

DISCUSSION QUESTIONS

1. To what extent are liberalism and democracy compatible concepts?
2. On balance, do you think there are more advantages or disadvantages to a federal system of government?
3. What are the three branches of government, and why do we separate power between them?
4. How are legislative and executive powers blurred in Australia? Why is this done?
5. What is the difference between representative and responsible government?
6. What is the difference between the 'formal' and 'substantive' requirements of the rule of law?
7. Which countries provide good examples of upholding the rule of law, and which provide bad examples? Why have you chosen those countries?
8. Which countries currently rank above Australia in the World Justice Project's Rule of Law Index?

NOTES

1 Yale Law School (2008). *The Avalon Project: Declaration of the Rights of Man – 1789* (2008). Retrieved from: https://avalon.law.yale.edu/18th_century/rightsof.asp.

2 Museum of Australian Democracy at Old Parliament House (2024). ***Defining democracy: what is democracy?*** Retrieved from: https://www.moadoph.gov.au/explore/democracy/defining-democracy.

3 Griffiths, K., & Chan, I. (2024). Big money was spent on the 2022 election – but the party with the deepest pockets didn't win. ***The Conversation***, 1 February.

4 Ibid.

5 Galligan, B. (2001). ***Parliament's development of federalism*** (Research Paper 26). Canberra: Parliament of Australia.

6 Galligan, B. (1995). ***A federal republic: Australia's constitutional system of government***. Cambridge University Press.

7 French, R. (2004) Co-operative federalism: a constitutional reality or a political slogan. ***Federal Judicial Scholarship***, ***21***.

8 Dee, J., & Menzies, J. (2023). With the COVID crisis easing, is the National Cabinet still fit for purpose? ***The Conversation***, 28 April.

9 Williams, G. (2018). Kavanaugh circus couldn't happen here but we can't be complacent. ***The Australian***, 9 October.

10 Bell, V. (2022). ***Report of the inquiry into the appointment of the former Prime Minister to administer multiple departments*** (Commonwealth Government) 6.

11 Department of the Prime Minister and Cabinet (2022). ***Solicitor-General opinion: in the matter of the validity of the appointment of Mr Morrison to administer the Department of Industry, Science, Energy and Resources*** (Commonwealth Government) 23.

12 O'Donnell, G.A. (2004). Why the rule of law matters. ***Journal of Democracy***, ***15***(4), 32-46.

13 World Justice Project (2023). ***Rule of law index: rankings***. Retrieved from https://worldjusticeproject.org/rule-of-law-index/global.

14 United Nations (2005). ***Rule of law and human rights***. Retrieved from https://www.un.org/ruleoflaw/rule-of-law-and-human-rights.

Chapter 7

Justice

In this chapter, you will learn about:

- Different meanings of justice: procedural, social and more
- Restorative justice and circle sentencing
- Challenges that people face accessing justice

Does Australia's system of law and government achieve **justice**? You can think about this from many different perspectives. Justice is a complex concept with no single definition, but it captures many ideas that are important to our way of life, including fairness and equality. It helps us determine how wrongs can be righted, and whether procedures and outcomes are fair. Everyone should be able to access justice equally, but unfortunately this is not the case in practice.

Justice: a complex concept which captures many different ideas relating to fairness and equality

1. WHAT IS JUSTICE?

There is no single, accepted definition of justice, but it is usually associated with ideas of fairness. There are several ways to think about this.

First, justice involves different responses when harm or another wrong is done in society. One basic type of justice is **retribution**. If someone hurts you or your family, you might want to see them punished, or you might even want to harm them back. We all know the saying: 'an eye for an eye'.

Retribution: punishment inflicted as repayment for a harmful act

DOI: 10.4324/9781003433408-9

Criminal laws were built on this idea: when someone breaks the law, the state punishes them. The punishment should also be fair or 'just', in the sense of it being proportionate to the crime committed (you might have heard the saying: 'the punishment should fit the crime'). An offender is punished more if they kill someone, and less if they hurt someone or steal something. Increasingly, though, the criminal law is relying on other meanings of justice, which involve rehabilitating offenders and repairing the harm done to victims.

Compensation: the payment of money to repair harm

National Redress Scheme: scheme established to provide compensation for victims of institutional child sexual abuse

Justice can also be achieved through **compensation**: the payment of money to repair previous harm. Compensation is often an imperfect means of repairing serious harm but symbolically it can be very important. For example, the Royal Commission into Institutional Responses to Child Abuse, which investigated the institutional cover-up of child sexual abuse in Australia, recommended that the federal government establish a **National Redress Scheme** to provide compensation to victims. In Chapter 5, you learned about the compensation paid to child prisoners who suffered abuse in the Don Dale youth detention centre.

We can therefore think about justice *as* retribution, rehabilitation, compensation and other responses to harm. But we can also think about justice *for* different groups and individuals. Justice for a victim, their family or society might mean a lengthy prison term for the offender and a large amount of compensation. Justice for victims also means recognising their interests in court processes, like presenting a **victim impact statement** which explains the harm that was done to them.

Victim impact statement: prepared statement presented to a court that explains the impact of a crime on a victim or their family

Justice from the perspective of the offender might mean something different. It might mean they are allowed to participate in a counselling or similar program to address the underlying reasons why they committed the crime in the first place. For example, someone who keeps committing robberies to pay for their drug habit might be given the opportunity to enrol in a drug rehabilitation program to help them not to reoffend in the future. Or, justice might mean overturning the decision of a lower court, if a guilty verdict depended on key evidence that was obtained unlawfully by police.

Another important distinction is between procedural and substantive justice. We have **procedural justice** when processes are fair, and **substantive justice** when outcomes are fair. These can overlap and support each other—fair processes often lead to fair outcomes—but they are not the same thing. For example, imagine a person is having trouble qualifying for a welfare payment from Centrelink. They might be treated fairly and transparently according to the letter of the law (procedural justice), but they are denied the payment when morally we think they should have it (a lack of substantive justice).

Procedural justice: when processes are fair

Substantive justice: when outcomes are fair

In policing research and practice, procedural justice refers to strategies used by police to build trust and legitimacy. **Procedural justice policing** is where police officers treat people with respect and give them an opportunity to have their voices heard. There is strong evidence that this makes people more likely to obey the law, and more likely to report crimes to the police.[1] This helps to reduce crime in society without the same need for harsh punishments.

Procedural justice policing: when police officers engage respectfully with communities and give people an opportunity to have their voices heard

Substantive justice means opportunities and outcomes are distributed fairly across society. This is usually called **distributive justice** or social justice. **Social justice** refers to efforts designed to remedy inequalities in society. This is not easy to achieve, because strategies for fixing inequality can seem unequal at first glance. There is a well-known cartoon, shown in Figure 7.1, that captures this idea.

Distributive justice: when resources, outcomes and opportunities are distributed fairly across society

Social justice: efforts to address inequalities in society

In the first frame (labelled 'equality'), all three characters have one box to stand on. Even with a box to stand on, the youngest boy still cannot see the game.

In the second frame ('labelled equity'), the man's box is given to the youngest boy. The man now has no boxes, but he can see over the fence anyway, so he does not need one. The middle boy has one box, which is just as much as he needs. His box did not need to be redistributed, and if it were, he would not be able to see over the fence. The youngest boy now has two boxes and can finally watch the game.

Figure 7.1 Equality vs equity.
Source: Interaction Institute for Social Change. Artist: Angus Maguire (2016)

On one level, the cartoon simply tells us that it was nice for the man to give his box to the boy. The boy can now see the game and everyone is happy. But there is a more complex, serious point: distributing things equally is not always the fairest thing to do, or the best way to fix problems in society. Formal **equality** means everyone has exactly the same thing or same amount, whereas **equity** means giving more to those who have less. The distribution of boxes is technically ***unequal***: the youngest boy has two boxes, the middle has one, and the man has none. But the result is fairer overall.

Equality: distributing things equally

Equity: redistributing things to address inequality

Of course, debating these kinds of issues for an entire country becomes much more complicated. Working out who has enough, who deserves more, and who needs the most help leads to many heated debates. Welfare schemes, scholarships and other financial payments can lead to criticisms that some groups are receiving special treatment. As in the cartoon, however, the purpose of special payments like these is precisely to make things more equal by reducing some existing inequality.

In lectures on this topic, I ask my students to imagine I have $1,000 to distribute between them. (I'm sure they would like it if this was not just a hypothetical exercise.) I give them two options: I could give them all $10 each (for 100 students) or I could give $1,000 to one student who proves to me that they really need it (because they cannot afford their textbooks, are suffering at home, or are experiencing some other hardship). Nearly every student in the class puts up their hand to support the second option (or they come up with a slight variation, like having two $500 scholarships). Gaining $10 is only a very small benefit to 99 students who don't really need it. With current rates of inflation, it would hardly buy you lunch. But $1,000 for one student who is struggling more than the others could help that student get through the trimester and eventually complete their degree. The first option is technically more equal, but the value of the $1,000 is lost if it is divided up into almost meaningless amounts.

Maybe I just have nice students (and I do), but the question also shows that dividing things equally is not always the fairest thing to do. There are still no easy answers, though, to these kinds of problems. When I increase the amount to $10,000 and ask my students if they would like $100 each, or a $10,000 scholarship for one student, I can see their hesitation. Most hands go halfway up, then pause. Some students put them back down. Some put them up more slowly than they did the first time. Some stay in the middle and don't commit either way. Many look around the room to see what others are doing. Perhaps there are limits to their kindness, but I think this has more to do with valid perceptions that the redistribution has 'gone too far'. Their hesitation comes from a more complex calculation they are making, some consciously, some subconsciously. Giving $100 to 100 students provides a relatively significant benefit to a lot of people. No one knows what the disadvantage to the one student involves, so maybe $10,000 is more than they need. They also don't know how that student would be chosen, and what kind of evidence might be needed to get the scholarship. If I handed out the money on the spot without thinking about it much, that would seem quite unfair.

They are right to hesitate, because it is very difficult to decide how resources can be distributed most fairly. A **utilitarian** perspective, associated with the philosopher Jeremy Bentham, would say that governments should aim to maximise happiness or advantage for the greatest number of people. In the examples above, this would normally mean giving $10 or $100 to each student. This sounds like a good idea because it maximises happiness overall. Still, though, giving $10 to everyone will not increase anyone's happiness very much. The fact that they all

Utilitarian: approach to decision-making that aims to maximise happiness for the most people

put up their hands to support the $1,000 scholarship suggests that most happiness would instead be gained by giving all the money to one student. Happiness is not increased only by receiving a benefit, but also by helping others.

The second example, giving $100 to each student, is more clearly utilitarian. On balance, it seems that most students would be happiest with $100 each, and some might even be annoyed if one student got $10,000. There may be many other students who would benefit from having that money but miss out. So it seems best to divide it up equally. However, we still can't accurately calculate how happy they would all be with $100, or how happy the one student would be with $10,000. It becomes even more complicated when we start weighing some people's unhappiness against the happiness of others. Perhaps a few people would be extremely unhappy to the point of anger and protest. Could that vocal minority outweigh the happiness of all?

So utilitarian approaches tend towards equal distribution, but in reality, it is much more complicated. An ongoing issue, whatever decision is made, is that the interests of the majority tend to outweigh those of smaller groups and individuals. We spoke about some of these risks with democracy in the previous chapter. Essentially, 99 students have the power to decide whether one other student gets the money or not. If they were less kind than my students, the 99 might not even care about the struggling student because they all want $100 or even $10. Unfortunately, human nature means that many people in society can be comfortable with this approach: if they get a benefit and are happy, it does not matter what happens to someone else. At its worst, a utilitarian approach can mean that minority groups are actively disadvantaged in favour of the majority. Strictly speaking, if removing the rights of a minority group would advantage most people, a utilitarian approach would say this is okay.

Deontology: branch of philosophy that focuses on ethics and the inherent morality of different choices

This is where deontology steps in. **Deontology** is a branch of philosophy that focuses on whether choices are good or bad, morally and ethically speaking, and not on their consequences. It is most closely associated with the German philosopher Immanuel Kant. Deontology is about the inherent fairness in the choices we make. It comes from the Greek word ***deon***, meaning 'duty'. In other words, as members of a common society, we have a duty to do the right thing to others. Deontology draws a 'line in the sand' that we should not cross, even if it would benefit us.[2] It is about respecting the inherent humanity of other people and valuing them as ends in themselves—not treating them as a means to some end that would benefit us.

A simple example relates to honesty. Many people believe we should never lie, even if we would gain some benefit from it. There is inherent good in honesty, and inherent bad in dishonesty, which provides us a sort of moral compass for a life well lived. Put another way, we should always try to do the right thing, even if it disadvantages us. Of course, agreeing on what these ethical rules are can be very difficult, and they differ across societies and over time. But this at least gives us an additional and different framework, beyond a utilitarian approach, to maximise fairness in society.

A leading modern philosopher on justice is Michael J Sandel, who gave famous lectures on the topic at Harvard University. In his book ***Justice: What's the Right Thing to Do?***, Sandel explains that 'morality means something more—something to do with the proper way for human beings to treat each other'.[3] He defines justice according to three themes: 'maximising welfare, respecting freedom, and promoting virtue'.[4] In other words, justice must mean something more than a cost-benefit analysis.

We can apply these ideas to the theories and principles we learned about in the previous chapter. Liberalism, democracy, the separation of powers, and the rule of law all have importance beyond their utilitarian value. We will also look at human rights in Chapter 9. An ethical approach says we should aim to uphold these ideals at all times, even if the consequences might involve some reduced practical benefit. Australia's counterterrorism laws, for example, impact on liberty, privacy, free speech and many other rights for the purposes of preventing terrorism. You will read more about these laws in Chapter 14. Even if a law helps us to prevent terrorism effectively, we must always ask whether it crosses a moral or ethical 'line in the sand'. At the same time, governments face difficult challenges in balancing our rights to liberty, privacy, and free speech against our rights to safety and security.

A famous idea can help us think more about what justice means and how societies can best achieve it. In *A Theory of Justice*, the philosopher John Rawls proposed a thought experiment known as the '**veil of ignorance**'. Forget everything you know about society and your place in it. Imagine you are creating a new one. You should debate with your friends or classmates what the rules of this new society should be, and how wealth and other benefits should be distributed. Importantly, when you create this society, you have no idea of who you will be or the cards you will be dealt. You could end up being the poorest person, the richest person, or anywhere in between. How would you design this

Veil of ignorance: thought experiment designed by philosopher John Rawls, where we imagine what a society would look like if we did not know our place in it society? Would it differ from the one we live in now? This is a useful exercise that has stood the test of time, because we could all have ended up in different circumstances to those we are in now. It helps us think about whether the society we live in is fair and how everyone should be treated.

2. DUE PROCESS

Procedural justice is achieved when processes and procedures are fair. This is particularly important when citizens deal with courts or government departments. In the court system, it is captured in the idea of due process. (In Australian law, it is technically more correct to say '**procedural fairness**' or '**natural justice**', but the more American term 'due process' has stuck.)

Procedural fairness: another name for due process

Natural justice: another name for due process

Due process: requirement that everyone should receive a fair hearing of their case in court

Due process is the requirement that people receive a fair hearing of their case in a court. As Chisholm and Nettheim explain, '[t]he fundamental rule of "due process" and "natural justice" is that no person shall be judged unheard. There must be a hearing, and the hearing must be fair'.[5] You might have heard about the right to a fair trial. This is very similar, but it comes from the common law (case law) instead of a human rights document.

Notice: requirement that everyone should know the case and evidence against them

Publicity: requirement that court proceedings should be open for everyone to see

Open court: a court that is open for everyone to see

Due process has many specific principles and requirements.[6] One is **notice**, meaning that individuals must know the case against them. In criminal trials, this means all the evidence from police and prosecutors must be disclosed to defendants so they can argue their innocence. In civil matters, such as divorce proceedings or a contract dispute, there is an exchange of documents between the parties. Another principle is **publicity**, meaning that courts should be open for everyone to see. There are some exceptions (like national security matters and children's courts) but otherwise it is an **open court** system. You can walk into any court in Australia and watch the proceedings. Members of the public with no connection to a case may not do this often, but the option is there. The idea is to create a transparent system of justice in which everyone can see what is happening.

In the courtroom, both parties present their case in front of a judge. This is known as an **adversarial system**. They must follow the rules of evidence, which determine the types of information that can and cannot be put before the court. For example, if police collected evidence from the defendant's house without first obtaining a warrant, that evidence would be considered prejudicial and excluded from the courtroom. **Prejudicial evidence** is evidence that unfairly suggests the defendant is guilty of a crime. There are other complex rules relating to hearsay, character witnesses, and expert opinion evidence, which you will read about in Chapter 11.

Adversarial system: a court system where parties oppose each other

Prejudicial evidence: evidence that would unfairly suggest a person is guilty of a crime

Standards of proof require that cases are proven to a high degree of reliability. In criminal matters, the prosecution must prove **beyond a reasonable doubt** that a person committed the crime. This is a very high standard that means a jury must be satisfied there is no reasonable doubt the person is guilty. The jury trial itself is another core aspect of due process.

Standards of proof: requirements that court cases be proven to a specified level of certainty

Beyond a reasonable doubt: standard of proof in criminal proceedings

In criminal matters, the **burden of proof** is placed on the prosecution. This means it is the prosecution's responsibility to prove that an accused person is guilty. The accused person is not required to prove their innocence. This is similar to the **presumption of innocence**. A person must always be considered innocent, unless and until a magistrate or jury has determined they are guilty of a crime.

Burden of proof: the responsibility to prove something in court

Presumption of innocence: the principle that everyone is considered innocent until they are found guilty in a court of law

In civil matters, cases are decided by a magistrate or judge (and, less often, a jury) on the **balance of probabilities**. This means, put simply, that the stronger of the two arguments should be preferred.

Balance of probabilities: civil standard of proof, which favours the stronger case

Impartiality requires that court cases are overseen by a magistrate or judge who acts like an independent referee. If a judge has a conflict of interest (for example, because they know one of the parties) they must

Impartiality: requirement that judges are independent and do not have conflicts of interest

Recuse: when a judge steps down from a case due to a conflict of interest

recuse themselves from the case. This means they step down and let another judge hear the case instead.

Appeal: challenge a decision in a higher court

When a case concludes, either party can **appeal** the decision. This means they challenge the decision in a higher court. There are complex rules that determine when parties can appeal a case. You will read more about these in Chapter 12.

Legal representation: having a lawyer to contest your case in court

Stayed: when a court case is delayed by a judge's order

Finally, there is no formal right to legal representation in Australia, but the common law protects it to some degree. Having **legal representation** means having a lawyer to contest your case. This is not strictly guaranteed, but a judge can elect to have a court case **stayed** (delayed) until adequate representation can be found. Under common law, this is considered an aspect of the right to a fair trial.

3. FROM RETRIBUTION TO REHABILITATION

Punishment and compensation are still common ways to achieve justice in Australia, but courts are increasingly relying on more nuanced approaches. In the criminal law, there is increasing recognition that putting people in prison is neither helpful in reducing crime nor cost effective. In 2023, the cost of detaining someone in prison for one year was $147,900—a lot more than most salaries![7] Australia has some of the highest recidivism rates in the world,[8] so this money is spent again and again, for no long-term benefit to the offender or community.

Recidivism: when people reoffend after being released from prison

Recidivism is when someone is released from prison, then reoffends and ends up back in prison. The more people who can be helped not to reoffend, the fewer crimes committed and the more money saved.

Therapeutic jurisprudence: court processes that promote the wellbeing of offenders and victims

An important idea that can help is therapeutic jurisprudence. **Therapeutic jurisprudence** (TJ) is a catch-all term for court processes that aim to address the underlying causes of crime by promoting wellbeing for both offenders and victims. Victims have a greater role to play in court processes, and offenders are required to participate in rehabilitation, counselling or other therapeutic programs to address underlying, contributing issues such as drug addiction, unemployment, and social isolation. Examples of therapeutic jurisprudence in practice include specialist drug and mental health courts, which aim to connect offenders with appropriate and individualised support services.

Another is **restorative justice**. Restorative justice (RJ) processes aim to repair the harms caused by crime. They typically involve mediation or dispute resolution processes between the victim and offender. When these involve other people as well, such as lawyers, police or family members, they are called **conferences**. RMIT's Centre for Innovative Justice usefully describes what RJ involves:

> As a practice, restorative justice processes most commonly bring together people affected by harm in a safe, structured and facilitated way, to talk about what happened, how they were impacted and how the harm can be repaired or addressed.[9]

Restorative justice: alternative means of resolving cases, usually through mediation and other dispute resolution processes

Conference: in restorative justice, a meeting between the offender, victim and other people which provides a safe place to talk about the crime

In other words, instead of a court simply punishing the offender and putting them in prison, RJ supports victims and offenders to work together for better outcomes. The overall goals are to repair the harm done, promote healing, and restore things to the way they were (as far as possible) before the crime was committed. Of course, this approach is more suitable for certain types of crimes, where both victim and offender are suitable candidates for conferencing and are willing to work together.

Similar approaches to TJ and RJ can be seen in Indigenous courts and **circle sentencing**. These have been developed across the country in both urban and remote areas. Circle sentencing is a mediation process based on traditional Indigenous practices. It was introduced into Canada's legal system in the early 1990s, and the first Australian trial took place on the south coast of NSW in 2002.[10] In circle sentencing, Indigenous elders and community members meet with lawyers and a magistrate to determine an appropriate sentence.

Circle sentencing: mediation process based on traditional Indigenous practices

Circle sentencing has aims beyond repairing harm and promoting healing,[11] so it is not strictly a TJ or RJ approach. However, it relies on a similar and more nuanced concept of justice compared to simple retribution. As Marchetti and Daly explain, a key purpose of Indigenous courts and circle sentencing is to provide a more culturally appropriate form of justice:

> The aim has been to make court processes more culturally appropriate, to engender greater trust between Indigenous communities and judicial officers, and to permit a more informal and open exchange of information about defendants and their cases. Indigenous people, organisations, elders, family and kin group members are encouraged to participate in the sentencing process and to provide officials with insight into the offence, the character of victim–offender relations, and an offender's readiness to change.[12]

This comment captures the complex, nuanced and culturally diverse nature of justice, beyond the basic idea of courts punishing people for their crimes.

Justice reinvestment: when governments redirect funds from prisons to community-based strategies which address the underlying causes of crime

A final, related concept is **justice reinvestment**. This is where governments redirect funds from prisons to community-based strategies so that people are less likely to commit crimes in the first place.[13] Justice reinvestment strategies can mean increased funding for health services, housing, and employment. To be classed as justice reinvestment (as many other government strategies invest in those areas), the funding should target communities judged to be at higher risk of criminal behaviour.

There is a growing body of evidence suggesting that justice reinvestment can reduce crime while delivering significant savings to government. A trial of justice reinvestment strategies in Bourke, in western NSW, saved nearly $3 million for the local economy while making significant gains in criminal justice.[14] Breaches of bail conditions fell by 14 per cent, the number of days people spent in custody decreased by 42 per cent, and the number of charges for the top five criminal offences fell by 38 per cent.[15] This shows again that justice can be achieved in many different ways, and that effective outcomes can be achieved outside recurring cycles of prisons and punishment.

4. ACCESS TO JUSTICE

It is essential for the rule of law that all Australians have equal opportunity to access the justice system. While courts and legal services are available to everyone in theory, in practice there are many barriers to accessing the legal system. Rice defined **access to justice** in these terms:

> The idea of 'access to justice' is ... the capacity to understand the law, to get legal advice, to get legal assistance and representation, and to use public legal institutions such as the courts. It requires an ability to, for example, understand, communicate, travel and pay, and also requires the means to overcome the inability to do any of those things.[16]

Access to justice: the ability of people to source legal advice and representation, and to use the court system

The most obvious barrier to accessing justice is not having enough money to pay for a lawyer. The cost of a lawyer can vary greatly but they are invariably expensive. A **solicitor** can cost a few hundred dollars per hour, and a junior **barrister** could charge up to $5,000 to represent you for one day in court. For an experienced Senior Counsel, you could even pay up to $10,000, just for a single day! Even at the lower end, these costs stack up very quickly. It is difficult to put a price on individual cases, as they vary in length and complexity. For example, though, an average family law matter might cost around $30,000; they often exceed $100,000, and complex cases can cost $200,000 and more. This is unaffordable even for people on good salaries. For those on a low income or unemployed, it is simply out of reach.

Solicitor: lawyer who briefs barristers on cases, but can also represent clients in court

Barrister: specialist advocate who represents clients in court

These very high costs prevent many Australians from accessing justice when they need it most. As the Law Council of Australia explains, the cost of legal services compounds disadvantage that people experience in housing, health and many other areas:

> The cost of legal services presents a barrier to justice for people experiencing economic disadvantage, many of whom will have public housing, health, social security and other needs. Legal fees and court costs can prevent people from obtaining legal advice and pursuing resolution of legal problems through the court system. This may compromise their safety, rights, or entitlements.[17]

In addition, many people experiencing economic disadvantage have personal and psychological issues that make accessing justice difficult. They may even fail to recognise and understand when they have a legal issue worth addressing:

> People experiencing economic disadvantage may fail to recognise legal problems or may not know how to respond if they do. They may have personal and psychological barriers which affect their capacity to resolve legal problems, or they may struggle with the complexity of relevant laws. They may also lack the time to deal with legal problems, particularly if they are primary caregivers.[18]

Beyond those experiencing economic disadvantage, there are many individuals and groups in Australia that struggle to access justice. These include older people, children, people who are homeless, the LGBTIQA+ community, migrants and refugees, prisoners and detainees, people with a disability, Aboriginal and Torres Strait Islander peoples, people who experience domestic and family violence, and people from rural, regional and remote areas.

Legal Aid: government-funded offices which provide free legal advice and services to people in need

Difficulties accessing justice are mitigated to some extent by Legal Aid. There is a government-funded **Legal Aid** office in each state and territory. These provide legal advice and services (including court representation) to people facing social and economic disadvantage. However, limited funding and high demand for their services mean that strict means tests (based on a person's salary and assets, like whether they own a car or house) are used to determine who can receive assistance.

There are many people in Australia who cannot afford a lawyer but also do not qualify for Legal Aid. This has been called the 'missing middle',[19] but it is not only middle- or even low-income earners who miss out. According to estimates by the Productivity Commission, 13% of Australians live below the poverty line, but only the bottom 8% of households are likely to meet Legal Aid's income and asset tests.[20] An economic analysis published in late 2023 found that $484 million was urgently needed for Legal Aid to avoid an 'immediate threat of supply failure'.[21] That is not even fixing the supply problem; it is just enough to stop the system from collapsing. Australia's Legal Aid services are facing a very real crisis.

Community legal centres: independent community organisations that provide legal advice and services to communities

Community legal centres (CLCs) also play a crucial role in improving access to justice, but they face similar limitations. CLCs are independent community organisations that provide free legal information, advice and services, especially to disadvantaged communities. They also contribute to law reform debates and policy development by producing reports and writing submissions to parliamentary inquiries.

Their services are particularly important when community members face systemic disadvantage compounded by one or more legal issues. CLCs work closely with different community organisations, such as mental health services, to address these compounding issues as early as possible. These significant benefits are also provided at a reasonable cost to government:

> The services provided by CLCs are … delivered at very low cost to government. CLCs are extremely efficient, leveraging volunteer and pro bono support to maximise the total hours, dollar value and range of services they provide. Despite this, there is significant unmet demand for legal assistance services which cannot be met without additional funding.[22]

Despite providing cost-effective benefits to communities, CLCs face a massive funding shortfall. In 2023, more than 200,000 people who sought help from CLCs were turned away due to a lack of funding and resources.[23] The problem is only likely to get worse with rising inflation and a cost-of-living crisis. Without more funding, the system simply cannot help everyone in Australia who needs to access justice.

5. THE ROLE OF GOVERNMENT

Funding Legal Aid and CLCs is just one of the many ways that governments can improve justice in Australia. Parliaments enact laws that shape many aspects of justice, including new offences for domestic and family violence, or court procedures that allow victims better outcomes.

Living in a democracy means we can expect governments to reduce these and other inequalities in society. They can do this by investing more money into health, education, employment and welfare. However, given that governments ultimately have limited resources, choosing where to invest those resources presents ongoing challenges with no easy solutions. Different political parties also tend to have very different ideas as to how taxpayer money should be spent.

We should continually ask whether Australia is a fair and 'just' society. Do we achieve justice, socially, legally, politically and economically? Do different groups in society have equal resources, opportunities and outcomes? Can everyone who needs to access the justice system afford it?

Compared to many other countries, Australia is a relatively fair society (we have often been called the 'land of the fair go'). However, it should be clear from the discussion above and a quick browse of the daily news that many groups in Australian society face ongoing disadvantage. These include people who are unemployed, people who are homeless, people with a disability, Aboriginal and Torres Strait Islander communities, refugee and migrant communities and many more. Justice means many different things, so how might justice for these groups be improved?

KEY POINTS

- Justice means many different things but is generally associated with ideas of fairness and equality. In the criminal law, it can simply mean retribution—punishing a person for a crime—but courts are increasingly recognising the need to repair harms and rehabilitate offenders.
- Due process is a core aspect of justice. It requires that a person knows the case against them and has their case heard in an impartial court according to the rules of evidence.
- The high costs of legal services and a lack of adequate funding for Legal Aid and community legal centres means that many Australians cannot afford to access the justice system.

DISCUSSION QUESTIONS

1. If a person harmed you or your family, what type of justice would you want?
2. What are some different ways justice can be achieved?
3. What are the requirements of due process?
4. Why is there a need to rehabilitate offenders rather than simply punishing them?
5. How could justice be improved in Australia for groups experiencing disadvantage?
6. Is Australia a fair and 'just' society compared to others around the world?

NOTES

1 Madon, N., & Murphy, K. (2021). Police bias and diminished trust in police: a role for procedural justice? ***Policing: An International Journal*, *44***(6), 1031-1045.

2 Stanford Encyclopedia of Philosophy (2020). ***Deontological ethics***. Retrieved from: https://plato.stanford.edu/entries/ethics-deontological/.

3 Sandel, M. J. (2009). ***Justice: what's the right thing to do?*** Farrar, Straus and Giroux.

4 Ibid.

5 Chisholm, R., & Nettheim, G. (2002). ***Understanding law: an introduction to Australia's legal system*** (6th ed.). LexisNexis Butterworths.

6 See ibid.

7 Schlicht, M. (2023). ***The cost of prisons in Australia: 2023***. Institute of Public Affairs. Retrieved from: https://ipa.org.au/research/rights-and-freedoms/the-cost-of-prisons-in-australia-2023.

8 Ibid.

9 Centre for Innovative Justice, RMIT University (2024). ***What is restorative justice?*** Retrieved from: https://cij.org.au/opencircle/what-is-restorative-justice/.

10 Potas, I., et al. (2003). ***Circle sentencing in New South Wales: a review and evaluation***. Judicial Commission of NSW and NSW Aboriginal Justice Advisory Council.

11 Marchetti, E., & Daly, K. (2004). Indigenous courts and justice practices in Australia (Trends & Issues in Crime and Criminal Justice, No. 277). Australian Institute of Criminology.

12 Ibid.

13 Willis, M., & Kapira, M. (2018). Justice reinvestment in Australia: a review of the literature (Research Report No. 9). Australian Institute of Criminology.

14 Allam, L. (2018). Aboriginal-led justice project saves rural town almost $3m. ***The Guardian***, 28 November.

15 Ibid.

16 Rice, S. (2011). Access to a lawyer in rural Australia: thoughts on the evidence we need. ***Deakin Law Review, 16***(1), 13-46.

17 Law Council of Australia (2018). ***The Justice Project: final report***. Canberra: Law Council of Australia.

18 Ibid.

19 Productivity Commission (2014). ***Productivity Commission inquiry report*** (No 72). Canberra: Australian Government.

20 Ibid.

21 Impact Economics and Policy (2023). ***Justice on the brink: stronger Legal Aid for a better legal system***. Retrieved from: https://www.nationallegalaid.org/resources/justice-on-the-brink/.

22 National Association of Community Legal Centres (2018). Submission to Australian Government – federal budget 2018-2019. National Association of Community Legal Centres.

23 Richards, S. (2024). 'Unprecedented' demand means Australia's community legal centres are having to turn people away. *ABC News*, 8 February.

Chapter 8

First Nations peoples and the law

In this chapter, you will learn about:

- Indigenous justice and sovereignty
- *Terra nullius*, settlement, and the High Court's *Mabo* decision
- The Voice referendum and constitutional recognition.

Diverse Aboriginal and Torres Strait Islander cultures have existed in Australia for at least 65,000 years. The Commonwealth of Australia has existed only since Federation in 1901: a little more 120 years ago.

Indigenous communities are our First Peoples with a rich culture and history, but they face ongoing disadvantage compared to Australia's population as a whole. There are many reasons for this, but a key part of the story is how Indigenous peoples have been treated under our legal system. Since Australia was colonised by Britain, the legal system has failed to adequately recognise Indigenous peoples and the important role they play in our society.

This chapter begins by explaining how Australia could achieve greater justice for its First Peoples. Next, it introduces the concept of sovereignty. This traditionally means power over a given territory but it has many other meanings. The remainder of the chapter focuses on the settlement of Australia by Britain, the High Court's landmark *Mabo* decision, and the 2023 referendum on a Voice to Parliament.

1. JUSTICE

Ideas about justice help us understand what is fair or 'right' and how inequalities in society can be reduced. In the previous chapter, we discussed social and distributive justice: whether opportunities and outcomes are spread fairly across

DOI: 10.4324/9781003433408-10

society. According to these and other meanings, it is clear that Australia's Indigenous communities face significant injustice. Indigenous peoples experience systemic disadvantage compared to the non-Indigenous population, including lower life expectancy, lower rates of literacy and numeracy, and higher rates of unemployment and preventable illness.

Closing the Gap: national agreement that sets out 19 targets across 17 areas to help reduce gaps in outcomes between Indigenous and non-Indigenous Australians

Closing the Gap is a national agreement that sets out 19 targets across 17 areas to help reduce these gaps between Indigenous and non-Indigenous Australians. All three levels of government (federal, state and local) are parties to the agreement. However, progress on reducing the gaps remains extremely slow, and on some measures the gaps have widened. In January 2024, the Productivity Commission released a damning report, finding that:

> governments are not adequately delivering on this commitment. Despite some pockets of good practice, progress in implementing the Agreement's Priority Reforms has, for the most part, been weak and reflects … business-as-usual approaches. The disparate actions and ad hoc changes have not led to improvements that are noticeable and meaningful for Aboriginal and Torres Strait Islander people. This raises questions about whether governments have fully grasped the scale of change required to their systems, operations and ways of working to deliver the unprecedented shift they have committed to.[1]

In March 2024, data from the Productivity Commission showed that only five of the 19 targets were on track to be met, and 4 had worsened over time.[2]

One of the worsening targets is imprisonment rates, which remain a 'national tragedy'.[3] Aboriginal and Torres Strait Islander Peoples make up less than 4 per cent of the Australian population, but 33% of the prison population.[4] Another way to measure imprisonment rates is how many prisoners there are per 100,000 of a given demographic background. For the Australian population as a whole, there are 202 prisoners per 100,000 people. For Aboriginal and Torres Strait Islander peoples, the figure is 2,442 per 100,000: around 12 times higher.[5] More than three-quarters (78%) of the Indigenous prison population had previously been imprisoned as adults.[6]

These startling figures result from intergenerational cycles of poverty, grief, and trauma. This began with the colonisation of Australia by Britain, which dispossessed Indigenous peoples from their lands and severed their traditional connections.[7] As the Closing the Gap targets show, Aboriginal and Torres Strait Islander peoples experience multiple, related forms of disadvantage. These experiences accumulate over a lifetime and are passed on through the generations, from one to the next.

A related problem is that Indigenous communities, particularly those in remote areas, face significant hurdles in accessing justice. A lack of available legal advice and fewer alternative sentencing options (such as drug and alcohol rehabilitation programs) contribute to these significantly higher rates of imprisonment.[8]

Further reducing these gaps would significantly improve justice for Indigenous peoples. Ideally, there will come a time where there are no gaps in outcomes and opportunities for Indigenous peoples compared to non-Indigenous Australians.

Importantly, however, achieving justice for Australia's First Peoples can mean something more. Justice can also mean that the Australian government recognises and apologises for past wrongdoing that fuels these ongoing cycles of disadvantage.

On 13 February 2008, Prime Minister Kevin Rudd made a formal apology to Australia's Indigenous peoples. He offered the apology in the federal parliament to a crowded public gallery watching on, with thousands more outside.

The apology focused on the **Stolen Generations**: successive generations of Indigenous children who were forcibly removed from their families and taught to adopt white culture. This was part of the Australian government's policy of assimilation: the idea that other cultures should reject their heritage and become part of the dominant white community. Under the policy of **assimilation**, up to 50,000 Indigenous children were forcibly taken by the state.[9]

Stolen Generations: successive generations of Indigenous who were forcibly taken from their families and taught to adopt white culture

Assimilation: government policy that said other cultures should reject their heritage and become part of the white community

The Stolen Generations are part of Australia's recent history. Indigenous children were still being removed from their families as late as the early 1970s, and some of the schools and missions housing the stolen children did not close until the 1980s.[10] Concerns about Indigenous children being removed from their families still continue, as the rate of Indigenous children in the child protection system is more than ten times higher than that for non-Indigenous children.[11] Child protection rates are another of the worsening Close the Gap targets.

In the apology, Prime Minister Rudd offered the following words:

> We apologise for the laws and policies of successive parliaments and governments that have inflicted profound grief, suffering and loss on these our fellow Australians.
>
> We apologise especially for the removal of Aboriginal and Torres Strait Islander children from their families, their communities and their country.
>
> For the pain, suffering and hurt of these stolen generations, their descendants and for their families left behind, we say sorry.[12]

These words were historic and significant. In the apology, Rudd admitted that words were not enough to address the significant and ongoing disadvantage faced by Indigenous communities. But this was the first time in Australia's history that the federal government had recognised its past wrongs and admitted the profound impact of its laws and policies on Indigenous communities.

Voice to Parliament: proposed representative body that would allow representatives of First Nations communities to advise the Parliament and executive government

It took 15 years for the federal government to take action this significant again. In October 2023, a referendum was held on whether an Indigenous **Voice to Parliament** should be created. The Voice was to be an advisory body that would allow First Nations representatives to speak to the Parliament and executive government on issues affecting their communities. Australians voted against this proposal, and so the Constitution still fails to recognise—or even mention—our First Peoples. Below, we will trace the history of Australia's legal system, including a referendum in 1967 that was successful but left work remaining to be done. Before we get to that detail, it will help to understand the concept of sovereignty.

2. SOVEREIGNTY

Monarch: King or Queen

Sovereign: a ruler with absolute power over a given territory, often used interchangeably with King or Queen

The French political theorist Jean Bodin, writing in 1576, defined sovereignty as 'supreme power over citizens and subjects unrestrained by the laws'.[13] This meaning is often used interchangeably with **monarch**, meaning a king or queen. A **sovereign** is a ruler with unrestrained executive power over people in a defined territory. (You might have even heard of a sovereign as a gold coin: a British one-pound coin with an image of the King or Queen on it.)

Today, sovereignty more commonly describes the legal and political power of a national government. In Chapter 6, you learned about Rousseau and the **social contract**, the hypothetical agreement where we agree to pass up our inherent lawmaking power to the sovereign. We also refer to **sovereign states** as members of an international community. Holding official status as a sovereign state enables a country to deal with other states through treaties and foreign policy. The United Nations is an international organisation made up of 193 member states. These are all recognised sovereign states which participate in the United Nations General Assembly. The General Assembly is similar to an international parliament, where sovereign states debate global law and policy issues including economic development, peace and security, and international law. You will learn more about international law in the next chapter.

Social contract: the hypothetical agreement we enter into as citizens living under a government, which grants us civil liberties

Sovereign state: an internationally recognised government that has legal and political power over its citizens within a defined territory

The power of sovereign states is not unlimited, but it can still help to think about **sovereignty** as absolute legal and political power, held by one government within a defined territory. Under international law and Australian law, it is not considered possible to have sovereignty residing in more than one body. This idea will help you understand the complex relationship between the sovereignties of the British government, the Australian governments, and our First Peoples.

Sovereignty: absolute legal and political power over a defined territory

Australian courts have been very clear that it is not possible to recognise Indigenous sovereignty in a legal system that already recognises the fundamental lawmaking authority of the Australian government. In ***Members of the Yorta Yorta Aboriginal Community v Victoria*** (2002) 214 CLR 422, Justices Gummow and Hayne held that there could be no 'parallel' system of law in Australia:

> what the assertion of sovereignty by the British Crown necessarily entailed was that there could thereafter be no parallel law-making system in the territory over which it asserted sovereignty. To hold otherwise would be to deny the acquisition of sovereignty and as has been pointed out earlier, that is not permissible.

In other words, according to the High Court, sovereignty is absolute or fundamental and not capable of being shared. British sovereignty, which became the sovereignty of the Australian government, is the only possible sovereignty that can exist within the territory of Australia. This is despite the High Court recognising in the landmark ***Mabo*** case that Indigenous peoples have traditional rights over land, known as native title. That decision is explained further below. In ***Coe v Commonwealth*** (No 2) (1993) 118 ALR 193, Chief Justice Mason held that Mabo is 'entirely at odds with the notion that sovereignty adverse to the Crown resides in the Aboriginal people of Australia'. In ***Wik Peoples v Queensland*** (1996) 187 CLR 1, Justice Kirby held that Mabo did not create a 'dual system of law', and that Indigenous rights must be sourced within the Australian legal system, not some prior authority or customary law.

This makes sense according to traditional meanings of sovereignty, which describe a fundamental lawmaking authority. If we think about sovereignty in this way, it is not possible for the Australian government to have full lawmaking authority over the land of Australia if the sovereignty of Indigenous peoples is also recognised. This is why Chief Justice Mason said that Indigenous sovereignty could not be recognised, or else it would be 'adverse to' (against or in competition with) that of the Australian government. According to the High Court, recognising these competing powers would undermine Australia's constitutional structure and its recognition as a sovereign state.

Institutional sovereignty: the legal and political power of institutions like Parliament

Popular sovereignty: the inherent lawmaking power of the people

However, this focus on sovereignty as fundamental lawmaking authority is overly simplistic. For a start, a distinction has long been drawn between **institutional sovereignty** and **popular sovereignty**.[14] Institutional sovereignty means the legal and political power of institutions like parliament and the executive branch of government. Popular sovereignty is the inherent lawmaking power that resides in all of us, the people. So, despite what the High Court has said, we already have more than one type of sovereignty in Australia. Fundamental lawmaking power resides in us, the voting public—not with parliament and the executive. Those institutions hold legal and political power, but only because we handed our power up to them. This tells us that Indigenous peoples, and all Australians, have an innate or inherent type of sovereignty that already coexists with that of the Crown.

According to leading academics and First Nations representatives, Indigenous sovereignty also means something more. It means a connection to the land, an innate sense of identity, legal and political justice, and a starting point for recognition and inclusion.[15] As Brennan, Gunn and Williams explain, sovereignty is 'the basic power in the hands of Indigenous people, as individuals and as groups, to determine their futures'.[16] This is a very different concept to those defined by Bodin and relied upon by the High Court. It captures a more spiritual notion, one that recognises the distinct culture and history of Australia's First Peoples and their ties to land and waters.

The **Uluru Statement from the Heart**, a statement on Indigenous rights and recognition published in 2017, captures this additional meaning of sovereignty:

> This sovereignty is a spiritual notion: the ancestral tie between the land, or 'mother nature', and the Aboriginal and Torres Strait Islander peoples who were born therefrom, remain attached thereto, and must one day return thither to be united with our ancestors. This link is the basis of the ownership of the soil, or better, of sovereignty. It has never been ceded or extinguished, and co-exists with the sovereignty of the Crown.[17]

Uluru Statement from the Heart: statement on Indigenous rights and recognition published in 2017 by the Referendum Council

Understanding sovereignty in this way gives a very different result to our starting definition. Instead of it not being possible to recognise Indigenous sovereignty, it is actually not possible to deny that it already exists. This meaning of sovereignty is also consistent with the human right to self-determination, as protected by article 1 of the *International Covenant on Economic, Social and Cultural Rights*. **Self-determination** means that everyone should have the right to 'freely determine their political status and freely pursue their economic, social and cultural development'.[18]

Self-determination: human right for communities to freely determine their political status and future development

There is no doubt that the self-determination of Indigenous Peoples could be recognised by the High Court and Australian government without it being 'adverse' to the sovereignty of the Crown. The bigger problem, as you will read about in Chapter 9, is that Australia's Constitution does not protect the right to self-determination or other human rights contained in international treaties.

3. SETTLEMENT AND FEDERATION

It is not possible to fully understand the disadvantage faced by Indigenous peoples today without tracing the history of Australia's legal system. This section provides a brief history of how Australia's legal system developed, beginning with the colonisation of Australia by Britain in 1788.

A. Settlement and *terra nullius*

Australia was just one of many countries colonised and ruled by Britain as part of the British Empire. There were three doctrines under colonial law that said how Britain and other colonial powers could take control of another country: a country could be (1) conquered, (2) ceded or (3) settled.

Conquer: to take a country by force

Cede: to surrender, give up or hand over

To **conquer** a country meant that Britain forcibly took control of an existing population using military force. For a country to be ceded meant that the existing population agreed to hand over control to the British government (to '**cede**' means to surrender or 'give up' something).

In either of these cases, Britain recognised that the country was owned and occupied by an existing population with an established system of law. The existing population and the new British presence would then coexist. The local legal system would remain in force until the laws were explicitly changed by Britain.

The third possibility, to settle a country, meant that the country had no existing population or legal system and Britain could simply claim the unoccupied land. This applied where the land was 'desert and uncultivated' (empty and undeveloped).[19]

Settlement: doctrine from colonial law that allowed a country to claim unoccupied land

A fundamental and ongoing issue is that the doctrine of **settlement** still applies in Australia, even though Indigenous peoples had lived on the land for at least 65,000 years before colonisation. Settlement meant that British law applied immediately in Australia. This began in 1788 when the First Fleet arrived in Sydney Cove and Governor Phillip raised a flag to claim the land in the name of the British Empire. Britain simply claimed the land as 'new' territory for itself.

Legal fiction: principle with legal force based on something that is factually inaccurate

Terra nullius is the legal fiction that allowed the doctrine of settlement to apply in Australia, even though Indigenous peoples were living on the land. A **legal fiction** is a principle that has legal force but is based on something that is factually inaccurate. ***Terra nullius*** means 'land belonging to no one'. It was based on the discriminatory idea that Indigenous people were 'so low on the scale of social organisation' as to not be considered people at all.[20] In other words, there were people physically present on the land, but those people were considered so primitive or barbaric as to not be recognised by British law. In 1837, a parliamentary committee reported to the House of Commons (the lower house of Britain's Parliament) that Australia's Indigenous population was so 'barbarous' and 'entirely destitute' that their claims to the land should be 'utterly disregarded'.[21] These discriminatory ideas were eventually overturned in *Mabo*, but the doctrine of settlement remains current law.

***Terra Nullius*:** the legal fiction that allowed Britain to settle Australia (means 'land belonging to no one')

B. To Federation and beyond

When Britain arrived in Australia, it did not create 'states' as we know them today. There were separate colonies, first in New South Wales and Van Diemen's Land (later called Tasmania), then Western Australia, South Australia, Victoria and Queensland. As these colonies matured, local courts and parliaments were established. For example, the *New South Wales Act 1823* created courts and a parliament for New South Wales. It established Van Diemen's Land as a separate colony with its own supreme court.

By the 1880s, the idea of joining the colonies together into a single country took hold. The colonies would become states, and a federal or national government would have power over all the land. Together, this arrangement created the Commonwealth of Australia (the single country we know today). In Chapter 6, we discussed some of the reasons for developing this federal system of government, including greater security, improved transport, and reduced taxes. Joining the colonies together also helped to recognise a growing sense of Australian identity, separate from Britain. In 1889, Henry Parkes delivered the famous **Tenterfield Oration**. In a speech in northern New South Wales, he made the case for a federal system of government to the Australian public. This is why Parkes is known as the 'father of Federation'.

Tenterfield Oration: speech given in 1889 by Sir Henry Parkes which made the case for Federation

In the 1890s, the text of the Australian Constitution was drafted at a series of **constitutional conventions**. The Constitution would become the founding document of the nation and establish a set of rules for how this

Constitutional conventions: meetings held in the 1890s to debate and draft the text of the Constitution

new system of government was to be run. Meetings to draft the Constitution were held in Adelaide, Sydney and Melbourne. They were attended by representatives from each of the colonies. Many of the delegates later became premiers of the states and judges of the High Court. The transcripts of these debates, known as the **Records of the Australasian Federal Conventions**, are a significant collection of historical documents. They provide important insights into how the Constitution was drafted, which helps to interpret it today.

Records of the Australasian Federal Conventions: transcripts of the constitutional conventions

In 1898, following the conventions, a draft constitution was put to a referendum (national vote) of the Australian people. This first attempt was unsuccessful but, after further changes, the text of the Constitution was approved in 1899. The Queen was asked to enact it in the British parliament. In 1900, it was enacted as the *Commonwealth of Australia Constitution Act 1900* (Imp). Today, our Constitution is still section 9 of this British legislation.

The Australian Constitution came into force on 1 January 1901. This was the moment of **Federation**, when the Australian colonies joined together as states to form the Commonwealth of Australia.

Federation: the moment on 1 January 1901 when the colonies joined together as states to form the Commonwealth of Australia

Leading up to Federation, views on Indigenous peoples had hardly improved. At the constitutional conventions, delegates debated whether Indigenous peoples should have the right to vote at federal elections. Isaac Isaacs (Australia's first Governor-General and later a Chief Justice of the High Court) claimed that Aboriginal people 'have not the intelligence, interest or capacity' to vote.[22] Henry Higgins, another future High Court judge, thought it 'utterly inappropriate … [to] ask them to exercise an intelligent vote'.[23] This reflected racist sentiments amongst the wider population—not just against Indigenous peoples but anyone not belonging to the white, British race. Sir John Forrest, a future Western Australian Premier, said 'there is a great feeling all over Australia against the introduction of coloured persons'.[24] James Howe, a South Australian delegate, said Australia should be 'a home for Australians and the British race alone'.[25]

At that time, Indigenous peoples held some voting rights. In the first federal election in 1901, Indigenous men could vote in all states except Queensland and Western Australia. In South Australia, Indigenous women could also vote. But it was not until 1962, following amendments to the *Commonwealth Electoral Act 1918* (Cth), that all Indigenous adults across Australia were entitled to vote at federal elections. In 1983, compulsory voting was extended to Indigenous peoples. This means full equality in voting rights was not achieved for all Australians until more than 80 years after Federation.

To understand how the legal and political status of Indigenous peoples could be ignored for so long, it helps to recognise that Australia was not legally an independent country from Britain for a long time after Federation. Originally, the state and federal parliaments were restricted by the doctrines of repugnancy and extra-territoriality. **Repugnancy** meant that Australian parliaments could not enact laws that conflicted with the laws of Britain, and **extraterritoriality** meant that Australia could not legislate outside its borders. This undermined Australia's status as a sovereign state and it meant that the British government still had legal and political power over the people of Australia.

Repugnancy: doctrine that applied in early Australian law, which said Australian Parliaments could not legislate inconsistently with British law

Extraterritoriality: doctrine that applied in early Australian law, which said that Australian Parliaments could not legislate outside their borders

The ***Statute of Westminster 1931*** (Imp), which was adopted in 1942 and backdated to the start of World War II in 1939, removed these limits on the federal parliament. From then on, Britain could legislate for Australia only with the 'request and consent' of the federal Parliament. However, it was not until the ***Australia Act 1986*** (Cth) that these limits were removed for state parliaments and Britain could no longer legislate for Australia in any circumstances. In ***ACT v Commonwealth*** (1992) 108 ALR 577, Chief Justice Mason held that the ***Australia Act*** 'marked the end of the legal sovereignty of the British parliament and recognised that ultimate sovereignty resided in the Australian people'. Even then, it was not until 1999, in the decision of ***Sue v Hill*** (1999) 163 ALR 648, that the High Court considered the UK to be a 'foreign power' for the purposes of Australian law. If 1986 is taken as the point of our true legal independence from Britain, the Commonwealth of Australia as a fully independent nation has existed for less than 40 years. If 1999 is taken as the point of full legal independence, our current system of law has been separate from Britain's for only 25 years!

4. *MABO* AND NATIVE TITLE

Mabo v Queensland (No 2) (1992) 175 CLR 1, commonly known as ***Mabo***, is probably the most famous High Court judgment. Proceedings for the case began in 1982, when Eddie 'Koiki' Mabo and other Meriam people made a claim to native title which asserted their traditional ownership of the Murray Islands in the Torres Strait. In 1992, the High Court delivered a landmark judgment that upheld the Meriam people's claim.

In their judgment, the High Court judges reached two significant conclusions. First was that ***terra nullius*** no longer applied. They said that the doctrine 'depended on a discriminatory denigration of indigenous inhabitants, their social organization and customs'.[26] The judges believed that Australian values had moved on from earlier times, and that an 'unjust and discriminatory doctrine of that kind' had 'no place in the contemporary law of this country'.[27]

Radical title: land ownership acquired by Britain upon colonisation, which is subject to native title claims

Native title: right to use lands and waters which derives from the traditional laws and customs of Indigenous people

Second was that Britain did not automatically acquire full legal ownership of the land when it colonised Australia. Rather, it acquired **radical title** to the land. This is less than full ownership, as the rights of the British (and now Australian) government are subject to valid native title claims. **Native title** is a property right to use land and waters, which derives from the traditional laws and customs of Indigenous groups.

A successful claim to native title can be made if an Indigenous group proves that it has maintained its traditional laws and customs in an area. The laws and customs must have existed before Britain colonised Australia. The traditional connection to the land must continue today and have never been 'extinguished'. The key test from Mabo is set out in these terms:

> Where a clan or group has continued to acknowledge the laws and (so far as practicable) to observe the customs based on the traditions of that clan or group, whereby their traditional connexion with the land has been substantially maintained, the traditional community title of that clan or group can be said to remain in existence ... However, when the tide of history has washed away any real acknowledgement of traditional law and any real observance of traditional customs, the foundation of native title has disappeared.[28]

The phrase 'tide of history' means that Indigenous groups who no longer practise their laws and customs in an area, or those who experienced a break in those customs, cannot make a valid claim. Given that colonisation dispossessed Indigenous peoples of their land and frequently severed that very connection, this is a major hurdle to making a successful claim.

Native title claims are now governed by the ***Native Title Act 1993*** (Cth), which the federal parliament enacted in response to ***Mabo***. That legislation recognises native title in statute. It specifies the process by which native title claims can be made, and it provides for other matters like compensation and **Indigenous Land Use Agreements** (ILUAs). These are voluntary but binding legal contracts between the traditional owners of land and a corporate or government interest. ILUAs relate to issues like mining, land development, and the employment of Indigenous workers.

Indigenous Land Use Agreements: binding legal contracts between traditional owners of land and a corporate or government interest

It is also important to recognise that native title does not grant Indigenous groups legal ownership of their land. Native title recognises that Indigenous groups have traditional connections to land and water. It can also grant **exclusive possession**, meaning traditional owners can be the only people on the land and using it. But Indigenous peoples do not strictly own the land they hold under native title. In fact, native title is extinguished by any grant of **freehold title**, which is the type of full legal ownership that applies to most privately held and residential land. Instead, native title provides usage rights that allow traditional owners to live on the area, erect shelters and structures, access the area for traditional purposes, visit places to hunt, fish and gather food, and teach law and customs.[29]

Exclusive possession: the sole right to live on and use land, to the exclusion of all others

Freehold title: full legal ownership that applies to most privately held and residential land

Mabo, then, represents a turning point in Australia's legal history. It achieved two fundamental things. First, the judges overturned *terra nullius*, a discriminatory idea that had applied for nearly 100 years since Federation. Second, the judges established a common law rule for native title, which allowed Indigenous peoples to assert their rights to traditional ownership over the land. These rights are enforceable in Australian courts. The decision rightly 'triggered widespread celebrations and fresh hope among Indigenous Australians'.[30]

However, it is worth considering the judgment's limitations. The judges overturned *terra nullius*, which provided the legal foundation for settlement, as it said that no one was present on the land. However, they managed at the same time to uphold the idea that Australia was settled by Britain. This seems unsustainable, and legally it is one of the weaker parts of the judgment. It means that the legal consequences of *terra nullius*—that Britain was able to claim the land because nobody legally occupied it—are still current law.

Another limitation, explained above in the section on sovereignty, is that *Mabo* and many later judgments failed to recognise Indigenous sovereignty. Recognising this would be a significant step forward in achieving justice for Indigenous peoples, but it seems beyond legal challenge. According to the High Court, the only relevant sovereignty in Australian law is that of the British and Australian governments.

Finally, native title rights are very significant for groups who can claim them successfully, but proving a claim in court can be very difficult. The High Court set a high bar by requiring evidence that pre-British laws and customs are still observed today. The reason that native title claims need to be made is because Indigenous peoples were dispossessed from their lands, but a claim cannot be successful if a group's traditional connection with the land has ever been broken. This test, and the difficulties of gathering evidence to prove that traditional laws and customs have been observed unbroken since colonisation, means that native title claims can take many years or even decades to succeed, if they do succeed at all.

5. CONSTITUTIONAL RECOGNITION

Australia's Constitution does not recognise—or even mention—our First Peoples. Attempts to achieve constitutional recognition remain an ongoing challenge. This section begins by explaining the 1967 referendum, which helped to advance Indigenous rights but did not go far enough. It then explains two more recent approaches to constitutional reform, including the unsuccessful referendum in 2023 to establish a Voice to Parliament.

Referendum: national vote on whether change the text of the Constitution

Double majority: requirement that changes to the text of the Constitution must be approved by a majority of Australians overall, and a majority of people in a majority of states

A **referendum** is a national vote on whether to change the text of the Constitution. For a referendum to take place, the federal Parliament must first approve a Bill containing the proposed change. All Australians then vote on whether they support it. For the referendum to succeed and the change to be made, there must be a double majority 'Yes' vote. The **double majority** means that a majority of the Australian people overall must vote 'Yes', as well as a majority of people in a majority of states. (In other words, 4 out of 6 states must approve the change, in addition to the overall count. The territories are included in the overall count, but not the state majority.)

These requirements are set out in section 128 of the Constitution. The double majority sounds like it is repeating the same thing, because a majority overall should mean that a majority of states approved it. However, it actually sets a very high bar. If 2 states vote 'No', it takes only one more state voting 'no' for the referendum to fail. If states with the largest populations vote 'Yes', that can help the overall count reach a majority, but they still only count as one when determining the additional, state majority.

A. 1967 referendum

When it was first enacted, the Australian Constitution made two references to Indigenous peoples. The first was section 127, which said that 'aboriginal natives' were not to be counted in any state or federal census. The second was in 51(xxvi), which is a head of federal lawmaking power known as the **races power**. As originally drafted, that section said that the federal parliament could make laws regarding 'the people of any race, other than the aboriginal race in any State, for whom it is deemed necessary to make special laws'. This meant the federal parliament could make special laws for any race, except Indigenous Australians.

Races power: head of power in section 51(xxvi) of the Constitution, which says that the federal Parliament can make special laws for the people of any race

A successful referendum held in 1967 removed both these discriminatory references. The 1967 referendum was the most successful in Australia's history, with a 'Yes' vote of 90.77%. Section 127 was removed completely, and the words 'other than the aboriginal race in any State' were deleted from the races power. That change meant the federal parliament had the power to make special laws for the benefit of Indigenous Australians.

The 1967 referendum showed there was overwhelming public support for supporting Indigenous rights. However, it has not proven to be the resounding success that it first appeared. As Appleby and McKinnon explain, 'the referendum fell far short in giving people what they thought they were voting for, and in giving Aboriginal people what they wanted from it'.[31] There is an ongoing myth that the referendum provided Indigenous peoples with equality before the law and protected them from discrimination, but this was not part of the changes made to the text of the Constitution.

The changes made in 1967 had two main limitations. The first, and most obvious, is that the Constitution now makes no reference to Indigenous peoples whatsoever. The changes removed discriminatory references to Indigenous peoples, but they did not insert anything in their place. The Constitution is simply silent on the place of Indigenous peoples in Australian law. Given the important culture and history of Australia's First Peoples, who have been living on the land for 65,000 years and counting, this is a major oversight.

The second limitation is that the races power, as amended in 1967, does not necessarily protect Indigenous peoples from discrimination. It merely allows the federal parliament to enact 'special laws'. This means that the laws must be specifically targeted at Indigenous groups, but it does not mean the laws must be intended for their benefit. The races power could be used to support racially discriminatory laws. This is why the 1967 referendum definitely did not achieve full protection for Indigenous peoples from discrimination.

A third, ongoing problem is that section 25 of the Constitution still contemplates discrimination against Indigenous peoples. Section 25 says that the people of any race who are disqualified from voting at state elections must not be counted in any census. The section does not explicitly mention Indigenous peoples, but it raises the possibility that Indigenous peoples (or the people of any race) could be prevented from voting at state elections and not counted as part of the Australian population. Even if this does not happen in practice, the fact that our Constitution contemplates that people would be denied voting rights on the basis of their race is startling.

B. Expert panel

There have been several moves, so far unsuccessful, to remedy these ongoing problems. In 2012, an important report was published by the Expert Panel on Recognising Aboriginal and Torres Strait Islander Peoples in the Constitution ('Expert Panel'). The Expert Panel included Indigenous community leaders, members of parliament, legal academics and others. It was appointed by Prime Minister Julia Gillard's government to consult and report on the best possible changes to recognise Indigenous peoples in the Constitution.

To some extent, the recommendations of the Expert Panel are now outdated, given that a more recent proposal to establish an Indigenous Voice to Parliament was put to the Australian people in a referendum. However, given that the Voice referendum was unsuccessful, the Expert Panel's views could still feed into future proposals for constitutional recognition. It is important, in any case, to understand the history of proposals for constitutional recognition, prior to 2023.

In its report, the Expert Panel made four main recommendations.[32] First, it recommended that section 25 and the races power in section 51(xxvi) be repealed. Second, it recommended that a new section 51A be inserted in place of the current races power. This new section would be similar to the races power, in that it would give the federal parliament power to make laws regarding Indigenous peoples. However, it would be accompanied by some preliminary text to ensure that any such laws must be for the benefit of Indigenous peoples. The Expert Panel recommended that section 51A be enacted in the following terms:

> **Section 51A Recognition of Aboriginal and Torres Strait Islander peoples**
> Recognising that the continent and its islands now known as Australia were first occupied by Aboriginal and Torres Strait Islander peoples;
> Acknowledging the continuing relationship of Aboriginal and Torres Strait Islander peoples with their traditional lands and waters;
> Respecting the continuing cultures, languages and heritage of Aboriginal and Torres Strait Islander peoples;
> Acknowledging the need to secure the advancement of Aboriginal and Torres Strait Islander peoples;
> the Parliament shall, subject to this Constitution, have power to make laws for the peace, order and good government of the Commonwealth with respect to Aboriginal and Torres Strait Islander peoples.

The preliminary text would be important both symbolically and legally. Symbolically, it would recognise the important place of Indigenous peoples in Australia's history in a way that the 1967 referendum failed to achieve. It would be similar to calls for a preamble to the Constitution, which the Howard government had earlier supported. A **preamble** is a section of introductory text to a constitution.

Preamble: opening statement to a constitution or international law instrument

In 1999, the poet Les Murray produced a draft preamble for the Howard government, but this was never put to the Australian people at a referendum. His draft text recognised that Indigenous peoples had occupied the land 'since time immemorial' and were 'honoured for their ancient and continuing cultures'.[33] The preliminary text in section 51A would be like a 'mini-preamble' within the text of the Constitution.

Legally speaking, the 'mini-preamble' in section 51A would be important because the High Court would need to take it into account in interpreting the scope of the federal parliament's lawmaking powers. It is not clear this would happen if the preamble was included only at the beginning of the Constitution (as in the Howard government's model). Using the text suggested by the Expert Panel would mean that the federal parliament would no longer have a constitutional power to enact laws that discriminated against Indigenous peoples. Any such laws could be struck down by the High Court under its power of judicial review.

Third, the Expert Panel recommended that a new section 116A be inserted into the Constitution. This would prohibit discrimination on the basis of 'race, colour or ethnic or national origin'. Finally, it recommended that a new section 127A be inserted. This would recognise that 'Aboriginal and Torres Strait Islander languages are the original Australian languages, a part of our national heritage'.

The Expert Panel's recommendations provided a legally sound, thoroughly considered and culturally appropriate model for achieving constitutional recognition of Indigenous peoples. Unfortunately, they were never put to the Australian people in a referendum. Several reasons likely contributed. Political infighting and leadership challenges within the two major parties (still) leads to delays. There can be a lack of political will to limit the lawmaking powers of the federal parliament, even if the idea of recognising Indigenous peoples in the Constitution has wider support. There were also concerns that the prohibition on racial discrimination went too far in creating something like a Bill of Rights. Concerns like those can stifle reforms, and still do, because changes will only succeed in a referendum if they are supported in their entirety. As the more recent experience with the Voice referendum shows, these and other reasons make achieving constitutional change for Indigenous peoples an ongoing challenge.

C. Voice to Parliament

In October 2023, all voting Australians had their say on whether they supported an Indigenous Voice to Parliament. The Voice was to be an advisory body that would allow representatives from First Nations communities to make representations to the federal Parliament and the executive government. Only 39.9% of voters supported the change, and no state had a majority 'Yes' vote.[34] This was seen by many, including around the world, as a devastating blow for constitutional recognition.

The question put to the Australian people was simply whether they supported a change to the Constitution that would establish an Aboriginal and Torres Strait Islander Voice. If the referendum was successful, it would have inserted a new section 129 into the Constitution:

129 Aboriginal and Torres Strait Islander Voice
In recognition of Aboriginal and Torres Strait Islander peoples as the First Peoples of Australia:

I. There shall be a body, to be called the Aboriginal and Torres Strait Islander Voice;
II. The Aboriginal and Torres Strait Islander Voice may make representations to the Parliament and the Executive Government of the Commonwealth on matters relating to Aboriginal and Torres Strait Islander peoples;
III. The Parliament shall, subject to this Constitution, have power to make laws with respect to matters relating to the Aboriginal and Torres Strait Islander Voice, including its composition, functions, powers and procedures.

Referendum Council: body appointed in 2016 to make recommendations on how Indigenous peoples could be recognised in the Constitution

This text was the product of a long consultation process. In 2016, Prime Minister Malcolm Turnbull and opposition leader Bill Shorten established a **Referendum Council** that built on the earlier efforts of the Expert Panel. Like the Expert Panel, the Referendum Council comprised expert representatives from a range of backgrounds (including Indigenous community leaders, academics, lawyers and former judges). The Council held 13 regional dialogues across Australia over a six-month period across 2016 and 2017. This culminated in a First Nations National Constitutional Convention, which was held at Uluru over four days in May 2017. The Convention was attended by more than 250 delegates, who came together to discuss proposals for constitutional reform.

The delegates to the Convention adopted and published the Uluru Statement from the Heart. This is an historic statement that recognises that 'Aboriginal and Torres Strait Islander tribes were the first sovereign Nations of the Australian continent and its adjacent islands'.[35] As we discussed at the start of this chapter, the Uluru Statement celebrates Indigenous sovereignty as a 'spiritual notion' and an 'ancestral tie' to the land. It recognises that Australia's Indigenous communities are 'the most incarcerated people on the planet', and that challenges like these can be overcome with meaningful constitutional reform.[36]

The Referendum Council made three key recommendations.[37] First, as was put to the Australian people, it recommended that the text of the Constitution be changed to establish an Indigenous Voice to Parliament. Second, it recommended that all Australian parliaments pass a 'Declaration of Recognition'. These would

Makarrata Commission: a truth-telling commission that would help to overcome previous harm and symbolise the restoration of peace

recognise the shared story of Indigenous peoples, the British institutions of government and 'our multicultural unity'. Third, it called for the establishment of a **Makarrata Commission**. 'Makaratta' is a word from the language of the Yolŋu people in Arnhem Land. As Noel Pearson, a prominent Indigenous lawyer, academic, activist and community leader, has explained:

> The Yolŋgu concept of Makarrata captures the idea of two parties coming together after a struggle, healing the divisions of the past. It is about acknowledging that something has been done wrong, and it seeks to make things right.[38]

A Makarrata Commission would facilitate a process of regional 'truth telling' between Indigenous communities and the Australian government. This would help to overcome previous harm and symbolise the restoration of peace. It would uphold a similar idea to restorative justice, which we discussed in Chapter 7.

In response to the Referendum Council's report, the Liberal government at the time established a joint parliamentary committee to consider the recommendations and other proposals for constitutional reform. This was seen by many as a weak and disrespectful response to an historic statement.[39] The Prime Minister Malcolm Turnbull and Attorney-General George Brandis did not help matters by saying that a referendum would not succeed, because the Voice 'would inevitably become seen as a third chamber of parliament'.[40]

A referendum was eventually put to the Australian people, under Prime Minister Anthony Albanese's Labor government, in October 2023. The reasons why the referendum failed are complex and warrant longer treatment, but some brief reasons are worth considering here. As a starting point, it helps to recognise that only 8 out of 44 referendums succeeded prior to the Voice referendum, and no referendum has ever succeeded with a 'No' campaign against it.[41] Referendum proposals are likely to succeed only if they have **bipartisan support**, meaning support from both the major parties. So the proposal was at a disadvantage from the start, which compounded once the Liberal Party under Peter Dutton as opposition leader came out against it. This is shown clearly in a study by researchers from the Australian National University (ANU).[42] According to the ANU survey, 39% of Coalition voters supported the Voice in January 2023, but this dropped to only 8% by the October referendum.

Bipartisan support: when a proposal is supported by both major political parties

The ANU survey showed that 'No' voters identified strongly with reasons put forward by the 'No' campaign and the Liberal and National parties. These included fears and conspiracies that the Voice would 'divide' the country or take land away from white Australians. Other views were clearly discriminatory, with some voters believing the Voice would not change anything because Indigenous disadvantage stems from a lack of 'effort'.[43] Other common complaints were that the government did not provide enough detail about the proposal, even though there was a 270-page report about it,[44] and that the Voice would have too much power over parliament. The idea of 'making representations' simply meant that the Voice could advise the parliament and the executive. It is the same as powers held by countless other parliamentary committees and advisory bodies. The government would not have been legally bound to follow its recommendations. But misinformation spread about the Voice's powers, and many other talking points all played a role in delivering a resounding 'No' vote.[45] How Australia will reflect on and regroup from the unsuccessful Voice referendum to achieve constitutional recognition remains to be seen.

KEY POINTS

- The significant disadvantage experienced by Aboriginal and Torres Strait Islander peoples stems from colonisation, the Stolen Generations, and intergenerational cycles of poverty, grief and trauma.
- The High Court's *Mabo* decision overturned *terra nullius* and recognised native title, but it did not recognise Indigenous sovereignty and it is still current law that Australia was settled by Britain.
- Following a resounding 'No' vote in the referendum to create an Indigenous Voice to Parliament, Australia's Constitution still makes no reference to Aboriginal and Torres Strait Islander peoples.

DISCUSSION QUESTIONS

1. How can justice for Australia's First Peoples be achieved?
2. How do Indigenous ideas about sovereignty differ from those relied upon by the High Court?
3. What were the major benefits of the *Mabo* decision, and what were some of its limitations?
4. How can an Indigenous group make a successful claim to native title?

5. What might be done to ensure that a proposal for recognising Indigenous peoples in the Constitution has the greatest chance of succeeding in the future?

NOTES

1 Productivity Commission (2024). ***Review of the national agreement on Closing the Gap: study report – volume 1.*** Australian Government.

2 Productivity Commission (2024). Closing the Gap: information repository. Retrieved from: https://www.pc.gov.au/closing-the-gap-data/dashboard.

3 Muir, M. (2017). A national tragedy: ALRC seeks views on Indigenous incarceration. ***Law Society Journal***, 1 August 2017.

4 Australian Bureau of Statistics (2023). ***Prisoners in Australia***. Retrieved from: https://www.abs.gov.au/statistics/people/crime-and-justice/prisoners-australia/latest-release.

5 Ibid.

6 Ibid.

7 Australian Law Reform Commission (2017). ***Incarceration rates of Aboriginal and Torres Strait Islander Peoples: discussion paper***. Australian Government.

8 Law Council of Australia (2018). ***The Justice Project: final report***. Law Council of Australia.

9 Read, P. (2014). Reflecting on the stolen generations. ***Indigenous Law Bulletin***, ***8***(13), 3-6.

10 Creative Spirits (2023). A guide to Australia's Stolen Generations. Retrieved from: https://www.creativespirits.info/aboriginalculture/politics/stolen-generations/a-guide-to-australias-stolen-generations.

11 Australian Institutes of Family Studies (2020). ***Child protection and Aboriginal and Torres Strait Islander children***. Retrieved from: https://aifs.gov.au/resources/policy-and-practice-papers/child-protection-and-aboriginal-and-torres-strait-islander.

12 Rudd, K. (2008). Full transcript of PM's speech. ***The Australian***, 13 February.

13 Sabine, G. H. (1920). The concept of the state as power. ***The Philosophical Review***, ***29***(4), 301-318.

14 Brennan, S., Gunn, B. & Williams, G. (2004). Treaty – what's sovereignty got to do with it? (Issue Paper No. 2). Gilbert + Tobin Centre of Public Law, UNSW.

15 Ibid.

16 Ibid.

17 Referendum Council (2017). ***Final report of the Referendum Council***. Canberra: Australian Government.

18 *International Covenant on Economic, Social and Cultural Rights*, 16 December 1966. Retrieved from: https://www.ohchr.org/en/instruments-mechanisms/instruments/international-covenant-economic-social-and-cultural-rights.
19 Secher, U. (2005). The *Mabo* decision – preserving the distinction between 'settled' and 'conquered or ceded' territories. *University of Queensland Law Journal, 24*(1), 35-71.
20 Ibid.
21 *Mabo v Queensland (No 2)* (1992) 175 CLR 1).
22 Williams, G. (2000). Race and the Australian Constitution: from Federation to reconciliation. *Osgoode Hall Law Journal, 38*(4), 643-665.
23 Ibid.
24 Ibid.
25 Rubinstein, K. (1997). Citizenship and the constitutional convention debates: A mere legal inference. *Federal Law Review, 25*, 295-316.
26 *Mabo v Queensland (No 2)* (1992) 175 CLR 1
27 Ibid.
28 Ibid.
29 Kimberley Land Council (2024). *What is native title?* Retrieved from: https://www.klc.org.au/what-is-native-title.
30 Keon-Cohen, B. (2017). Reforms are urgently needed to the native title scheme. *Sydney Morning Herald*, 1 June.
31 Appleby, G., & McKinnon, G. (2017). Lessons of 1967 referendum still apply to debates on constitutional recognition. *The Conversation*, 22 May.
32 Expert Panel on Recognising Aboriginal and Torres Strait Islander Peoples in the Constitution (2012). *Recognising Aboriginal and Torres Strait Islander Peoples in the Constitution: report of the Expert Panel*. Australian Government.
33 Lambert, H. (2003). A draft preamble: Les Murray and the politics of poetry. *Journal of Australian Studies, 27*(80), 5-14.
34 Biddle, N., et al. (2023). Detailed analysis of the 2023 Voice to Parliament referendum and related social and political attitudes. ANU Centre for Social Research Methods.
35 Referendum Council, n. 17.
36 Ibid.
37 Ibid.
38 Pearson, N. (2017). Uluru Statement practical on indigenous recognition. *The Australian*, 27 May.
39 Hunter, F. (2017). Government rejection of referendum proposal sends 'shockwaves' through Indigenous community. *Sydney Morning Herald*, 27 October.
40 Wahlquist, C. Indigenous voice proposal 'not desirable', says Turnbull. *The Guardian*, 26 October.

41 Williams, G., & Hume, D. (2010). ***People Power: The History and Future of the Referendum in Australia***. Sydney: UNSW Press.

42 Biddle et al., n 34.

43 Ibid.

44 Langton, M., & Calma, T. (2021). ***Indigenous Voice co-design process: final report to government***. National Indigenous Australians. Agency.

45 Appleby, G., Lindell, G., McGlade, H. Ten questions about the Voice to Parliament – answered by the legal experts. ***The Conversation***, 19 June.

Chapter 9

International law and human rights

In this chapter, you will learn about:

- The United Nations and human rights treaties
- Rights protection in Australian law
- Models for achieving national human rights protection

Australia's Constitution has two major gaps: it does not recognise our First Peoples, and it does not mention human rights. **Human rights** are core protections and freedoms that all human beings should be afforded. All liberal democracies except Australia protect human rights in a bill of rights or similar national document.[1] This chapter explains more about human rights and how Australia could achieve greater protections in the Constitution or national legislation.

Human rights: core freedoms that all human beings should be afforded to respect their dignity and wellbeing

Bill of Rights: part of a country's constitution that provides legal protection for human rights

To understand rights protections in Australia, it helps first to understand the essentials of international law, including human rights treaties and their influence on domestic law.

1. INTERNATIONAL LAW

International law provides rules that states must uphold when they interact with each other and to protect their own citizens. (Here and throughout this chapter, state means the national government of a country.) However, it is important to understand that international law is not enforceable on states to the same degree that domestic law is enforceable on citizens. A major criticism of international law is that states do not often face consequences for breaching it. International

DOI: 10.4324/9781003433408-11

law provides critically important standards to uphold dignity, equality, and human rights, but sovereignty remains 'the paramount principle'.[2]

As the legal theorist Costas Douzinas has written, weak implementation of international law means that 'the shield of national sovereignty is not seriously pierced, unless the interest of the great powers dictates otherwise'.[3] What he means is that the legal and political power governments hold within their own territories is upheld as the most important principle in the international system. This poses a major obstacle to them being held accountable by the system governing them all. He wrote those words more than 20 years ago, but they are still just as relevant today.

A. Branches and sources

Private international law: rules that help to resolve disputes between companies and citizens in different countries

Conflict of laws: another name for private international law

Public international law: system of rules that states must abide by when interacting with each other, and to protect their own citizens

A key distinction in international law is between public international law and private international law. **Private international law** governs disputes involving companies or individuals from different countries. For example, if an Australian company enters into a contract with a foreign company, and there is a dispute over it, it would not be clear which set of domestic laws apply. For this reason, private international law is also called **conflict of laws**. It has more to do with differences between domestic legal systems, than with overarching rules governing the international community.

Public international law governs interactions between the governments of different countries, and between those governments and their own citizens. The distinction between private and public international law is broadly similar to that between private or civil law in Australia (which governs how individuals and companies interact) and public law (which governs the state and its relationship with citizens). In this chapter, we focus on public international law.

The main branches of public international law include:

- International human rights law;
- International refugee law;

- International humanitarian law;
- International criminal law;
- International environmental law;
- International trade law;
- Law of the sea;
- Air and space law.

Below, we will focus on international human rights law. However, as with the branches of domestic law, there is significant overlap between these areas.

In each of these areas, we find legal rules across different sources. You can think about this in a similar way to the sources of law within Australia. In domestic law, we have legislation (including regulations) and case law (including tribunal decisions). Where do we find the legal rules that make up international law? This becomes a bit more complicated. The main sources we look to for information about human rights are treaties and declarations, which are supported by other sources.

Treaties (also called **conventions**) are legally binding, written agreements between states. A **bilateral** treaty is between two states, and a **multilateral** treaty between three or more. Treaties are first negotiated, then signed by the states who agree to them. The state parties then **ratify** the treaty. This can happen some time (even years) later, once approvals are sought within a country or domestic laws are enacted. The act of ratification is when the executive government indicates to the other parties and the world that the state intends to be bound the treaty. This usually involves depositing an **instrument of ratification** (essentially, a brief, signed statement) with the **United Nations**. In other words, signing the treaty indicates an intention to be bound by the treaty, and ratifying it confirms that intention.

States can ratify a treaty that was earlier negotiated and signed by other states (in other words, they can join it later). This is called **accession**: they accede to a treaty that already exists. States can also make **reservations** to a treaty when signing, ratifying, or acceding to it. These are exceptions or qualifications to the treaty's terms; the

Treaty: a formal, written agreement between two or more countries that is governed by international law

Convention: another name for a treaty

Bilateral: between two states

Multilateral: between three or more states

Ratify: confirm intention to be bound by a treaty

Instrument of ratification: signed statement deposited with the United Nations which confirms a government's intention to be bound by a treaty

United Nations: international organisation dedicated to international peace, security, and human rights

Accession: when a state ratifies a treaty that was earlier negotiated and signed by other states

Reservation: exception or qualification to the articles of a treaty

Declaration: a non-binding treaty

Implement: recreate a treaty provision in domestic legislation

state says it will be bound by most of the treaty but not those specific articles. A reservation cannot, however, be incompatible with the overall aims of the treaty.

Declarations are similar to treaties, but they are not legally binding and states do not sign and ratify them. They are written agreements that express international principles, goals or aspirations, as opposed to legally binding conditions. This sounds like they are less important than treaties, but they can be very important, morally and symbolically. The Universal Declaration of Human Rights, for example, was the founding document of the international human rights movement. The United Nations Declarations on the Rights of Indigenous Peoples is another example. We will return to these further below.

It is important to recognise that the rules found in treaties (and declarations) do not have any legal effect in Australian law, unless and until they are also enacted in domestic legislation. This is true even if the Australian government has ratified a treaty. The federal government needs to **implement** (recreate) those protections in domestic law for an argument to be made about them in an Australian courtroom, or for the Australian government to be held legally accountable for breaching them.

In addition to treaties and declarations, there are also:

- *Decisions by international courts and tribunals*. This is essentially case law at the international level. It includes decisions of the International Court of Justice and the International Criminal Court, which are both explained below.

Customary international law: fundamental rules based in state practice rather than treaty law

***Opinio juris*:** intention to be bound by a rule, which forms part of customary international law

- ***Customary international law***. These are fundamental rules of custom that arise from state practice instead of treaty law. Whether a rule amounts to international custom depends on whether there is evidence of two things: (1) consistent state practice in accordance with a rule, and (2) a belief that states recognise that rule as legally binding. The second of these is known as ***opinio juris*** (a shortened version of the phrase '*opinio juris sive necessitatis*', which means 'an opinion of law or necessity').

- *Opinions of expert scholars*. More so than in domestic law, the opinions of highly qualified, esteemed legal scholars can be taken into account when bodies interpret international law or determine ***opinio juris***. This includes practising international lawyers who write about the law and professors of international law. They are often called publicists or **jurists**.

Jurists: highly qualified and esteemed international law scholars

- ***Resolutions***. Resolutions are expressions or statements of opinion, intention or agreement by international bodies. They are not technically a source of legal rules in the same way as the categories above, but they provide an important record of statements by international bodies and they can have fundamental effects, like determining whether countries can legally go to war. Resolutions issued by the United Nations General Assembly are not binding on states, but those issued by the United Nations Security Council can be, depending on how they are written.

Resolution: statement of opinion or intention by the United Nations General Assembly or Security Council

Opinio juris is a very complicated area of international law, because it requires evidence of states abiding by implicit rules over a long period of time. It can also be confusing as some of the rules are also written down in treaties. Essentially, customary international law refers to the fundamental rules of international law, which all states must abide by, regardless of whether they are written down. One example is *non-refoulement*: a principle that forbids states from returning refugees to places where they will face persecution, torture, or other mistreatment. This is recognised as customary law, but it is also codified in article 33 of the United Nations Convention on the Rights of Refugees and other instruments that prohibit torture.

B. United Nations

The United Nations (UN) is the main international organisation dedicated to peace, dignity, and equality for all people around the world. It was created at the end of World War II by its founding treaty, the ***United Nations Charter 1945*** (UN Charter). The UN Charter established the six **organs** (parts or bodies) of the UN. It mandates, among many other things, that member states must settle international disputes peacefully, and not use or threaten force that violates each other's political independence. The UN

Organ: word used to describe the six main parts of the UN

Charter was implemented in Australia via the *Charter of the United Nations Act 1945* (Cth).

General Assembly: the United Nation's main representative forum, in which all member states deliberate on issues affecting world peace and security

The six organs of the UN are as follows. First is the **General Assembly**, which is the main deliberative and representative forum. All 193 members of the UN have seats. The General Assembly functions sort of like an international parliament, but its decisions and resolutions are not legally enforceable on member states in the same way that domestic laws are enforceable on citizens.

Security Council: United Nations organ with primary responsibility for maintaining international peace and security

Second is the **Security Council**, which has primary responsibility for international peace and security. It has five permanent members (France, China, Russia, the United States and the United Kingdom) and 10 non-permanent members who rotate on two-year terms. Australia has been a non-permanent member of the Security Council on five occasions, most recently in 2013–14.

Veto: power to prevent a law being enacted or a resolution being issued

Each of the permanent members holds a **veto** power, meaning they can stop any Security Council resolution from being issued. This is a major obstacle to achieving international agreement on matters involving security, terrorism, and armed conflict. For example, in 2022, Russia vetoed a Security Council resolution that called for it to immediately and completely withdraw its troops from Ukrainian territory. Of course, this seems like an obvious design flaw: why would anyone create a system where no action can realistically be taken against five of the most powerful countries in the world? The answer is that they were the most powerful victors in World War II, and the chances of changing the veto system or expelling any of those five members are equally remote. Those actions would need Security Council approval, and so would each be able to veto the change.[4]

International Court of Justice: the United Nation's main court

Advisory opinion: judicial statement of legal advice

Third is the **International Court of Justice** (ICJ). The ICJ sits in The Hague in the Netherlands. It is the principal judicial organ of the UN, meaning its main court. States can bring cases in the ICJ against each other, and it can also issue **advisory opinions**. These are judicial statements of legal advice provided to one of the other UN organs or a specialised agency (including the World Health Organisation and the International

Monetary Fund). In 2023, the Australian academic Professor Hilary Charlesworth, an eminent international law scholar, was re-appointed as a judge on the ICJ after first being elected in 2021.

Like many other aspects of international law, the ICJ's ability to act effectively depends on whether states consent to its jurisdiction. States often withdraw their consent when they know another state will bring a case against them. Australia did this in 2002 to avoid the compulsory settlement of maritime boundaries relating to oil and gas reserves in the Timor Sea.[5] That relates to a larger, ongoing controversy in which the Australian Secret Intelligence Service (ASIS) bugged offices of the Timor-Leste government, in an operation authorised by the Foreign Affairs Minister Alexander Downer, to gain an unfair advantage in treaty negotiations.[6] The only people charged in relation to that operation were the ASIS officer who revealed that it happened, and his lawyer who tried to take action against the Australian government under international law.[7] Like the prosecution of David McBride you read about in Chapter 5 on the media, this is another example of how whistleblowers and even their lawyers can face severe consequences for trying to do the right thing, while the people involved in allegedly criminal acts remain free.

The United States has continually avoided the ICJ's jurisdiction since the 1980s. The original trigger was a landmark decision, which found that the US violated customary international law by supporting military and paramilitary actions by Contra rebel groups at war with the Nicaraguan government.[8]

The UN's fourth organ is the Economic and Social Council. It reviews policies, makes recommendations, and monitors state progress on economic, social and environmental issues. It has 54 members in overlapping 3-year terms. It is responsible for implementing and monitoring state progress with the United Nations **Sustainable Development Goals** (SDGs). The SDGs are a collection of 17 goals, with 169 specific targets, to create a better world by 2030. SDG 16 aims to 'promote peaceful and inclusive societies for sustainable development, provide access to justice for all and build effective, accountable and inclusive institutions at all levels'.[9] This includes promoting the rule of law at the national and international levels. Most other SDGs relate to human rights, including goals to end poverty, end hunger, achieve gender equality, promote health and wellbeing, provide clean water and sanitation, and ensure inclusive education.

Sustainable Development Goals: 17 goals developed by the UN Economic and Social Council to create a better world by 2030

The remaining two organs are the Trusteeship Council and the Secretariat. The Trusteeship Council was designed to help a small number of colonies and territories transition to self-government after World War II. Its main activities were suspended in 1994 after that job was done, and so the council is now largely obsolete. The UN Secretariat comprises the Secretary-General and the many thousands of staff that are responsible for the UN's daily functioning.

The six UN organs are supplemented by other bodies that enforce international law. The **International Criminal Court** (ICC) has jurisdiction to hear cases on genocide, war crimes, crimes against humanity, and (since 2017) crimes of aggression. **Genocide** includes any acts designed to destroy, in whole or part, a national, ethnic, racial or religious group. **War crimes** are acts committed by individuals against international law during armed conflict, including the murder, rape, and torture of civilians. **Crimes against humanity** are those and other acts conducted as part of a widespread or systematic attack on a civilian population. **Crimes of aggression** are, essentially, when one state unlawfully invades another.

International Criminal Court: international court established under the Rome Statue which hears cases on genocide, war crimes, crimes against humanity and crimes of aggression

Genocide: attempts to destroy, in whole or part, a national, ethnic, racial or religious group

War crimes: acts committed by individuals against international law during armed conflict

Crimes against humanity: systematic criminal acts against civilian populations during armed conflict

Crimes of aggression: when one country invades another contrary to international law

Rome Statute: treaty that established and governs the International Criminal Court

Ad hoc tribunal: court set up for a time-limited purpose, usually to prosecute individuals for war crimes

The ICC is governed by a treaty called the Rome Statute of the International Criminal Court 1998 (known as the **Rome Statute**). Similar to the ICJ, the ICC's jurisdiction is impacted if states decide to withdraw their consent. In 1998, the United States was one of only seven countries—including China, Israel, Iraq, Libya, Yemen, Qatar—who voted against the Rome Statute and the creation of the ICC.[10]

Historically, **ad hoc tribunals** have been set up to prosecute individuals for war crimes and other acts violating international criminal law. This began with the Nuremberg and Tokyo war crimes tribunals held following World War II. In the 1990s, two ad hoc tribunals were set up by the Security Council: the International Criminal Tribunal for the former Yugoslavia and the International Criminal Tribunal for Rwanda. In comparison to the ICJ and ICC as permanent courts, ad hoc tribunals are created for a single, time-limited purpose arising from a specific conflict.

These aspects of international criminal law, and key provisions of the UN Charter, overlap with international humanitarian law (IHL). IHL might sound like rules relating to humanitarian aid, but it refers to the laws of armed conflict. It has two main components: *jus ad bellum* and *jus in bello*. ***Jus ad bellum*** are the laws *of* war. They say when it is lawful to engage in armed conflict. War is not always unlawful; it is permitted in self-defence under section 51 of the UN Charter, or where a country has prior authorisation from the Security Council (there is a third possible ground, which does relate to humanitarian crises, but there is not the same consensus on it). Crimes of aggression breach *jus ad bellum*.

Jus ad bellum: laws of war

Jus in bello are laws *in* war. A war can be lawful overall, but acts done within it can still be criminal. Put another way, the legality of a war and the legality of the acts done within it are two separate questions. *Jus ad bellum* is relevant at all times, as it governs decisions to go to war, but *jus in bello* is triggered only in situations of armed conflict. There are two main types of conflict for the purposes of IHL: **international armed conflict** (between two or more countries) and **non-international armed conflict** (such as a civil war between two opposing factions within the same country). Genocide, war crimes, and crimes against humanity all breach *jus in bello*.

Jus in bello: laws in war

International armed conflict: war between two countries

Non-international armed conflict: war within a country

The **Geneva Conventions** are a collection of 4 treaties and 3 **optional protocols** (additional, related agreements) which set out fundamental rules that must be followed in armed conflict. They protect people who are not taking part in the conflict, including civilians and medics, wounded and sick soldiers, and prisoners of war. Common article 3, found in each of the 4 conventions, prohibits murder, torture, mutilation and any other cruel, humiliating or degrading treatment.

Geneva Conventions: series of 4 treaties and 3 optional protocols that protect non-combatants in armed conflict

Optional protocols: additional agreements that relate to a primary treaty

Two key principles of *jus in bello* are proportionality and distinction. **Proportionality** means that military attacks must not be excessively harmful compared to the military advantage sought, while avoiding unnecessary (but not all) collateral damage to civilians. **Distinction** means that military attacks must

Proportionality: in sentencing, the principle that punishments should be appropriate in type and severity to the crime committed, or in international law, that military attacks must not be excessive compared to the military advantage sought

distinguish between military and non-military targets, and between combatants and civilians.

2. HUMAN RIGHTS

To understand exactly what a human right is, it is important to first understand what it means to have a 'right'. A right is a justified claim to something. For example, if you lend your computer to someone, you have a right to have that property returned to you. If you paid too much tax during the financial year, it's your right to have that money returned to you by the tax office.

To fully be considered a right, the other party must have a correlating (matching) duty to give the thing to you.[11] If the other party is not morally or legally required to give it to you, you don't strictly have a right to it. Rights are 'enforceable moral claims'.[12] (You might still, however, have a right to make a claim to the thing, even if you are not guaranteed to get it.)

Human rights are enforceable moral claims against governments to provide us with the things we need to live a life of dignity. They typically include the rights to life, liberty, security, privacy, free speech, a fair trial, and the freedoms from slavery, torture and discrimination.

This might sound familiar from the chapter on liberalism, when we discussed civil liberties. Human rights and liberalism certainly overlap, but they are different concepts with different origins. Under the seventeenth-century philosophy of liberalism, we are entitled to civil liberties because we are citizens living under a liberal-democratic government. Our civil liberties include rights to liberty, privacy, security and private property.

Human rights are based in this liberal tradition, which values individual rights and freedom from government. However, we are entitled to human rights simply because we are human beings (regardless of the type of government we live under). Human rights are universal, and they are more fundamental than civil liberties, because they are derived from a source higher than all governments: our common nature as human beings. Human rights have more contemporary origins than the philosophy of liberalism, and they extend beyond civil liberties to include things like freedom from slavery and torture.

Like much of the international law system, the history of human rights is generally dated to the years following the Second World War. Following the Holocaust and other atrocities that led to tens of millions being killed, there was worldwide recognition that human beings must be afforded minimum standards of dignity.

These standards were agreed upon and issued in December 1948 by the General Assembly as the Universal Declaration of Human Rights (**UDHR**). The UDHR is a founding document of the human rights movement. Its **preamble** (opening statement) refers to 'barbarous acts' committed during the Second World War, from which all people must be protected:

UDHR: Universal Declaration of Human Rights, the founding document of the Human Rights movement, published in 1948 by the UN General Assembly

> Disregard and contempt for human rights have resulted in barbarous acts which have outraged the conscience of mankind, and the advent of a world in which human beings shall enjoy freedom of speech and belief and freedom from fear and want has been proclaimed as the highest aspiration of the common people.[13]

Preamble: opening statement in a constitution or international law instrument

The UDHR sets out 30 **articles**, which are like sections of legislation. Article 1 starts by saying that 'All human beings are born free and equal in dignity and rights'. The remaining articles set out various other protections, including the rights to life, liberty, security, and freedom from slavery and torture.

Article: a section of a treaty or other international law document

A selection of rights from the UDHR is set out in Figure 9.1. Many of these relate directly to issues we have been talking about in this book, including the right to a fair trial (article 10) and the right to elect a democratic government (article 21).

Many other treaties protect human rights. The major human rights treaties have been issued by the United Nations General Assembly. These set out agreed international standards on many human rights issues, including the rights of children, women and people with disabilities.

Australia is a party to the seven core human rights treaties:

- *United Nations Convention Against Torture* (UNCAT);
- *United Nations Convention on the Rights of the Child* (UNCROC);
- *International Covenant on Civil and Political Rights* (ICCPR);
- *International Covenant on Economic, Social and Cultural Rights* (ICESCR);
- *Convention on the Elimination of All Forms of Discrimination Against Women* (CEDAW);

- *International Convention on the Elimination of All Forms of Racial Discrimination* (CERD);
- *Convention on the Rights of Persons with Disabilities* (CRPD).

Universal Declaration of Human Rights (1948)

Article 1
All human beings are born free and equal in dignity and rights. They are endowed with reason and conscience and should act towards one another in a spirit of brotherhood.

Article 3
Everyone has the right to life, liberty and security of person.

Article 4
No one shall be held in slavery or servitude; slavery and the slave trade shall be prohibited in all their forms.

Article 5
No one shall be subjected to torture or to cruel, inhuman or degrading treatment or punishment.

Article 7
All are equal before the law and are entitled without any discrimination to equal protection of the law. All are entitled to equal protection against any discrimination in violation of this Declaration and against any incitement to such discrimination.

Article 9
No one shall be subjected to arbitrary arrest, detention or exile.

Article 10
Everyone is entitled in full equality to a fair and public hearing by an independent and impartial tribunal, in the determination of his rights and obligations and of any charge against him.

Article 11
(1) Everyone charged with a penal offence has the right to be presumed innocent until proven guilty according to law in a public trial at which he has had all the guarantees necessary for his defence.

Article 12
No one shall be subjected to arbitrary interference with his privacy, family, home or correspondence, nor to attacks upon his honour and reputation.

Article 13
(1) Everyone has the right to freedom of movement and residence within the borders of each State.

Article 14
(1) Everyone has the right to seek and to enjoy in other countries asylum from persecution.

Article 18
Everyone has the right to freedom of thought, conscience and religion; this right includes freedom to change his religion or belief, and freedom, either alone or in community with others and in public or private, to manifest his religion or belief in teaching, practice, worship and observance.

Article 19
Everyone has the right to freedom of opinion and expression; this right includes freedom to hold opinions without interference and to seek, receive and impart information and ideas through any media and regardless of frontiers.

Article 20
(1) Everyone has the right to freedom of peaceful assembly and association.

Article 21
(1) Everyone has the right to take part in the government of his country, directly or through freely chosen representatives.

Figure 9.1 Universal Declaration of Human Rights.
Source: United Nations (2024)

There is some debate as to whether social and cultural rights, like those found in the ICESCR, should be considered human rights. Economic rights include the rights to work, fair pay, and adequate housing. Social and cultural rights include the right to participate in cultural activities and experience the benefits of scientific progress. These are sometimes classed as 'second-class' rights.[14] This is not to say they are unimportant, but they are often seen as secondary to life, liberty, freedom from torture and slavery, and other civil and political rights that are necessary for our immediate physical wellbeing.

The drafters of the UDHR certainly considered economic, social and cultural rights to be core human rights. The declaration includes the rights to work and fair pay (article 23) and to experience culture and science (article 27). Another core economic, social and cultural right is the right to self-determination, which is found in article 1 of the ICESCR. As we discussed in the previous chapter, **self-determination** means that communities should 'freely determine their political status and freely pursue their economic, social and cultural development'.

Self-determination: human right for communities to freely determine their political status and future development

Treaties contain many important protections for human rights but, unfortunately, like most aspects of international law, their enforcement ultimately depends on 'buy-in' from governments. As mentioned above, human rights treaties are not automatically incorporated into Australian law. The Australian government must enact domestic legislation that implements the specific protections.

Another problem is that human rights are not **inalienable**. An inalienable right is one that cannot be taken away. You might assume that the fundamental nature of human rights means they can never legally be taken away from us or breached by governments. However, nearly all human rights can be derogated from in times of emergency. To **derogate** from a human right means to suspend or interrupt its protection, usually for a defined period of time. This means that a government can legally fail to protect a human right, even if it is fundamental to our human dignity.

Inalienable: not able to be taken away

Derogate: suspend or interrupt a legal obligation

Only a small number of rights are non-derogable. **Non-derogable** rights are those that cannot be suspended or taken away, even in times of emergency. They include the right to life and the freedoms from torture and slavery. However, even these are not absolute: the right to life can be taken away in times of war or by

Non-derogable: not able to be suspended

a lawful death penalty, the freedom from torture does not prevent all coercive interrogation, and freedom from slavery does not protect people from forced labour in times of emergency.

The possibility of derogating from human rights means that governments can reduce or suspend human rights protection to counter serious threats to our security, such as terrorism. This is allowed even under the world's strongest human rights instruments—though any derogation must be necessary, reasonable and proportional to the current threat. For example, article 15 of the European Convention on Human Rights says that governments may derogate from human rights '[i]n time of war or other public emergency threatening the life of the nation', provided that the derogation is limited 'to the extent strictly required by the exigencies of the situation'.[15]

3. RIGHTS PROTECTION IN AUSTRALIAN LAW

Australia remains the only liberal-democratic nation without legal protection for human rights at the national level.[16] This section explains more about our Constitution and the rights it does contain, the power of courts to strike down legislation that is incompatible with the Constitution (known as judicial review), and other ways that human rights are protected in Australia.

A. The Constitution

The Constitution does not mention human rights. Yet, according to one survey, 61 per cent of Australians believe that Australia has a bill of rights similar to that found in the United States (US) constitution.[17] A bill of rights is part of a country's constitution that provides legal protection for human rights.

The belief that we have a bill of rights in Australia may be because popular culture often refers to protections found in the US bill of rights. For example, suspects often 'plead the fifth' (exercise their right to silence) in American police dramas. However, there is definitely no bill of rights in the Australian Constitution (nor has there ever been).

There are two main reasons why human rights were not included when the Constitution was drafted. The first is that legal protections were seen as unnecessary, because the fairness and good sense of our politicians would be sufficient. For example, at the constitutional conventions, Dr Alexander Cockburn (later Premier of South Australia) said that a bill of rights would 'be a reflection on our civilisation'. He believed people would say, 'Pretty things these States of Australia; they have to be prevented by a provision in the Constitution from doing the grossest injustice'.[18] There is some truth to his argument, in that Australian politicians are not likely to sanction gross human rights abuses like genocide or slavery. However, it is also clear that relying on the fairness and good sense of politicians has never been sufficient to ensure that human rights are protected, either in Australia or around the world.

The second reason for not protecting human rights was more overtly racist. There was concern among the drafters that protecting human rights would prevent the Australian government from discriminating against minority and ethnic communities. For example, when Henry Higgins (later a Justice of the High Court) heard a suggestion at the constitutional conventions for including a human rights clause, he asked: '[i]t protects Chinamen too, I suppose, as well as negroes?'.[19]

These attitudes from the late nineteenth century shaped the founding law of our nation, which is essentially in the same form today. Because the Constitution is so difficult to change, the document is in many ways out of date.

The Constitution protects a few limited rights. Section 80 protects the right to trial by jury in criminal trials for indictable offences under federal law (you will read more about indictable offences in Chapter 10). Section 116 protects the right to freedom of religion, but this has been interpreted narrowly by the High Court. Section 117 prohibits discrimination on the basis of which state somebody lives in, but not on the grounds of race, religion or sexuality. Section 51(xxxi) provides some protection for private property, as it says that property can be acquired by the Commonwealth only 'on just terms' (this was made famous in the movie *The Castle*).

Implied rights: rights that are not expressly protected, but the High Court has developed by interpreting other words in the Constitution

There are also two **implied rights**: a right to vote and a freedom of political communication. An implied right means that the Constitution does not explicitly protect these things, but the High Court has upheld these rights by interpreting words in other sections of the Constitution. The right to vote, for example, has been derived from the requirement (found in sections 7 and 24) that the houses of parliament be 'directly chosen by the people'.[20] Parliament is allowed to restrict the right to vote for some categories of people (like temporary visa holders, those with a severe mental illness, those convicted of treason, or prisoners serving lengthy prison terms). However, it could not enact a law that removed (for example) the right to vote for people of a particular religion or ethnic group.

The implied freedom of political communication protects speech relating to government and political matters. Parliaments cannot enact legislation that unduly restricts what people can say, publish or broadcast about ministers or government policy. Being able to discuss, critique and criticise our elected representatives is a core aspect of our democracy.

The test used by the High Court to determine whether a law breaches the implied freedom of political communication has three limbs.[21] First, the court asks whether the law burdens freedom of communication about government or politics. Second, it asks whether the purpose of the law is legitimate and compatible with our system of representative and responsible government. Third, it asks whether the means adopted by the law are proportionate to that legitimate end. The third question is complex but is essentially an assessment of proportionality and fairness. If the law restricts political speech in a way that is disproportionate to achieving some legitimate aim, the law will be struck down.

It is important to realise that this does not fully protect our human right to freedom of speech and opinion. The implied freedom only protects speech about political matters; it does not protect artistic, commercial, personal or academic expression, except where those relate in some way to government policy or the election of candidates to parliament. The implied freedom is not even strictly a right at all; it is a restriction on the lawmaking power of Australian parliaments. This is very different to having a constitution that formally protects human rights to freedom of speech, opinion and expression.

B. Judicial review

Judicial review: power of the High Court to strike down legislation that is incompatible with the Constitution

Read down: when the High Court interprets a section of legislation so it is consistent with the Constitution

The High Court has the power to strike down legislation that is inconsistent with these rights or any other section of the Constitution. This power is known as **judicial review**, and it means the High Court can declare a law null and void—as if it were never enacted by parliament. Where possible, the High Court will **read down** a section of legislation (interpret it in a way that is consistent with the Constitution) instead of striking it down completely, but judicial review is a common feature of High Court judgments.

The power of judicial review has been inferred from the text of the Constitution; it is not referred to explicitly. The High Court, drawing on the famous US Supreme Court case ***Marbury v Madison***, considered judicial review to be 'axiomatic' to our constitutional system.[22] This means it is a core, self-evident feature of how our legal system is meant to work. There would be little point in having a constitution as the founding document of our nation if parliaments could simply legislate against it.

However, because the Constitution does not refer to human rights, the High Court cannot strike down legislation that undermines liberty, free speech or other fundamental protections. This means that Australian parliaments can enact laws that impact on human rights and there is nothing that can be done about this in a court. In theory, the federal parliament could even enact a law authorising torture, and the High Court could not strike it down for that reason. The High Court might fundamentally disagree with the legislation, but the constitutional grounds for invalidating it simply are not there. There may be an alternative way to strike down the law (for example, the law might not be authorised by the heads of power in section 51, or it may breach the separation of powers) but these do not ensure that human rights are considered and protected.

A recent, landmark decision provides a key example of how the High Court must focus on constitutional and not human rights issues. In ***NZYQ v Minister for Immigration, Citizenship & Multicultural Affairs*** [2023] HCA 37, the High Court held that legislation supporting the indefinite detention of refugees was invalid. This overturned precedent that had stood for nearly two decades. Around 140 individuals in immigration detention were immediately released. However, despite findings by the UN Human Rights Committee that Australian immigration detention amounts in many cases to torture,[23] this judgment had nothing to do with human rights and international law. Rather, it revolved around questions about the separation of powers and whether indefinite detention is punitive or not. Issuing punishment is solely within the power of courts, so the laws were said to give an invalid power to detain someone punitively with no prospect of either staying in Australia or being deported.

This might seem surprising but, without a national human rights instrument, there are simply no legal grounds for challenging legislation on the grounds of human rights or international law. Even if parliament enacted a law authorising torture or allowing some form of slavery, you could not lodge a claim in the High Court on the grounds of human rights. You would instead need to make an argument based on the separation of powers, or that the legislation does not fall within the heads of power in section 51 of the Constitution. Of course, the Australian government is not likely to enact such laws, but it is shocking that the legal grounds for challenging them do not even exist. This is what puts Australia out of line with all other liberal democracies.

C. Statutes and committees

Australia's Constitution does not formally protect human rights, but there are other ways human rights are protected in Australia. First, there is a presumption that courts will interpret legislation in a way that is consistent with fundamental rights, unless it clearly says something to the contrary. This is a principle of statutory interpretation known as the **principle of legality**. In *Potter v Minahan* (1908) 7 CLR 277, the High Court held it 'improbable' that parliament 'would overthrow fundamental principles, infringe rights, or depart from the general system of law, without expressing its intention with irresistible clearness'. In *Coco v The Queen* (1994) 179 CLR 427, the High Court clarified that any interference by parliament with fundamental rights 'must be clearly manifested by unmistakeable and unambiguous language'.

Principle of legality: judicial presumption that parliament did not intend to interfere with fundamental rights and freedoms

According to ***Minister for Immigration and Ethnic Affairs v Teoh*** (1995) 183 CLR 273, this includes interpreting legislation wherever possible in line with international human rights treaties. However, the obvious limitation with this approach is that it does not prevent human rights or international law from being violated; it merely says that any violations must be written in clear and unambiguous language.

Thankfully, there are several pieces of legislation that do protect human rights in Australia. Examples passed by the federal parliament include the:

- *Racial Discrimination Act 1975* (Cth);
- *Sex Discrimination Act 1984* (Cth);
- *Disability Discrimination Act 1992* (Cth);
- *Age Discrimination Act 2004* (Cth);
- *Privacy Act 1988* (Cth);
- *Australian Human Rights Commission Act 1986* (Cth).

The ***Australian Human Rights Commission Act 1986*** (Cth) established the Australian Human Rights Commission (AHRC), which advocates for greater human rights protection in Australia. The AHRC can investigate complaints about how individuals have been treated and how government departments have acted. These complaints can be taken all the way to the United Nations Human Rights Committee (UNHRC), which can investigate further and make recommendations to the federal government.

Ultimately, however, the UNHRC cannot make Australia comply with its recommendations. At times the government has even treated it with disdain. For example, after a report suggesting that Australia's treatment of asylum seekers breached the right to freedom from torture, former Prime Minister Tony Abbott claimed that Australians were 'sick of being lectured to' by the United Nations.[24]

Even if legislation does protect human rights, it is weaker than constitutional protection, as it can simply be amended or repealed by parliament. This happened in 2007, when sections in the ***Racial Discrimination Act 1975*** (Cth) were suspended by the Howard government to allow the Northern Territory National Emergency Response (commonly called the Northern Territory Intervention). The Northern Territory Intervention was designed to protect Indigenous children from sexual abuse and neglect, but it caused controversy for several reasons, including a lack of consultation with Indigenous communities and the deployment of military troops on Australian soil.[25]

In 2011, the federal parliament enacted the *Human Rights (Parliamentary Scrutiny) Act 2011* (Cth), which created a **Parliamentary Joint Committee on Human Rights** (PJCHR). The PJCHR examines legislation as it goes through parliament and reports back on whether it complies with human rights. However, it cannot force parliament to amend a Bill; it can only make recommendations. In addition, the committee has a majority of government members, which means most of them are likely to support the government's position. In practice, this means legislation that undermines human rights can be enacted with little substantive change.[26]

Parliamentary Joint Committee on Human Rights: parliamentary committee that examines whether legislation complies with human rights

Stronger legal protections for human rights exist in the Australian Capital Territory, Victoria and Queensland. The *Human Rights Act 2004* (ACT), the Victorian *Charter of Human Rights and Responsibilities Act 2006* (Vic) and the *Human Rights Act 2019* (Qld) protect a long list of human rights, including those to liberty, security, freedom of movement and freedom of expression. This model of human rights protection is known as a **human rights act**, because the rights are sourced in

Human rights act: piece of legislation which allows courts to declare legislation incompatible with human right

legislation (an Act of Parliament) rather than a constitution. Other states may well follow.

These human rights acts do not allow courts to strike down legislation that is incompatible with them. Rather, they allow a state or territory supreme court to issue a **declaration of incompatibility** (in Victoria this is called a 'declaration of inconsistent interpretation'). This means the court finds in a judgment that the legislation is incompatible with human rights, but the legislation remains constitutionally valid. This is known as a **dialogue model** of human rights protection, because it creates a conversation between the courts and parliament. The court pronounces judgment on the legislation, and parliament can respond by fixing it. Ultimately, it is up to the politicians in parliament to choose whether they amend the legislation or not.

Declaration of incompatibility: statement issued by a court under a human rights act which says a piece of legislation is incompatible with human rights

Dialogue model: model of human rights protection in which courts can declare legislation incompatible with human rights

In the other Australian states and federally, there are essentially no legal hurdles to enacting legislation that undermines human rights. There has been some discussion in the courts about a 'deep rights' doctrine—the idea that there may be legislation so terrible that even a parliament could not enact it—but this has never been fully developed, and there is no legal basis for it. Ultimately, governments that introduce rights-infringing legislation must be held accountable by the people. If we dislike the legislation a government introduces, we can vote them out at the next election. This is an important feature of our democracy, but it provides much weaker protection than constitutional law, which would render the legislation invalid.

The lack of human rights protection in Australia is significant because it allows Australian parliaments to enact legislation that would be unthinkable in many other countries. For example, many of Australia's counter-terrorism laws would not be possible to enact in countries that constitutionally protect the rights to silence, freedom of speech and freedom from arbitrary detention.

D. Models for change

There are two main ways human rights could be legally protected at the national level in Australia. First, Australia could establish a constitutional bill of rights similar to that found in the United States. The US bill of rights is contained in the first ten amendments to the US constitution. It protects free speech, religion and assembly (1st amendment), freedom from unreasonable searches and seizures (4th amendment), due process and the privilege against self-incrimination (5th amendment), and the right to a fair trial (6th amendment). The second amendment is famous for protecting the right to 'keep and bear arms' (i.e., own and carry weapons).

Australia could amend its Constitution to protect human rights in a similar way (though we would not protect the right to bear arms). This would allow the High Court to strike down legislation on human rights grounds, using its power of judicial review. Achieving this would, however, require a **referendum**. Only 8 out or 45 proposals for constitutional change have succeeded. This is partly due to the onerous **double majority** requirement, which requires a majority of the Australian people voting yes overall, and a majority of people in a majority of states. A bill of rights would also be difficult to change if we later wanted to add new rights or change existing ones. Any minor change to the text of the Constitution would require another referendum. It would be very important to get it right the first time, and debating different models can create the kinds of divisions and disagreements that cause referendums to fail.

Referendum: a vote of the Australian people to change the text of the Constitution

Double majority: requirement that changes to the text of the Constitution must be approved by a majority of Australians overall, and a majority of people in a majority of States

Second, the federal parliament could enact human rights legislation similar to that found in Victoria, Queensland, and the ACT. An overseas example can be found in the United Kingdom's ***Human Rights Act 1998*** (UK). That legislation incorporates the European Convention on Human Rights into UK law. It provided the template for the ACT, Victorian and Queensland legislation, and so provides a similar model. It allows the UK Supreme Court to issue declarations of incompatibility, which the British parliament can respond to by choosing to keep or change rights-infringing legislation.

A different model can be found in New Zealand. The New Zealand ***Bill of Rights Act 1990*** (NZ) provides that laws must be interpreted consistently with human rights wherever possible. New Zealand's Attorney-General must report to its parliament whenever a Bill appears to be inconsistent with human rights. This provides similar protections to the principle of legality and Australia's Parliamentary Joint Committee on Human Rights.

A statutory model would be easier to enact and change, but it would provide weaker protection for two reasons. First, it would be easier for a government to suspend or even repeal it in times of emergency. Second, if existing models were followed, the legislation would not provide the High Court with a power of judicial review. It would allow people to challenge legislation on human rights grounds, but we would ultimately still depend on the good faith of politicians to decide whether human rights should be protected.

Ultimately, given the difficulties of achieving constitutional change, a national human rights act remains the more likely possibility. However, there is little hope of this being achieved, at least in the short-term. In 2009, Prime Minister Kevin Rudd's government established a National Human Rights Consultation led by Father Frank Brennan. The consultation received 35,000 written submissions, and 87 per cent of them supported a bill of rights or human rights act.[27] The consultation recommended that the federal parliament enact legislation to protect human rights, but the government never took action.

Still, even without a bill of rights or human rights act, there are many actions the Australian government can take to improve its compliance with international law. The United Nations Declaration on the Rights of Indigenous Peoples (**UNDRIP**), for example, is a comprehensive instrument that recognises, protects and promotes Indigenous rights, including to self-determination. Australia formally endorsed the UNDRIP in 2009, but its compliance in practice has been piecemeal.[28] The Voice referendum was a missed opportunity for Australia to advance the UNDRIP's agenda, but governments must still take action to improve outcomes for Australia's First Peoples.

UNDRIP: the United Nations Declaration on the Rights of Indigenous Peoples, a comprehensive instrument that recognises, protects and promotes Indigenous rights

KEY POINTS

- Human rights are core protections and freedoms that all human beings should be afforded. They include rights to life, liberty, security, free speech, self-determination, and freedoms from torture, slavery and discrimination.
- Australia's Constitution does not protect human rights, and international treaties do not automatically apply in Australia if they are not implemented in domestic legislation. The High Court cannot strike down a law on the grounds that it violates human rights or international law.

- There are two main ways human rights protections could be improved in Australia: they could be inserted into the Constitution following a referendum, or the federal parliament could enact legislation protecting human rights. A human rights act remains the more likely possibility, but it would provide weaker protection.

DISCUSSION QUESTIONS

1. Can you find a copy of the international human rights treaties listed near the beginning of this chapter (like the United Nations Convention on the Rights of the Child)? Which rights do these treaties protect?
2. Do you think economic, social and cultural rights should be categorised as human rights? Are they necessary to ensure human dignity?
3. Which rights are protected in the Australian Constitution?
4. What is an implied right, and which two of these have been recognised by the High Court?
5. What is the difference between a bill of rights and a human rights act? What are the advantages and disadvantages of each?
6. Can human rights be adequately protected in Australia without national protection in the constitution or a human rights act?

NOTES

1 Hume, D., & Williams, G. (2013). ***Human Rights under the Australian Constitution*** (2nd ed.). Oxford: Oxford University Press.

2 Douzinas, C. (2000). The end of human rights: critical legal thought at the turn of the century. Hart.

3 Ibid.

4 Paige, T.P. (2023). Stripping Russia's veto power on the Security Council is all but impossible. Perhaps we should expect less from the UN instead. ***The Conversation***, 21 September.

5 Saul, B. (2016). On Timor, Australia looks like it's denying an impoverished neighbour its birthright. ***The Guardian***, 29 August.

6 Knaus, C. (2019). Witness K and the 'outrageous' spy scandal that failed to shame Australia. ***The Guardian***, 10 August.

7 Ibid.

8 ***Military and Paramilitary Activities in and against Nicaragua (Nicaragua v United States of America), Jurisdiction and Admissibility***, Judgment, ICJ

Reports 1984, p. 392. Retrieved from: https://www.icj-cij.org/sites/default/files/case-related/70/070-19841126-JUD-01-00-EN.pdf.

9 United Nations Department of Economic and Social Affairs (2024). ***16***. Retrieved from: https://sdgs.un.org/goals/goal16.

10 Human Rights Watch (2020). ***Q&A: The International Criminal Court and the United States***. Retrieved from: https://www.hrw.org/news/2020/09/02/qa-international-criminal-court-and-united-states

11 Ernst, G., & Heilinger, J. (2011). ***The Philosophy of Human Rights: Contemporary Controversies.*** Berlin: de Gruyter.

12 Ivison, D. (2008). ***Rights***. London: Routledge.

13 Universal Declaration of Human Rights, 10 December 1948. Retrieved from: https://www.un.org/en/about-us/universal-declaration-of-human-rights.

14 Byrnes, A. (2010). Second-class rights yet again? Economic, social, and cultural rights in the report of the National Human Rights Consultation. ***University of New South Wales Journal***, ***33***(1), 193-238.

15 European Convention on Human Rights, 4 November 1950. Retrieved from: https://www.echr.coe.int/documents/d/echr/Convention_ENG.

16 Hume & Williams, no. 1.

17 Ryan, E. (2017). University dean addresses nationwide human rights debate. ***Lawyers Weekly***, 24 July.

18 Beazley, M. J. (2017). The principle of legality and the protection of human rights in Australia. The Hon Barry O'Keefe Memorial Lecture, Australian Catholic University, 15 February.

19 Hume & Williams, no. 1.

20 ***Roach v Electoral Commissioner*** (2007) 233 CLR 162.

21 ***McCloy v State of New South Wales*** [2015] HCA 34.

22 ***Australian Communist Party v Commonwealth*** (1951) 83 CLR 1.

23 Doherty, B., & Hurst, D. (2015). UN accuses Australia of systematically violating torture convention. ***The Guardian***, 10 March.

24 Cox, L. (2015). Tony Abbott: Australians 'sick of being lectured to' by United Nations, after report finds anti-torture breach. ***Sydney Morning Herald***, 10 March 2015.

25 Perche, D. (2017). Ten years on, it's time we learned the lessons from the failed Northern Territory Intervention. ***The Conversation***, 26 June.

26 Williams, G., & Reynolds, D. (2015). The operation and impact of Australia's parliamentary scrutiny regime for human rights. ***Monash University Law Review***, ***41***(2), 469-507.

27 Branson, C. (2009). The National Human Rights Consultation: Outcomes. Sydney: Australian Human Rights Commission. Retrieved from: https://www.human-

rights.gov.au/news/speeches/president-speech-national-human-rights-consultation-outcomes.

28 Law Council of Australia (2022). Australia must formally adopt UN Declaration on Rights of Indigenous Peoples. Retrieved from: https://lawcouncil.au/media/media-releases/australia-must-formally-adopt-un-declaration-on-rights-of-indigenous-people.

Part 3
Criminal justice

Chapter 10
Criminal responsibility

In this chapter, you will learn about:

- Different types of crime
- What it means to be guilty of a crime
- Specific defences, including self-defence and provocation

A core function of the legal system is to protect communities from harm. It does this by punishing people who commit crimes. A crime is conduct that causes harm or is morally wrong and attracts a penalty of imprisonment under the law.

This chapter explains what a crime is, different types of crimes, and how courts determine whether someone is guilty of a crime.

1. WHAT IS A CRIME?

A **crime** is something a person does (or, sometimes, fails to do) that attracts a penalty of imprisonment under the law. We find crimes in legislation, which specifies the conduct involved and a penalty. In Australia's federal system of government, criminal law is primarily a state responsibility, but there are also many offences in the federal *Criminal Code Act 1995* (Cth).

Crime: conduct that causes harm or is morally wrong and attracts a penalty of imprisonment under the law

The crime of robbery, for example, involves using (or threatening to use) violence to steal something. In Queensland, this is defined in section 409 of the *Criminal Code 1899* (Qld):

DOI: 10.4324/9781003433408-13

> **409 Robbery**
> (1) Any person who steals anything, and, at or immediately before or immediately after the time of stealing it, uses or threatens to use actual violence to any person or property in order to obtain the thing stolen or to prevent or overcome resistance to its being stolen, is said to be guilty of 'robbery'.

The penalty is set out in a separate section:

> **411 Punishment of robbery**
> Any person who commits the crime of robbery is liable to imprisonment for 14 years.

Any person who does the conduct in section 409 (steals something by using or threatening violence) is liable to the penalty in section 411 (14 years imprisonment). Often, the definition of a crime and its penalty will be in the same section.

Liable: legally responsible for

Being **liable** means the person is legally subject to that penalty. This does not mean everyone who commits robbery will be imprisoned for 14 years. The penalty is a maximum penalty: a person who is found guilty of the crime might receive a prison sentence of any length, up to and including that amount. They might even receive a different type of penalty altogether (you will read more about sentencing and punishment in Chapter 12).

This is an easy, practical way to define a crime: a crime is something that attracts a penalty under the law. The more difficult question is: why are certain types of conduct considered worthy of criminal punishment? In other words, why does society and the government consider certain types of conduct to be a crime?

To answer these questions, we can define a crime in three ways. A useful account of this is given by Findlay, Odgers and Yeo, who describe three different approaches to the criminal law: the individual autonomy approach, the community welfare approach and the moral wrongness approach.[1]

Murder: the intentional or reckless killing of another person

First, crime is conduct that causes harm to individuals. **Murder** and assault are the clearest examples of this, as they involve killing or physically harming someone.

Sometimes, however, the harm is indirect. For example, when a person sells illegal drugs, the exchange of money for a product does not immediately hurt the buyer—but taking the drugs later can be harmful to their health. Some assaults do not even require direct contact: an **act of indecency**, for example, is where an unwanted sexual act is done in the presence of another person. These different types of crime, including drug offences and assaults, are discussed further below.

Act of indecency: sexual act done in front of another person without their consent

Second, crime is conduct that causes harm to a community. Drugs can harm individuals, but they also have a wider impact on society. Drugs have a significant impact on a user's family, friends and other relationships. They add costs to health services, reduce productivity in the workplace, and increase crime and other anti-social behaviour.

Another category of offences, known as **public order offences**, target harmful conduct that is done in a public place: such as loitering, urinating in public, being publicly drunk, or using offensive language. These acts do not usually cause harm to anyone in the moment, but a community would not be a nice place to live in if these sorts of acts continually affected other people going about their lives.

Public order offences: offences involving harmful conduct done in public, such as loitering, urinating in public, or using offensive language

Third, crime is conduct that is morally wrong. Killing or assaulting a person not only harms them directly; it is also against the values and beliefs that are important in our society. We believe that everyone should have the right to live a full life and go about their daily business without being harmed by others. Other criminal offences, such as those for illegal gambling and prostitution, target conduct more directly for moral reasons. These are sometimes called paternalistic offences, because the government is deciding on the moral standards we should live by.

These three ideas overlap, and crimes will not always fit neatly into any one of them. Murder harms an individual victim, it impacts on our society, and it is contrary to our beliefs and values. Drugs can harm a person, they have a wider impact on society, and you could argue that taking them is morally wrong because they artificially alter our bodies (some major religions believe this).

The three ideas also do not explain why some harmful conduct is ***not*** considered criminal. Alcohol is a drug that can harm individuals and communities by fuelling violence and reducing available resources in health services. But it is legal for adults over the age of eighteen to purchase and drink alcohol, and many people drink alcohol daily or weekly. It has also been known for a long time that cigarette smoking causes lung cancer. Arguably, the harms caused by tobacco are more extensive than those caused by marijuana. But governments have instead chosen to use taxation, education and advertising campaigns to address that problem, rather than making it illegal to purchase tobacco. Decisions as to whether harmful conduct will be prohibited, permitted or regulated are often complex and involve competing interests across governments, companies, and the wider community.

These three ways to define crime are simply useful lenses for thinking about what a crime is and why governments punish people for doing things. They raise questions that are especially useful to ask when government propose to create new crimes in legislation. When a new crime is proposed in parliament, you can ask: should this conduct be a crime? First, does it harm a person? Second, does it harm society? Third, is it morally wrong? If the answer is yes to any of these, how much punishment does it deserve?

Because criminal laws are enacted by parliaments, decisions as to what should be a crime can be heavily influenced by politics and the media. This dynamic is captured well by Nicholas Cowdery AM QC, a former Director of Public Prosecutions for New South Wales. Sometimes the lawmaking process works very well, but at other times it can be heavily influenced by politics and media reporting:

> Crimes are created by politicians—they legislate to proscribe certain conduct and to create penalties for breach of those proscriptions. The process by which that is done can be sound, aided by thorough research and expert input and evaluation; or it can be deeply unsatisfactory, depending as it may upon the political priorities and perceived urgency of the legislators and their assessment of what we deserve, often filtered through the tabloid media.[2]

Politics and perceived urgency have certainly influenced the enactment of many laws to prevent terrorism, which you will read about in Chapter 14. Mandatory minimum sentences introduced in response to alcohol-fuelled violence, which you will read about in Chapter 12, are another clear example. This does not mean laws to address those problems are not needed or effective, but the politics involved can mean their enactment is rushed. This reduces the ability of parliaments, committees, and others in society to scrutinise them properly and make sure we have the best laws in place.

2. TYPES OF CRIME

There are many different types of crime. The sections below explain the major categories, including homicide, assaults, property offences and drug offences, as well as the difference between summary and indictable offences.

A. Homicide

When people think of serious crimes, they often think of murder. Murder is a type of unlawful **homicide**. Homicide means the killing of one person by another. Unlawful homicide includes murder (the intentional or reckless killing of another person) and manslaughter (the unintended or negligent killing of another person). The reason we say ***unlawful*** homicide is because there can be situations (including in self-defence, or for medical reasons) where killing another person is not always criminal.

Homicide: the unlawful killing of another person

There are two types of **manslaughter**. Manslaughter by unlawful and dangerous act is where a person intends to commit another offence—like assaulting a person or stealing something from them—and kills someone in the process. The act must have carried an 'appreciable risk of serious injury'.[3] Manslaughter by criminal negligence is where a person causes death by falling greatly short of the standard of care required of a reasonable person. There must also be a high degree of risk of death or serious bodily harm. For example, parents who neglect to feed or look after a newborn child could be guilty of manslaughter if the child dies as a result.

Manslaughter: the accidental or negligent killing of another person

B. Assault

In its most basic form, an **assault** is any touching of another person without their consent. An assault also happens where a person threatens someone else and causes an apprehension of serious harm (scares them). Traditionally, unwanted contact with another person was called **battery**, but assault has become the more common term for both these situations.

Assault: unlawful contact with another person

Battery: contact with another person without their consent

Common assault can involve punching a person and causing minor bodily harm, like bruising and a bloody nose. A serious assault could involve cutting a person with a knife, which leads to major bleeding or disfigurement. Many other assaults involve unwanted sexual contact. Rape (also called **sexual assault**) is where a person penetrates a person's bodily orifices without their consent. Still other assaults involve giving people substances without their consent (for example, by spiking their drink to drug or poison them). These acts are still considered assaults because they interfere with a person's bodily freedom and integrity, even though the offender does not make always make physical contact with the victim.

Sexual assault: penetrating another person's bodily orifices without their consent

The type and seriousness of an assault depends on the method used and the level of harm caused. Trivial harm, like being pushed and having clothes dirtied on the ground, would not usually attract a criminal penalty. An assault generally requires more serious harm. However, this is not the case for **indecent assault**, which involves unwanted contact with sexual connotations. Touching a person's genitals or another private area without their consent can involve no physical harm, but it still constitutes an assault because it violates the victim's privacy and creates fears that more unwanted sexual contact will follow.

Indecent assault: unwanted contact with sexual connotations

Actual bodily harm refers to harm that is real but not trivial, such as significant bruising or a broken bone. **Grievous bodily harm** means very serious harm that causes disfigurement or disablement, or would endanger the victim's life if they did not receive medical treatment. Examples of conduct causing grievous bodily harm would include cutting an artery or pouring a corrosive liquid like acid on a person's skin. **Wounding** is where a blade or other instrument cuts the interior layer of a person's skin.

Actual bodily harm: harm that is real but not trivial

Grievous bodily harm: very serious harm that causes disfigurement, disablement, or would endanger the victim's life if they did not receive medical treatment

Wounding: when a blade or other instrument cuts the interior layer of a person's skin

There are specific offences and penalties for all these types of assaults. Which of these applies will also depend on whether the person intended to cause harm or did so recklessly. Under the law, **recklessness** means the offender is aware there is a substantial risk of harm, but continues the act anyway. For example, throwing large rocks off a bridge at oncoming cars could

Recklessness: where an offender is aware of a substantial risk of harm, but continues the act anyway

be an assault that recklessly causes grievous bodily harm, if a driver or passenger was seriously injured as a result. (Or, if someone died as a result of the same act, this reckless act could be charged as manslaughter.)

Assault is an interesting type of crime because a person's consent determines whether the physical contact is a serious crime or an everyday, valued activity. Clearly, there are many situations in daily life where we have physical contact with others. We shake hands with people we meet and bump into strangers on public transport. People have sex daily as an enjoyable activity. We even pay good money to watch sports stars like footballers, boxers and mixed martial artists repeatedly tackle, grapple, punch and kick each other. This causes bruises, bloodied noses and even broken limbs. A dangerous football tackle can mean that a player is disabled for the rest of their life. In mixed martial arts (cage) fighting, fighters are routinely knocked unconscious and even punched repeatedly in the head once they are already on the ground. The referee will step in, but the fighters are not charged with a crime, and the crowds keep on cheering. There is a lot of conduct in society that could be a serious assault in different circumstances, and yet we actively encourage and even celebrate it.

How do we know, then, what is an assault, and what is not? This is where consent comes in. **Consent** means that a person knows what the contact involves and agrees to it. In sports, players agree to a set of rules that include different types of contact. Provided a tackle or punch is within the expected behaviour of the sport, and is not clearly outside the rules and intended to cause serious harm, they will not be charged with assault. In a healthy relationship, both parties consent to having sex, so there is no sexual assault. We all implicitly consent to incidental contact with others as we go about our daily lives. If someone bumps you with their backpack on a bus, or walks into you while texting on their phone, they will not be charged with assault. Society could not function if we needed to avoid contact with each other at all times.

Consent: when a person understands what something involves and agrees to it

Consensual contact is not assault, then, but determining consent in many cases can be difficult. For example, it can be difficult in sexual assault cases for defence lawyers to convince a jury that the victim did not consent to sex, especially if the victim consented to one sexual act but not another, or agreed at first but then withdrew consent. This leads to drawn-out debates in the courtroom as to whose account of events—the victim's or offender's—is more accurate. It can involve a loss of privacy for victims, as text messages, photos and medical records can all be admitted into evidence to determine whether they consented. Cross-examination on the witness stand—designed to cast doubt on their version of

Affirmative consent: rules that require people participating in a sexual act to check that the other person is consenting

events—can also be retraumatising for many victims. For these and other reasons, Australian states have moved towards an **affirmative consent** model. This requires people participating in a sexual act to check whether the other person is consenting. A defendant cannot say they thought or assumed the person was consenting to sex; they must have taken active steps to find out.

Aggravated assault: assault with an additional element involving greater likely harm, which attracts a higher maximum penalty

Assaults, including sexual assaults, attract higher maximum penalties if a weapon is used, a drug is given to a victim without their knowledge or consent, or there is a group of offenders. These are called **aggravated assaults**, meaning there is some additional factor that makes the offence worthy of higher punishment.

C. Property offences

Property offences: crimes that involve stealing things or fraudulently acquiring them

Property offences are criminal acts that involve stealing things or acquiring them from others fraudulently. This category does not normally include damaging property, though there are other specific offences for vandalism and related acts.

Theft: another name for stealing

Larceny: another name for stealing

Stealing: taking something from another person without their consent, with an intention to permanently deprive them of the thing

The starting point is a basic offence that involves taking something from someone without their consent. This is called different things in different states—in Victoria, it is called '**theft**', in New South Wales it is called '**larceny**' and in Queensland, it is called '**stealing**'—but the essential definition is the same. Stealing involves taking a thing that belongs to someone else without their consent, where the offender intends to 'permanently deprive' the person of that thing (i.e., not give it back). This sounds simple, but it can raise complex questions, depending on who owns the thing that was stolen, and whether the offender intended to keep, borrow, or use it. For example, what if someone is borrowing a car from a friend, leaves the keys in it accidentally while parking it, and someone takes it for a joyride? Did they steal the car or not?

A step up from theft is robbery. **Robbery** is where someone uses force or violence to steal something. A basic robbery could involve wrestling a backpack from a person, pushing them to the ground, and running off with it. A more serious example could involve an offender threatening a bank teller with a gun and demanding them to hand over money. This would be an **armed robbery**, an aggravated version of the offence which attracts a higher penalty.

Robbery: stealing something with force of violence

Armed robbery: an aggravated version of robbery where a weapon is used

Fraud involves stealing something dishonestly. This often involves false statements that induce somebody to hand over large amounts of money. For example, an offender could convince someone to hand over thousands of dollars for an investment scheme that does not exist, then run off with their money. Online fraud has become increasingly common. In online dating scams, for example, an offender will often convince a victim to hand over substantial amounts of money for fake medical operations or other made-up emergencies (you will read more about these sorts of scams and other types of cybercrime in Chapter 13).

Fraud: stealing something dishonestly

D. Drug offences

Drug offences fall into four main categories: use, possession, supply, and production. How serious the offence is depends on complicated rules about different types of drugs and their quantity. Broadly speaking, drugs like heroin, cocaine and amphetamines (including ice and ecstasy) are treated more seriously than opioids (like morphine and oxycodone) and cannabis (marijuana). Using an illegal drug includes swallowing, smoking or injecting it.

Possessing a drug means being in control of it. This is separate to ownership. Drugs can be owned by one person and possessed by another. This can happen, for example, if someone who owns drugs asks someone else to hide or store them. In these cases, the owner is said to be in **constructive possession** of the drugs, even though they are not technically in control of them. There are also offences for possessing drug paraphernalia, such as bongs, pipes and syringes.

Possess: have physical control over something

Constructive possession: principle that says an owner of goods can still be in possession of them, even if they are held by another person

Trafficking: supplying drugs on a large scale

Supplying drugs does not simply mean selling them; it could involve giving them out for free, transporting them, or distributing them in any other way. Where supply is done on a large scale, it is known as **trafficking**. This is an offence under both state and federal law. There are also federal offences for importing and exporting drugs.

Produce: in relation to drug offences, to manufacture, prepare or package illegal drugs

Producing drugs means manufacturing them, or preparing or packaging them for distribution. Common examples would include running a 'meth lab' to manufacture crystal methamphetamine (ice) or using a hydroponic system to cultivate large amounts of marijuana. However, illegal drugs can also be produced on a much smaller scale (for example, growing a single cannabis plant in a backyard).

E. Other offences

The categories above capture the main types of serious criminal offences. There are many hundreds of criminal offences in state and federal law—far too many to list or discuss at length. Some other categories of crimes include:

- *Public order offences*—e.g., loitering, urinating in a public place, being publicly drunk, using offensive language, and being a public nuisance.
- *Road traffic offences*—e.g., dangerous driving, driving under the influence, driving without a licence or exceeding the speed limit.
- *Occupational health and safety offences*—e.g., exposing workers to a risk of death or serious injury by failing to maintain safety standards in a workplace.
- *Environmental offences*—e.g., dumping chemicals in a protected marine area or causing excessive pollution.
- *Paternalistic offences*—e.g., unregulated gambling and prostitution.
- *Offences against the state*—e.g., terrorism, espionage and treason.

F. Summary and indictable offences

All the crimes above fall into one of two overarching categories: they are either a summary or an indictable offence. These terms explain how serious a crime is and which court it is prosecuted in.

Summary offences are less serious and usually attract a maximum penalty of two years' imprisonment or less. Trials for summary offences are held in the local (magistrates') court.

Summary offence: a less serious offence punishable by two years imprisonment or less

Indictable offences (pronounced 'indightable') are more serious offences. They usually attract a maximum penalty of three or more years imprisonment. According to section 80 of the Constitution, a jury must decide whether a person is guilty of an indictable offence. Jury trials for indictable offences are held in the district and supreme courts. However, some indictable offences can be **heard summarily**, meaning they are treated like a summary offence . You will read more about the different trial processes for summary and indictable offences in Chapter 11.

Indictable offence: a more serious offence that attracts a penalty of three years imprisonment or more

Heard summarily: when an indictable offence is heard by a magistrate in the local court

3. WHEN IS SOMEONE GUILTY OF A CRIME?

A person will be guilty of a crime if a court finds that they have committed the elements of the offence beyond a reasonable doubt. This is a very high standard and means there must be no reasonable doubt that the accused person is guilty.

A. Physical and fault elements

The **elements** of an offence are the components or ingredients that need to be proven **beyond a reasonable doubt**. For example, in Chapter 2, we looked at the crime of murder in NSW, found in section 18 of the *Crimes Act 1900* (NSW). We distilled the elements of this crime by bolding the key words in the legislation. This gave us the following list of ingredients:

Elements: the components or ingredients of legal tests

Beyond a reasonable doubt: standard of proof in criminal proceedings

1. An act or omission causing death; AND
2. Intent to kill; OR
3. Intent to inflict grievous bodily harm; OR
4. Reckless indifference to human life

Physical elements: elements that describe the offender's conduct

Actus reus: the physical or conduct elements of a crime (means 'guilty act')

We can divide these into the physical and mental elements of the offence. The **physical elements** describe the actions or conduct involved: in other words, the 'doing' of the crime. The physical elements for murder are an act or omission that causes a person's death. For other crimes, the physical elements might include causing grievous bodily harm, stealing property, or using a weapon. The physical elements are also known as the **conduct elements** x or the ***actus reus*** (Latin for 'guilty act').

Mental elements: elements that describe the offender's state of mind

The **mental elements** describe the offender's state of mind at the time the offence was committed. Generally, this means that a person intended to commit the act. However, the mental elements can refer to any state of mind, including having knowledge of something, or being reckless as to different consequences. The mental elements are the intending, thinking or knowing behind the crime.

Fault elements: another name for the mental elements of a crime

Mens rea: the mental or fault elements of an offence (means 'guilty act')

The mental elements for murder require that the offender either intended to kill, intended to inflict grievous bodily harm, or was recklessly indifferent to human life. These are alternatives, meaning that any one of them will satisfy the mental elements of the offence. Just one of them is needed. The mental elements are also known as the **fault elements** or the ***mens rea*** (which is Latin for 'guilty mind').

We can organise the list of elements above into these categories for easier use:

Actus reus

1. act or omission causing death; AND

Mens rea

2. intent to kill; OR
3. intention to inflict grievous bodily harm; OR
4. reckless indifference to human life.

A person will be guilty of a crime when both the *actus reus* and *mens rea* are proven beyond a reasonable doubt. If either of these (or any single required element) is not proven, the person will be found not guilty and **acquitted**.

Acquit: find that a defendant is not guilty

The *actus reus* and *mens rea* must also coincide: they must occur at the same time. This is not normally an issue, but it can be in some unusual cases. For example, in *Thabo Meli v R* (1954) 1 WLR 228, two offenders struck a person on the head, intending to kill him. Thinking he was dead, they pushed him off a cliff to make it look like an accident. The victim did not actually die from the blow to the head or the fall, but he later died from exposure to the weather. The offenders argued that they could not be found guilty because their intention to kill did not coincide with the victim's death. Their argument was ultimately unsuccessful, but the case shows how important the ideas about *actus reus* and *mens rea* are to the criminal law. Together, these concepts represent the core philosophy of the criminal law as to when a person is considered guilty of a crime. A crime occurs when a guilty act and guilty mind coincide, and all necessary elements of the offence are proven beyond a reasonable doubt.

B. Inchoate and accessorial liability

Even if a person does not complete the *actus reus*, they can still be found guilty of an **attempt**. This is an example of **inchoate liability** because the crime was left incomplete (inchoate means 'not fully formed or developed').

Attempt: when someone starts committing a crime but fails to complete the *actus reus*

Inchoate liability: legal responsibility for attempt and conspiracy (means 'not fully formed or developed')

For a person to be found guilty of attempt, they must do some initial act towards completing the *actus reus*. Technically speaking, they must do something that is 'more than merely preparatory' to the offence.[4] Preparing for a crime might be morally wrong and create a risk of harm, but it does not ordinarily attract a penalty. A person could buy a gun, clean it, load it and practise shooting at a target so they can later kill someone, but none of those acts would constitute attempted murder.

To be found guilty of attempted murder, an offender must try to kill another person and fail for some reason. For example, they could shoot another person but the victim does not die from their wounds. The shooter could pull the trigger but the gun misfires or the bullet misses the target.

Conspiracy: agreement between two or more people to commit a crime

Another type of inchoate liability is **conspiracy**. This is where two or more people agree to commit a crime at some future time. Under state law, this does not require that the offenders do some act towards completing the *actus reus*. Instead, it is the agreement itself that is punished. Merely agreeing to do something does not harm anyone, but conspiracy is treated specially because of the added risk of harm when multiple offenders are involved.

Accessorial liability: extended criminal liability that applies to people who aid, abet, counsel or procure the commission of an offence

A related concept is **accessorial liability**. This means a person can be found guilty even though a different offender completed the *actus reus*. A person is complicit in the commission of a crime if they aid, abet, counsel or procure the commission of the offence. This means a person can be found guilty if they encourage, assist, instruct or otherwise facilitate another person to commit a crime. For example, they might supply the murder weapon, or instruct someone how to kill.

Complicity: liability for assisting, providing instruction in, or otherwise facilitating the commission of a crime

According to laws of **complicity**, a person can also be found guilty if they agree to commit a crime, and then encourage or assist other offenders by being present when it is committed. For example, imagine two friends agree to break into a warehouse at night and steal something. One of them keeps watch outside while the other cuts the fence, breaks the window and steals something from inside. In this case, the friend who keeps watch did not complete any physical elements of the offence, but they could still be found guilty for the same crimes (robbery, trespassing, breaking and entering) as the primary offender.

C. Defences

The concepts above help us determine when somebody is guilty of a crime. There are also legal tests that help us determine when someone is ***not*** guilty of a crime.

Defence: a specific legal argument that excuses or partially justifies a crime

A **defence** is a specific legal argument that justifies or excuses why a person committed a crime. In other words, the person technically committed the crime, but there is some special reason why they should be not considered criminally responsible or should face a lesser penalty. This is different from arguing that the person did not commit the crime altogether (though, broadly speaking, any argument presented for the accused can also be called a defence).

When we talk about 'defences' in criminal law, we usually mean a category of specific legal arguments, such as self-defence or insanity. Similar to offences, these defences have elements or tests that must be established in the courtroom. However, there are some differences as to how offences and defences are proven. The prosecution's main task is to prove the elements of the offence beyond a reasonable doubt. For a defence to be established successfully, the defendant must first raise enough evidence to suggest it is relevant in the case. The prosecution must then prove beyond a reasonable doubt that the elements of the defence were ***not*** present. In other words, the prosecution must prove the ***absence*** of any defence at issue in the case (they are not required to disprove every possible defence). Defences act sort of like 'negative' elements in the prosecution's case.

A common defence is **self-defence**. This is where a person believes on reasonable grounds that another person will kill or seriously hurt them, and they use reasonably necessary force to protect themselves. For example, a homeowner might kill an intruder with a kitchen knife during a home invasion because they believe their life is at risk. Self-defence allows a person to protect a third party (such as a friend, bystander or family member) in the same way.

Self-defence: when a person reasonably believes another person will kill or seriously harm them and responds with reasonably necessary force

Self-defence is a **full defence**, meaning the accused person will be found not guilty. Of course, there are usually difficult questions as to whether the force used was reasonably necessary. Being present during a home invasion is a traumatic experience, but it does not necessarily mean the homeowner's life is in danger. There is certainly no general rule that a homeowner can kill anyone who comes into their house without permission, even if they are stealing something. A homeowner could still end up facing charges for murder or manslaughter, and the outcome of the case could be determined by whether the force they used was reasonable in all the circumstances. Even if a homeowner is eventually found not guilty, they can still face a long battle in the courts trying to establish that their actions were justified.

Full defence: a defence that fully justifies a criminal act, meaning the defendant is acquitted

Another common defence is **provocation**. This is where a person kills someone after being provoked and losing self-control. It is a **partial defence** to murder, meaning that the accused will be found guilty of manslaughter instead.

Provocation: a partial defence to murder, where a person kills someone after being provoked and losing self-control

Laws on provocation around the country have recently been amended following criticisms that they were excusing horrific crimes. In *R v Singh* [2012] NSWSC 637, a man was sentenced to six years for manslaughter after slashing his wife multiple times with a boxcutter and slitting her throat. His defence of provocation was based on the fact that his wife told him she was leaving him for someone else. In NSW, provocation can now no longer be made out where someone threatens to leave a relationship.

Partial defence: a defence that reduces a charge from murder to manslaughter

In a Queensland case, a man was bashed to death by two offenders in the yard of a church. The offenders argued provocation on the basis that the victim made unwanted homosexual advances towards them. They later dropped the argument, but the charges were still downgraded from murder to manslaughter. The case led to an online petition to abolish the so-called 'gay panic' defence. The petition was signed by nearly 300,000 people and led to the Queensland parliament changing the law.[5] Provocation can no longer be made out in Queensland where the victim made an unwanted sexual advance.

Other defences relate to a person's mental impairment. The most well-known of these is **insanity**. A defence of insanity will be made out where the accused person could not understand what they were doing, could not control their actions, or could not understand right from wrong. These elements are known as **M'Naghten's rules** (pronounced McNorton) from an old British case. They set a very high bar and are not argued lightly, as the result can be a special verdict where the offender is found not guilty but placed in mental health detention.

A related defence is **substantial impairment**. This is a partial defence to murder on the basis that the person was operating under an 'abnormality of mind'. The abnormality must have significantly reduced their ability to understand what they were doing, control their actions or determine right from wrong. This is similar to insanity but satisfied to a lower threshold.

Insanity: defence that can be made out where an offender could not understand what they were doing, could not control their actions, or could not understand right from wrong

M'Naghten's rules: common law rules relating to the defence of insanity

Substantial impairment: defence that can be made out where the offender was operating under an abnormality of mind

D. Young offenders

A final question about criminal responsibility relates to when children can be held legally responsible for a crime. Across Australia, children aged ten years and over can be charged with a criminal offence. The exception to this is the Northern Territory, which raised the minimum age to 12 following the Don Dale Royal Commission.

Children aged between ten and thirteen years fall under a rule called ***doli incapax*** (which means 'incapable of crime'). This is a common law presumption which says children in that age range lack the capacity to understand the difference between right and wrong. In other words, they lack the necessary ***mens rea*** or intention to be held criminally responsible. However, that presumption can be rebutted by the prosecution, so children as young as ten years old can be convicted.

Doli incapax: presumption that children aged 10–13 years do not have the maturity to be considered criminally responsible

In a major human rights review, the United Nations reported that 14 should be the minimum age of criminal responsibility.[6] A national 'Raise the Age' campaign, combining the efforts of more than 130 organisations, is advocating for this to be achieved across Australia. Tasmania was the first state to commit to raising it. Given the very high rates of recidivism in Australia (over 60%), we know that putting people in prison leads to problematic cycles of reoffending. Raising the age of criminal responsibility would help Australia meet its international human rights obligations while helping to ensure that children have the best possible chance to avoid those cycles in the future.

KEY POINTS

- Crimes are harmful acts that attract a penalty of imprisonment under the law. Common categories of crime include homicide, assault, property offences, and drug offences.
- A person will be found guilty of a crime where they have committed the elements of the offence beyond a reasonable doubt. This requires proving both *actus reus* (guilty act) and *mens rea* (guilty mind).
- Defences are specific legal arguments that excuse or justify why a person committed a crime. Common defences include self-defence, provocation, and insanity.

DISCUSSION QUESTIONS

1. When is a person legally responsible for a crime?
2. What is the difference between stealing, robbery, and fraud?
3. Should possessing drugs be a crime? Does it matter which type of drugs are involved?
4. Can you think of harmful activities in society that are not considered a crime?
5. What is the difference between ***actus reus*** and ***mens rea***?
6. What is inchoate liability? Do you think a person should be punished for doing something even if no harm is caused to others?
7. In what circumstances might it be justified for a person to kill someone who broke into their home in the middle of the night to steal things?
8. Do you think someone should face a lesser penalty of manslaughter, rather than murder, if they are provoked to kill someone?

NOTES

1 Findlay, M., Odgers, S., & Yeo, S. (2014) ***Australian criminal justice*** (5th ed.). Oxford University Press.

2 Cowdery, N. (2014). Mandatory sentencing. Speech delivered to Sydney Law School distinguished speakers program, 15 May.

3 *Wilson v The Queen* (1992) 174 CLR 313.

4 *Criminal Code Act 1995* (Cth) s 11.1.

5 Burke, G. (2017). Gay panic defence scrapped by Queensland Parliament after lobbying by Catholic priest. *ABC News*, 22 March.

6 Davis, C. (2022). The minimum age of criminal responsibility in Australia: a quick guide. Retrieved from: https://www.aph.gov.au/About_Parliament/Parliamentary_Departments/Parliamentary_Library/pubs/rp/rp2122/Quick_Guides/MinimumAgeCriminalResponsibility.

Chapter 11

Investigation and trial

In this chapter you will learn about:

- Discretion and police powers
- Bail, meaning the release of an accused person before they face trial
- Criminal trials for summary and indictable offences

The **criminal justice system** is the collection of institutions and processes that impose penalties on people for committing crimes. The phrase usually refers to police, courts, and prisons.

Criminal justice system: collection of institutions and processes that impose penalties on people for committing crimes

This chapter explains police powers, charge, bail, and the criminal trial. The next chapter explains punishment, sentencing and appeals. Figure 11.1 sets out these stages of the criminal justice process.

A key concept guiding the criminal justice system is discretion. Having **discretion** means that decision-makers (including police, prosecutors, and judges) can choose between different courses of action.

Discretion: the ability to choose between multiple courses of action that are lawfully available

DOI: 10.4324/9781003433408-14

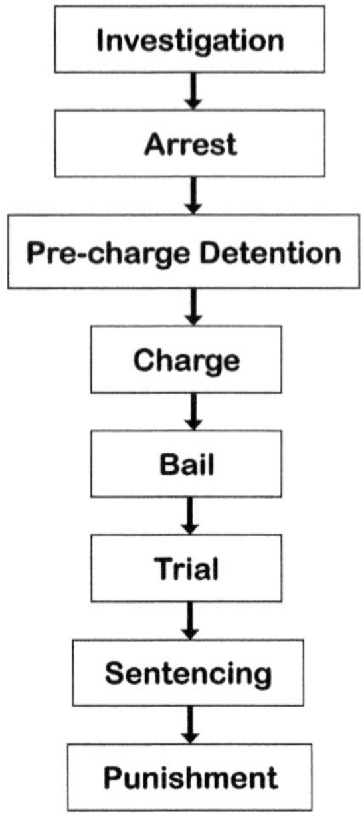

Figure 11.1 Stages of the criminal justice process

1. DISCRETION

If someone has the discretion to do something, it means they can choose between options that are available to them. In the legal system, this usually means choosing whether to use a power or not, or weighing up various factors when making decisions that affect individuals. Kenneth Culp Davis, a leading American legal scholar, said that a 'public officer has discretion whenever the effective limits on his power leave him free to make a choice among possible courses of action or inaction'.[1]

In the criminal justice system, law rarely specifies a single course of action that must be done. Instead, it allows police officers, judges and magistrates to make decisions: which powers should be used, whether a power should be used at all, and what is an appropriate punishment. In these ways, discretion is 'inbuilt within the formal and structure of policing, sentencing and punishment'.[2]

In other words, discretion involves the exercise of judgment by decision-makers, rather than a strict, mechanical application of legal rules. It often depends on their expertise, experience and intuition—or else anyone could be put in the position of a judge, or police officer, and arrive at the same decision.

This has many benefits, especially as it allows decision-makers to make fair choices in individual cases. Imagine a police officer pulls over a speeding driver, but the driver is speeding to see a family member in hospital. The officer could choose not to issue an infringement notice—even though the driver is technically breaking the law.

At the sentencing stage of a criminal trial, if one offender has had a difficult upbringing or has drug addictions and mental health problems, and another is purely greedy and exploits others who are more vulnerable, a judge can punish those two people differently, even if they committed the same crime. This means the law can account for different motives, backgrounds, experiences, and life histories.

At the same time, too much discretion can lead to inconsistent decisions. One police officer might choose to let off the speeding driver, but a different officer might have issued the fine. Too much discretion can also make it difficult to know how decisions are made. On what basis did one officer decide to issue the speeding ticket, but not the other? For a speeding ticket the consequences are not so severe. In a criminal trial, a judge can determine whether a person is imprisoned for a short or long time, or whether they end up in prison at all.

2. POLICE POWERS

Police officers have many special powers that allow them to investigate crimes. They can search for evidence, question suspects, and arrest a person for committing a crime. Legislation defines when these powers can be used, how they must be used, and what the power allows an officer to do. The law both creates and limits these powers. It aims to strike a balance between allowing police to investigate crimes and protecting the rights of suspects. Police powers also help to protect public safety, but most police work involves collecting evidence to prove the elements of offences in court.

Each state has legislation that regulates police powers. Some details differ but they are all broadly similar. The legislation is supplemented by regulations, which provide more details on how the powers must be used.

A. Searches

One common power is to search people, vehicles, homes and other premises. According to different rules, these searches can be made with or without a warrant. A **warrant** is an order issued by a judge that says police can use a special power that impacts on individual rights.

Warrant: an order issued by a judge that allows police to use a special power

Searching a person's private home or other premises generally requires a search warrant (there are only a few exceptions for emergency situations). For example, section 41 of the ***Criminal Investigation Act 2006*** (WA) says that police officers can apply for a search warrant to look for evidence relating to the commission of an offence. Section 42 says that a magistrate can issue the warrant if there are reasonable grounds for suspecting the evidence will be found on the property. A search warrant gives police quite extensive powers: to enter and search the property, open anything that is locked, detain and search people, use electronic equipment and take photographs.

Stop and search: power that allows police to stop somebody on the street and search them for illegal materials

Police can search people in certain circumstances without seeking a warrant. This is known as a **stop and search** power. Section 29 of the Queensland legislation allows police to stop, detain and search a person without a warrant if the officer 'reasonably suspects' that 'prescribed circumstances' exist.[3] The person could possibly be carrying a weapon, explosives, unlawful dangerous drugs or stolen property.[4] The same reasons can be used to justify police searching a vehicle without a warrant.

There are important protections relating to personal searches. According to section 32 of the *Law Enforcement (Powers and Responsibilities) Act 2002* (NSW), a search must be conducted in a way that preserves the person's dignity and privacy. The person must be asked for their cooperation, and the search must be done wherever possible by a police officer of the same gender as the person being searched.

B. Questioning

To investigate a crime, police can simply ask people in the community questions, but the rules become more complex when they start questioning someone they suspect has committed a crime. Police officers must **caution** a person if they suspect the person has committed an indictable offence. Cautioning means that the officer must inform the person that they have a right to remain silent and that anything they do say may be used as evidence against them in court.

Caution: when police inform a person of the right to silence, and also an official warning issued by police

The officers must inform the person that they are allowed to phone a friend or relative and a lawyer. The officer must record the questioning wherever possible, and any confessions or admissions need to be recorded or signed in writing. A **confession** is made when the suspect admits they committed the entire crime. An **admission** is any other statement that suggests the person is guilty. Police officers cannot obtain a confession or admission by threat, force, or promise.

Confession: when somebody admits to committing a crime

Admission: when somebody makes a statement that suggests they are guilty

The **right to silence** and the **privilege against self-incrimination** mean that suspects can refuse to answer police questions that would reveal information suggesting they are guilty. This is a core element of the burden of proof, meaning it is up to police to prove that a crime was committed, and not the accused person to prove their innocence.

Right to silence: requirement that people do not need to answer questions put to them by police

Privilege against self-incrimination: right that means suspects can refuse to answer police questions that would reveal information suggesting they are guilty

These rights are protected by legislation, and a person's silence cannot be used as evidence against them in court. However, there are some exceptions. The *Evidence Amendment (Evidence of Silence) Act 2013 (No 9)* (NSW) allowed negative inferences to be drawn in some circumstances when a person refuses to answer police questions. Under this law, a jury can infer from a defendant's silence that they are trying to hide their guilt. The law was enacted in response to a series of drive-by shootings and applies to serious indictable offences punishable by five or more years in prison.

The Australian Security Intelligence Organisation (ASIO), Australia's domestic intelligence agency, has special powers that undermine the right to silence. Under a questioning warrant, a person who refuses to answer one of ASIO's questions will face five years in prison.[5] You will read more about these powers in Chapter 14.

C. Arrest

Arresting a person means taking them into police custody for the purposes of a criminal investigation. This does not always mean that the person is put in handcuffs; the person might already be at the police station and cooperating with police. However, police

Arrest: to take a person into police custody to investigate a crime or have a court determine whether they committed one

officers may use handcuffs and any other reasonably necessary force to make an arrest (or to use any of their powers). An officer must inform the person that they are under arrest and identify the crime they are suspected of committing. An arrest can be made with or without a warrant.

A person can be arrested without a warrant where an officer reasonably suspects the person has committed or is committing a crime, and the arrest is reasonably necessary for some additional purpose, such as to prevent a crime, gather evidence, establish the person's identity or prevent the person from fleeing. If none of these reasons are valid, there are alternatives to arrest, such as issuing a **summons** or **notice to appear**. These notify a person that they must appear in court on a certain date.

Summons: order issued by police that requires a person to attend court at a later date

Notice to appear: order issued by police that requires a person to attend court at a later date

A general principle is that an accused person must be taken before a magistrate as soon as possible. In *Williams v R* (1986) 161 CLR 278, the High Court held that it is unlawful for police to delay taking an arrested person before a court in order to investigate a crime.

However, this common law rule has been modified by statute. Following arrest, police have a limited time to ask additional questions for the purposes of investigating the crime and gathering evidence. This period is known as **pre-charge detention**. The period of detention is typically for a reasonable time not exceeding eight hours, but this can be extended for more complex and serious crimes.

Pre-charge detention: the limited time available for police to question a suspect after arrest and before charge

D. Charge

If police believe there is sufficient evidence a person has committed a crime, they can **charge** the person. Charging a person is an administrative decision which signals that the police intend to prosecute the crime in court. This is done by presenting the person with a document (called a charge sheet or bench charge sheet). The charge sheet specifies the offence with a brief description of the facts and circumstances involved.

Charge: an administrative decision to prosecute a person in court

At this stage, the police usually work closely with a prosecution service to determine if there is sufficient evidence to charge the person and, if so, which offence or offences are the most appropriate. A **prosecution service** is an office of lawyers working for the government who pursue criminal charges in court. The **prosecutor** is the lawyer assigned to the case that tries to prove in court that the offence has been committed beyond a reasonable doubt. For less complex matters, the prosecutor will often be a police prosecutor. A **police prosecutor** is a police officer who has undertaken additional legal training.

Prosecution service: office of lawyers working for the government who pursue criminal charges in court

Prosecutor: government lawyer that pursues charges against a defendant in court

Police prosecutor: a police officer with legal training that pursues criminal charges in court

Sometimes it will be clear which offence the person has committed, but there can be difficult choices involved. As discussed in the previous chapter, for example, there are many different types of assaults, each with specific requirements relating to harm and intention.

Generally, the police and prosecution will charge the offender with the most serious crime that is available on the evidence. However, they need to be careful with this decision: if they try to prosecute the person for a more serious offence that is not available on the evidence, the case will fail.

A person should only be prosecuted where it is in the public interest. If an elderly person shoplifts to feed themselves, they might have technically broken the law, but it would hardly be in the public interest to pursue charges in court. Where prosecution would not be in the public interest, there are several alternatives. For less serious offences, police can issue a **caution** (an official warning not to do it again) or an **infringement notice** (a ticket that requires the payment of money as a fine). They could also divert the person to restorative justice programs, such as mediation or counselling.

Caution: when police inform a person of the right to silence, and also an official warning issued by police

Infringement notice: ticket that requires payment of money as a fine

E. Misuse of police powers

If police misuse any of their powers, there are multiple ways they can be held accountable. The most common consequence is that any evidence they collected unlawfully will be excluded from the courtroom. For example, if police officers obtain a confession by threatening a suspect, or search a suspect's home without a warrant, a judge could refuse to have the confession or any physical evidence from the house admitted into evidence. If the evidence is important to proving the charge, the prosecution could fail as a result. It is crucial, for the criminal justice system to be fair and effective, that police collect evidence and question suspects according to the letter of the law.

If police engage in more serious conduct—such as using excessive force to make an arrest, or coercing a suspect into a confession—more serious consequences are available. The suspect can make a complaint to the police station, a state ombudsman, or an anti-corruption body such as Queensland's Crime and Corruption Commission. An **ombudsman** is an office that investigates complaints by members of the public against government departments and employees. These avenues could lead to the officer's employment being suspended or terminated (i.e., they could be 'fired').

Ombudsman: office that investigates complaints against members of government departments

Where someone is mistreated seriously by police, the person can make a civil claim for **damages** (compensation). For example, if a person was physically harmed or detained without lawful reason, a police officer may have committed **torts** of assault or false imprisonment. Ultimately, criminal charges for assault, manslaughter or murder remain a possibility if a police officer causes harm that is sufficiently serious, reckless or intentional. This is a key requirement of the rule of law: everyone in Australia—including police officers—are subject to the same criminal laws.

Damages: payment awarded by a court as compensation

Tort: an unlawful but non-criminal harm

3. BAIL

After a person is charged, a difficult question arises: what should they be allowed to do while they await trial? For minor offences, a person can be taken to the magistrates court the next morning, or they can be released from police custody and attend court at a later date on summons. However, for more serious offences, the accused might pose a risk to public safety or flee from the authorities if released. These people are held on **remand**, meaning they are detained in a prison while they await their court date. They are usually, but not always, held in a separate section to convicted offenders.

Remand: when somebody is held in prison after they are charged and before the criminal trial

Prison populations fluctuate daily, but at any given time, more than one-third of Australian prison's population is being held on remand. In 2023, 38% of prisoners had not yet been sentenced for any crime.[6] That such a large number of prisoners have not yet been found guilty of anything may come as a surprise to many people. And the rates are continually rising. Between 2012 and 2017, the remand population increased by 87%, likely due to more people being refused bail and a backlog in court cases.[7] In 2023, the remand population increased by 7% on the previous year.[8]

For less serious offences, or where the accused person does not pose a risk, they are often released on bail. **Bail** is the release of an accused person from police custody before they face trial. The release is **conditional**, meaning that the person is placed under restrictions and obligations to ensure that they remain accountable to the police and attend court at the later date. The example most people think of (possibly after watching American TV shows) is the payment of money as a bond, which will be forfeited if they fail to attend court. This does happen, but there is no requirement that bail must involve payment of money. In most cases, offenders do not have enough money to offer it as a guarantee. That requirement is used more often for wealthy, high-profile offenders. Most of the time, bail orders include requirements like surrendering a passport so the person cannot leave the country, and reporting to the local police station several times a week.

Bail: the conditional release of a person after they are charged and before the criminal trial

Conditional: when a person's release is subject to restrictions and obligations, like reporting to a police station

Bail can be granted by the police, but for more serious offences, decisions about bail are usually made by a magistrate in the local court. Legislation in each state guides how these decisions are made. The starting point is a presumption that bail will be granted and the person released. Bail will be refused, and the person held on remand, if there is an 'unacceptable risk' they will fail to appear before the court, commit another crime, harm themselves or someone else, or tamper with evidence. In Victoria and Queensland, magistrates must now also consider risks of family and domestic violence.

A recurring issue is that some offenders commit crimes while they are released from custody. Some high-profile examples of this have led to state bail laws being amended. For example, the gunman who held eighteen people hostage during the 'Sydney Siege' was on bail at the time for more than 40 sexual assault charges and a charge relating to the murder of his ex-wife. Following those tragic events, NSW's bail laws were amended to deny bail to anyone involved in terrorism unless 'exceptional circumstances exist'.[9] Victoria's bail laws were also tightened following the Bourke Street Mall attack in 2017. That offender drove his car into pedestrians, killing 6 and injuring nearly 30 more. At the time of the attack, he was on bail for several domestic and family violence offences.

It is crucial for courts to refuse bail if an accused person poses a threat to other members of the community. At the same time, bail remains an important aspect of due process and the presumption of innocence. Nobody should be detained as guilty of a crime until their guilt has been decided by a judge or jury of their peers. In ***Williamson v DPP*** (1999) QCA 356, Thomas J explained this difficult compromise, that bail remains a core aspect of due process but also creates a risk of harm:

> No grant of bail is risk free. The grant of bail however is an important process in civilised societies which reject any general right of the executive to imprison a citizen upon mere allegation or without trial. It is a necessary part of such a system that some risks have to be taken in order to protect citizens in those respects.

4. THE CRIMINAL TRIAL

A criminal trial is a series of court proceedings in which a magistrate or jury determines whether a person accused of a crime is guilty or not guilty.

Defendant: the accused person in a criminal trial

During a criminal trial, the person accused of the crime is known as the **defendant** because they are defending the charge against them. For less serious offences, the prosecutor is often a police prosecutor. For more serious offences, the prosecution is a team of lawyers from a state or federal prosecution service.

A. Pre-trial

There are important stages before the trial itself.

Disclosure: pre-trial process where the prosecution informs a defendant of the evidence against them

Pre-trial **disclosure** is where the prosecution informs the defendant about the evidence to be led against them. The general rule (with limited exceptions) is that the defendant does not need to disclose anything to the prosecution. This is another aspect of the **burden of proof** and the **presumption of innocence**: it is up to the prosecution to prove the defendant is guilty, and not for the defendant to prove their innocence.

Burden of proof: the responsibility to prove something in court

Presumption of innocence: principle that everyone is considered innocent until they are found guilty in a court of law

Committal hearings take place before trial for many indictable offences. A **committal hearing** is a preliminary hearing of the prosecution's case in a local court. The purpose of a committal hearing is for the magistrate to decide whether there is sufficient evidence against the accused to commit (send) the case to a full trial in a higher court. Depending on how serious the crime is, the higher court will be the district or supreme court.

Committal hearing: initial proceedings held in a local court to determine whether a criminal case should be heard in a higher court

Committal hearings give the defence an opportunity to hear the case against them. They allow the court system to weed out cases that lack sufficient evidence, and they allow the defence and prosecution to agree on the key legal issues for trial. However, there is a trend away from full committal hearings due to the added time and cost involved.

B. Summary trials

How a criminal trial proceeds depends on whether the person is accused of a summary or indictable offence. For summary offences (or if an indictable offence is heard summarily) the case is heard by a magistrate in a local court. The first step is for the defendant to be arraigned. The **arraignment** is where the charge is read out to the defendant, and the defendant enters a **plea** of guilty or not guilty. This means the defendant declares to the court whether they accept or contest the charge. If the defendant pleads guilty, no evidence is presented and the case proceeds straight to sentencing.

Arraignment: when a judge or magistrate reads out a criminal charge to a defendant

Plea: declaration by the defendant that they will or will not contest the charges

If the defendant pleads not guilty, a **summary trial** takes place. The prosecution presents evidence against the accused. The defendant contests that evidence and presents additional evidence to defend the charge. In a summary trial, the magistrate alone determines

Summary trial: criminal trial in the local court, which is decided by a magistrate alone whether the person has committed the elements of the offence beyond a reasonable doubt.

C. Jury trials

For indictable offences, the case is heard by a judge and jury in the district or supreme court. This is required for offences under federal law by section 80 of the Constitution. Prosecutions for indictable offences under state law can be heard by judge alone, though this is rare and normally requires the consent of both parties.

Jury trial: criminal trial held in district or supreme court, where a jury decides the defendant's guilt

Enter a plea: when a defendant claims to the court that they are guilty or not guilty of the crime

Empanel: to select and enrol the members of a jury

Peremptory challenge: when the prosecution or defence challenges the enrolment of a juror without giving a reason

At the start of a **jury trial**, the defendant is arraigned and **enters a plea**. If they plead guilty, the case proceeds straight to sentencing. If they plead not guilty, a jury trial takes place. This begins with the jury being **empanelled**. A jury is made up of members of the public (usually 12) who are chosen randomly from the electoral roll. A larger group of people is required to turn up to the courtroom because some ask the judge to be excused and others are challenged by the defence or prosecution lawyers.

Lawyers from both sides can challenge a small number of jury members without giving a reason. This is called a **peremptory challenge**. Once the jury is finalised, the members are asked to take an oath or affirmation that they will perform their job faithfully.

A jury trial is similar to a summary trial, in that the prosecution presents evidence against the accused, the defendant contests the charge, and the judge acts as a referee or umpire. However, the major difference in a jury trial is that the jury—not the judge—determines whether the person is guilty or not guilty. The jury must be satisfied, as a question of fact, that the person committed the elements of the offence beyond a reasonable doubt. They do this by listening to the evidence presented, then retiring (meeting separately) to consider their decision as a group.

The role of the judge in a jury trial is to answer questions of law (not questions of fact). The judge does not decide 'what happened' and whether the accused person is guilty or not guilty. Rather, judges preside over proceedings and determine important questions about how the case is run. They determine the meaning of legal words and tests from legislation and case law and explain these to the jury. Importantly, they determine which evidence can be put before the jury for its consideration. For example, if police officers have collected evidence unlawfully, that evidence could be excluded from the courtroom. Lawyers from both sides will make arguments (while the jury is not present) about whether the evidence should be admitted.

At the end of the trial, the jury presents its verdict to the court. The **verdict** is the jury's decision as to whether the defendant is guilty or not guilty. It is announced by the **foreperson**, who is appointed as a leader and representative for the jury. Usually, the verdict must be **unanimous** (i.e., all 12 people agree that the person is guilty or not guilty). However, there is some provision for **majority verdicts** where a jury cannot reach a decision. This requires 11 out of 12 jury members to agree. It is not available in trials for offences under federal law.

Verdict: magistrate or jury's decision whether a person is guilty or not guilty

Foreperson: a jury member appointed as its leader and spokesperson

Unanimous: agreed or supported by every member in a group

Majority verdict: a decision that 11 out of 12 jury members agree on

Jury trials enhance due process and help protect the right to a fair trial. Defendants can be convicted of serious offences only if a group of their peers (people from the community) are satisfied they are guilty beyond a reasonable doubt. This reflects our democratic values, because the decision is made by a group of people who (in theory) represent the rest of the population. Decisions about criminal guilt are made by a magistrate only for minor offences in the local court.

But the system is not perfect. Like anyone, jurors are capable of getting things wrong. It is also very difficult to prevent jurors from accessing information outside the courtroom. In theory, jurors are not meant to know anything else about the case, so they can determine the person's guilt objectively based only on the evidence presented in court. However, in the age of social media and a 24/7 news cycle, it is very difficult to shield a jury completely from the outside world. The risk is that jury members can see media reports or other information that suggests the defendant is guilty, when that information would not meet the requirements to be presented as evidence. Some jurors have even posted their decision on social media before all the evidence has been heard.[10]

D. Evidence

In both summary and jury trials, complex rules govern the types of information and physical evidence that can be put before the court. The items of evidence presented could include witness statements, photographs, medical assessments, DNA and fingerprint evidence, CCTV footage, and many other things. The starting point for any evidence is that it must have **probative value**: it must be relevant to a rational assessment of whether the offence was committed.

Probative value: relevance to a rational assessment of whether the defendant is guilty

Evidence can be excluded from courts for many different reasons. This is ultimately up to the judge's discretion. Evidence that is collected unlawfully or improperly will generally be excluded, though it can still be admitted if the probative value of the evidence is significant and the wrongdoing was minor.

Any other evidence that would cause 'unfair prejudice' to an accused can be excluded. **Prejudicial evidence** is evidence that would unfairly suggest the defendant is guilty or lead the jury to make an irrational or emotional decision. For example, showing excessively graphic images or video footage of a murder scene to a court could make a jury more likely to believe the defendant is guilty of wrongdoing, even if the evidence was not otherwise strong, because it would generate feelings of fear and disgust.

Prejudicial evidence: evidence that would unfairly suggest the defendant is guilty

Hearsay and **opinion** evidence are also typically excluded. **Hearsay** is essentially when a person hears something second-hand (i.e., they heard somebody say something). It is not considered a reliable account of events to say 'Steve told me that Jake killed someone', so these kinds of statements are generally excluded from evidence. (The exception would be if this statement had probative value for the fact that it was made, and not for the truth of the information contained in the statement. These sorts of fine distinctions make evidence a very difficult area of law!)

Opinion: another name for a judgment, or in evidence law, a belief that something was likely to happen

Hearsay: statements that are heard second-hand

A person's opinion that something was likely to happen is also not considered reliable. Steve might think that Jake is the kind of person who would commit murder, but this is irrelevant to a court. The major exception is **expert evidence**. This can be given, for example,

Expert evidence: opinion evidence given by a suitably trained and experienced expert

where a person is trained and experienced in a relevant discipline like psychiatry or forensic pathology. A psychiatrist could give valid evidence in court, based on a prior assessment, that Jake had a diagnosis which explains his state of mind and helps to establish the mental elements or a defence.

E. Witnesses

A core aspect of the criminal trial involves hearing evidence from witnesses. A **witness** is someone who presents oral (spoken) evidence in the courtroom, usually in response to questions put to them by the lawyers or the judge. These can be expert witnesses, like the psychiatrist example above, or eyewitnesses who saw the crime took place. Witnesses can be called by the prosecution or defence. When a witness 'takes the stand', it means they step into a witness box to give their testimony. **Testimony** is a formal statement to the court that explains their interpretation of events.

Witness: a person who presents testimony to the court

Testimony: a formal statement made by a witness to the court which explains their interpretation of events

There is a specific procedure used when witnesses give evidence. First is the **evidence-in-chief**. This is where the lawyer who called the witness to the stand asks a series of questions to elicit the testimony. Next is the **cross-examination**. This is where lawyers from the opposing side ask the witness questions. Usually, the questions are designed to undermine the accuracy of the testimony. For example, the defence lawyers might ask an eyewitness whether they could clearly see the crime taking place. The final stage is **re-examination**. This is where lawyers from the side that called the witness can clarify any confusion arising from the cross-examination. This helps the side who called the witness restate the main points in the testimony.

Evidence-in-chief: initial statement of witness testimony

Cross-examination: when lawyers ask questions to undermine the accuracy of testimony presented by a witness who was called by the opposing side

Re-examination: the final stage of questioning a witness, when the side that called the witness asks questions to reinforce the testimony

This process is repeated over and over until all evidence from both sides has been presented. For complex criminal trials, this can take many months. Lawyers for both sides then present a **closing statement** that sums up their key evidence and arguments.

Closing statement: final speech made by a lawyer to the court, which sums up their major evidence and arguments

After all the evidence is presented, if the magistrate or jury returns a verdict of not guilty, the defendant is free to leave the courtroom. There is no legal basis to hold them in custody any longer. If, on the other hand, the defendant is found guilty, then the trial proceeds to sentencing. In a relatively simple trial, sentencing can happen straight away, but it is more common for a judge to set a later date for a dedicated sentencing hearing.

KEY POINTS

- Police have many special powers to investigate crimes. These powers are set out in legislation, which both creates the power and limits it. Common police powers include arrest, search, pre-charge detention, and questioning.
- Bail is the conditional release of a person charged with a criminal offence, before they face trial. There is a presumption that bail will be granted, unless there is an unacceptable risk the person will fail to appear before court, commit another crime, harm anyone, or tamper with evidence.
- How a criminal trial proceeds depends on whether the accused is charged with a summary or indictable offence. Trials for summary offences are heard in the local court by a magistrate alone. Trials for indictable offences are heard in the district or supreme courts, where a judge decides questions of law and a jury decides whether the person is guilty or not guilty.

DISCUSSION QUESTIONS

1. On balance, does discretion enhance or undermine fairness in the criminal justice system?
2. What are some examples of discretion at different stages of the criminal justice process?
3. In what circumstances will a person be denied bail, and held on remand?
4. Should all people charged with criminal offences be held on remand, to avoid the risk that any of them could commit another offence while on bail?
5. How does the criminal trial process differ depending on whether the accused is charged with a summary or indictable offence?

6. What types of information can be presented before a court as evidence of a crime being committed, and what types are usually excluded from consideration?
7. Are jury trials a fair system for deciding whether a defendant is guilty or not guilty?

NOTES

1 Davis, K. C. (1969). ***Discretionary justice: a preliminary inquiry***. Louisiana State University Press.

2 Findlay, M., Odgers, S., & Yeo, S. (2014) ***Australian criminal justice*** (5th ed.). Oxford University Press.

3 ***Police Powers and Responsibilities Act 2000*** (Qld) s 29.

4 ***Police Powers and Responsibilities Act 2000*** (Qld) s 30.

5 ***Australian Security Intelligence Organisation Act 1979*** (Cth) s 34GD.

6 Australian Bureau of Statistics (2023). ***Prisoners in Australia***. Retrieved from: https://www.abs.gov.au/statistics/people/crime-and-justice/prisoners-australia/latest-release.

7 Russell, S., & Baldry, E. (2017). Three charts on: Australia's booming prison population. ***The Conversation***, 14 June.

8 Australian Bureau of Statistics, n 6.

9 ***Bail Act 2013*** (NSW) s 22A.

10 Bartels, L. (2013). Jurors and social media: Is there a solution? ***The Conversation***, 31 July.

Chapter 12
Sentencing and appeals

In this chapter, you will learn about:

- Purposes of punishment and principles of sentencing
- Sentencing approaches for Indigenous offenders
- Appeals against conviction and sentence

When a defendant pleads guilty, or is found guilty by a magistrate or jury, they are sentenced for the crime. This is where a magistrate or judge determines the type and severity of the punishment. For offenders who are convicted and imprisoned, they can later apply for release on parole.

A person found guilty of a crime can appeal against their conviction or sentence. This means challenging the decision in a higher court. There are complex rules relating to when a court's decision can be appealed, which help to avoid—but do not prevent all—wrongful convictions.

1. PUNISHMENT AND SENTENCING

There are many types of orders, other than imprisonment, that courts can deliver as punishment when a person pleads or is found guilty of a crime. In determining an appropriate sentence, judges and magistrates must consider the purposes of punishment, principles of sentencing, and any aggravating and mitigating factors. These are all weighed up together in a method called 'instinctive synthesis'.

A. Types of punishment

It is important to recognise that courts are not required to imprison every convicted person (or even to register a conviction). While imprisonment is a

DOI: 10.4324/9781003433408-15

common punishment for serious offences, there are many other options. Courts can issue fines, require compensation to be paid, or impose a **community service order** that requires the offender to complete a specified number of hours volunteering in the community.

Community service order: an order issued by a court that requires a convicted offender to complete a specified number of hours volunteering in the community

Probation is where an offender is released on conditions such as reporting regularly to a corrective services officer and participating in counselling and rehabilitation programs. A **suspended sentence** is a prison term that is not served immediately but can be triggered if the person commits another crime. Probation and suspended sentences usually involve a **good behaviour bond**, which is essentially a promise not to commit other crimes. If the offender breaches the good behaviour bond, a prison sentence may then be triggered.

Probation: when a convicted offender is released on conditions, such as reporting to a correctional services officer at regular times

Suspended sentence: a prison term that is not served immediately but can be triggered if the offender commits another crime

Good behaviour bond: order issued by a court that requires an offender to promise they will not commit another crime

B. Purposes of punishment

Sentencing judges and magistrates need to consider many different factors. First are the **purposes of punishment**. These are the reasons why the court is punishing the person. They include **retribution**: the need simply to punish the person for the harm they caused. Another is **rehabilitation**: helping the person address the underlying reasons they committed the crime in the first place (such as a history of drug addiction). Another is **deterrence**, which has two types. **General deterrence** means the court signals to the entire community that a crime will be treated severely, which may prevent others from engaging in the same conduct. **Specific deterrence** means the court signals to the individual offender that their actions will be treated severely, which may prevent them from reoffending in the future.

Purposes of punishment: reasons why courts punish offenders, which are considered while sentencing them

Retribution: punishment inflicted as repayment for a harmful act

Rehabilitation: helping an offender address the underlying reasons why they committed a crime

Another purpose is **denunciation**. Courts play a role in society by denouncing ('calling out') conduct that is harmful or morally wrong, which highlights its negative impact. For example, there is purpose in punishing offenders who are guilty of committing domestic and family violence as a signal to the wider community that this conduct is unacceptable. Finally, **incapacitation** means protecting the community from further harm. When a person is imprisoned, they are incapable of committing further crimes.

Deterrence: signalling to an individual or the community that committing a crime will attract punishment, to encourage them not to offend

General deterrence: signalling to community members that committing a crime will attract punishment, to encourage them not to offend

Specific deterrence: signalling to an offender that their actions will be treated severely, to encourage them not to reoffend

Denunciation: declaring that conduct is morally wrong

Incapacitation: putting a person in prison to protect the community from further harm

These purposes of punishment are set out in legislation, and judges are required to take them into account in weighing up the type and severity of punishment.

A key issue is that these purposes of punishment do not always point in the same direction. Retribution, incapacitation, denunciation and deterrence suggest that a penalty should be more severe, whereas rehabilitation suggests that a penalty should be less severe. In *Veen (No 2)* (1988) 164 CLR 465, the High Court explained that the purposes may conflict with each other and are simply 'guideposts' to help judges determine an appropriate sentence:

> The purposes of criminal punishment are various: protection of society, deterrence of the offender and of others who might be tempted to offend, retribution and reform. The purposes overlap and none of them can be considered in isolation from the others when determining what is an appropriate sentence in a particular case. They are guideposts to the appropriate sentence but sometimes they point in different directions.

C. Principles of sentencing

Principles of sentencing: general rules that explain how a judge should arrive at an appropriate sentence

Sentencing judges must also consider **principles of sentencing**. These are a series of concepts that help judges arrive at an appropriate punishment. The first is **proportionality**, meaning that the punishment should bear an appropriate relationship to the conduct being punished. In other words, 'the punishment should fit the crime'. Another is **parsimony**, meaning the judge should favour the least severe sentence that is appropriate. A third is **totality**, which is relevant where an offender is being sentenced for multiple crimes. While the maximum penalties could theoretically be added up to deliver a crushing sentence, the offender should receive a sentence that is proportionate overall. For example, if an offender is facing ten counts of common assault, each attracting a maximum penalty of two years imprisonment, they would theoretically be facing twenty years in prison for ten minor assaults. In a case like this, the overall sentence should reflect the defendant's moral responsibility, and not reach the total maximum penalty.

A fourth principle is **consistency**, which means that similar cases should be treated in a similar way. Sentencing judges are not required to follow precedent in the same way as trial judges, but there is a need for overall consistency between decisions. A fifth principle is **parity**, meaning that multiple offenders being punished for the same offence should receive a similar sentence. However, a final principle is **individualised justice**, which means that courts should impose sentences that are appropriate in all the circumstances of an individual case.

D. Aggravating and mitigating factors

To achieve individualised justice, sentencing judges must take into account all relevant aggravating and mitigating factors. An **aggravating factor** is any information that suggests a punishment should be more severe. This could include details about how the offence was committed, whether the offender used a weapon, or who the offender targeted as a victim. For example, an assault against a child, or an elderly or disabled person, would be treated more severely. Aggravating factors can also relate to the offender's motive for

Proportionality: in sentencing, the principle that punishments should be appropriate in type and severity to the crime committed, or in international law, that military attacks must not be excessive compared to the military advantage sought

Parsimony: favouring the least severe sentence that is appropriate in the circumstances

Totality: principle that a sentence for multiple crimes should be fair overall

Consistency: principle that sentencing judges should treat similar cases in a similar way

Parity: principle that multiple offenders should receive a similar sentence for the same crime

Individualised justice: principle that a punishment should be fair in all the circumstances of an individual case

Aggravating factor: any piece of information that suggests a sentence should be more severe

committing the crime (for example, if the crime was committed for greed or revenge, or to exploit vulnerable people).

It is important to distinguish between aggravating factors in sentencing, and specific elements that make a crime an 'aggravated offence'. As you learned in Chapter 10, a person could be charged with an aggravated assault, which attracts a higher penalty than a common assault, if they used a weapon to attack another person. The use of a weapon is an element of the substantive offence that needs to be proven beyond a reasonable doubt. This could also be considered as an aggravating factor in sentencing, but it has already been accounted for to some degree by the higher penalty. More likely, specific facts about the weapon and its usage (such as the type of weapon, how it was used, and the injuries it caused) would be considered as aggravating factors in sentencing. Aggravating factors in sentencing suggest the penalty should be on the higher end for any given offence. This is equally true for aggravated offences and minor offences. If, for example, someone punched a vulnerable victim multiple times while shouting abuse at them, they might still be charged with a basic assault, but the punishment would be at the higher end of the available maximum penalty.

Mitigating factor: any piece of information that suggests a sentence should be less severe

A **mitigating factor** is any piece of information that suggests punishment should be less severe. These typically include details from the offender's background that excuse or justify their conduct to some degree. It might be, for example, that the offender has a history of being sexually abused, or problems with alcohol or drug addiction, which influenced their violent nature over the course of their life. Mitigating factors will also be taken into account where the offender has pleaded guilty, cooperated with police, or expressed remorse (guilt) about committing the crime. Mitigating factors are not the same as defences, such as self-defence or provocation. Those are specific legal arguments that reduce or remove the offender's criminal responsibility at the trial stage, before the sentencing hearing.

E. Evidence

Evidence rules are much more flexible at sentencing compared to trial. At trial, all evidence presented must be relevant to a rational assessment of whether the crime was committed. An offender's personal history and their motives in committing the crime are irrelevant to the *actus reus* and *mens rea*. The trial aims only to prove or disprove that the offender did the act with the required intention.

In a sentencing hearing, there are few limits on the kinds of information that could be presented to the sentencing judge or magistrate. Any relevant information about the offender (such as their age, employment history, relationships with family members, or involvement in the community) can be considered. This information has no bearing on the person's guilt, which has already been established. However, it can be useful for the court to determine an appropriate punishment.

Section 9 of the ***Penalties and Sentences Act 1992*** (Qld) sets out many factors that courts must take into account in sentencing. These include:

- The maximum and any minimum penalty for the offence.
- The nature of the offence and the seriousness of the offender's conduct.
- Any physical, mental or emotional harm done to a victim.
- The extent to which the offender is to blame for the offence.
- The offender's character, age and intellectual capacity.
- Any aggravating or mitigating factor.
- The prevalence of the offence (how often it occurs).
- How much assistance the offender gave to law enforcement agencies.
- Any other relevant circumstance.

You can see from this list that the information relevant to sentencing can far exceed the evidence used at trial to determine whether the defendant is guilty. In a sentencing hearing, many different types of documents (including psychologist reports, character references, letters of apology, or evidence of participation in rehabilitation programs) can all be tendered as evidence.

Another key piece of information, presented in many sentencing hearings, is a **victim impact statement**. This is where the victim explains how the crime has impacted on them. The statement can be written or oral. The harm described might be physical, psychological, or involve negative impacts on employment or personal relationships. For example, an assault in a domestic violence case may cause not only physical harm (like bruising or broken bones) but also ongoing depression and anxiety that impacts on the victim's ability to hold down a job or enjoy socialising with others. Following a murder or other homicide, family members can present a victim impact statement to present a picture of who the victim was and explain the loss they have suffered. Many of these details would not be allowed at trial because they are not relevant to whether the offence was committed, but they can help the court arrive at an appropriate sentence.

Victim impact statement: prepared statement presented to a court that explains the impact of a crime on a victim or their family

Victim impact statements also serve an important purpose, beyond this practical value, by giving victims and their families a greater role in criminal justice processes and acknowledging their grief and pain. The two parties in a criminal trial are the state and the defendant: the victim can give evidence, but they are not party to the proceedings. Victim impact statements mean that the experiences of victims, including their families, are voiced and acknowledged in the courtroom. This can play a role in healing and closure, by allowing victims to find a greater sense of justice and resolution.[1]

F. Instinctive synthesis

The overarching task for a sentencing judge or magistrate is to determine an appropriate punishment. They do this by weighing up the offender's conduct in combination with many other factors: the purposes of punishment, the principles of sentencing, aggravating and mitigating factors, the impact on victims and anything else that is relevant. This is a complex decision-making process involving significant discretion.

Instinctive synthesis: overall process followed by sentencing judges, in which they weigh up all relevant factors

This method is called **instinctive synthesis**. A judge conducts what is largely an intuitive exercise in each case, guided by the various principles and factors explained above. This has been criticised for being too vague and subjective.[2] However, it remains the decided method that sentencing judges should rely upon. The High Court has firmly rejected a 'two-tier approach', in which some objectively determined punishment (such as a predetermined number of years in prison) is tweaked up or down depending on the circumstances.[3] A two-tier approach is considered too significant a restriction on a judge's discretion.

Guideline judgment: judgment that explains the typical punishment for an offence

Judges do have significant discretion in sentencing hearings, but there are still important constraints. Legislation prescribes the factors they must consider when making their decisions. They must aim for consistency in similar cases. And, if a sentence is overly harsh or inadequate, the offender or prosecutor can appeal. Appeal courts in some jurisdictions can also issue **guideline judgments** that explain the typical punishment for an offence or how a sentence should be decided.

Most states also have a **sentencing advisory council** that conducts research and produces advice on sentencing matters. Sentencing councils publish statistics on sentencing, educate communities about sentencing, and test community views as to whether different punishments are fair. For example, Victoria's Sentencing Advisory Council has developed an interactive online program called 'You Be the Judge'.[4] Community members can hear offenders' stories, decide on an appropriate punishment, and compare their sentence with that given by the actual judge.

Sentencing advisory council: state body that conducts research, produces advice and educates communities about sentencing

G. Mandatory minimums

Criminal offences usually have a maximum penalty, which the sentencing judge cannot exceed. The judge can impose any penalty of imprisonment up to and including that amount, or they can issue an alternative type of punishment (such as probation, a good behaviour bond or a community service order).

Occasionally, criminal laws set a fixed or minimum penalty that the court must impose and not drop below. This is common for many minor offences, like exceeding the speed limit, which attracts a fixed penalty (the payment of money as a fine and a specified number of demerit points).

Minimum punishments become problematic when parliament sets one for a more serious crime. Setting a minimum penalty of imprisonment removes the discretion of the sentencing judge to recognise and account for factors specific to an individual case. It does not matter if there are lots of mitigating factors; a judge must impose a minimum penalty of imprisonment.

Mandatory minimum sentencing caught public attention after state parliaments began introducing new offences to address alcohol-fuelled violence and 'one-punch' attacks. In 2014, the NSW Parliament introduced an offence of 'assault causing death' into the *Crimes Act 1900* (NSW). Where an offender is over 18, intentionally strikes a person while intoxicated, and causes the person's death, the court must impose a minimum sentence of eight years' imprisonment.

Mandatory minimum: minimum penalty set in legislation for a criminal offence

Those changes followed the death of Thomas Kelly, an 18-year-old Sydney boy who was assaulted by a stranger on a night out in Kings Cross. Kelly was knocked unconscious by a single punch and later died from injuries to the brain. Another high-profile case contributing to the new laws was the death of 18-year-old Daniel Christie in Kings Cross on New Year's Eve in 2013.

There is no evidence to suggest that mandatory minimums act as an effective deterrent or help reduce crime over the long term.[5] They also undermine the separation of powers. Instead of a court deciding on an appropriate penalty, politicians in parliament have decided in advance what a punishment must require.

Mandatory minimums also have a disproportionate impact on Indigenous offenders due to their increased contact with the criminal justice system. In Western Australia and the Northern Territory, mandatory minimums apply to a range of property offences and serious assaults. In one case, a 15-year-old orphaned Aboriginal boy was imprisoned under a minimum penalty for stealing around $50 worth of pens and stationery from a council building.[6] He later committed suicide in prison. As Hilde Tubex from the University of Western Australia rightly commented, 'a system can't be fair or just if the marginalised and the vulnerable are the first to be affected by it'.[7]

H. Sentencing Indigenous offenders

Circle sentencing: a mediation process based on traditional Indigenous practices

Courts sentencing Indigenous offenders face additional challenges and responsibilities. In Chapter 7, we briefly discussed Indigenous courts and **circle sentencing**, which recognise more traditional forms of justice and involve Indigenous communities in the sentencing process. These approaches are designed in part to address the over-representation of Indigenous people in prison.[8]

According to regulation 39 of the Criminal Procedure Regulation 2017 (NSW), the aims of circle sentencing are to:

- include members of Aboriginal communities in the sentencing process;
- increase the confidence of Aboriginal communities in the sentencing process;
- reduce barriers between Aboriginal communities and the courts;
- provide more appropriate sentencing options for Aboriginal offenders;
- provide effective support to victims of offences by Aboriginal offenders;
- provide for the greater participation of Aboriginal offenders and their victims in the sentencing process;

- increase the awareness of Aboriginal offenders of the consequences of their offences on their victims and the Aboriginal communities to which they belong, and
- reduce recidivism in Aboriginal communities.

The first Indigenous court (the Nunga Court) was created in Port Adelaide in 1999. The first trial of circle sentencing began in Nowra, on the New South Wales south coast, in 2002. Since then, Indigenous courts and circle sentencing practices have expanded across all Australian states and territories. While specific practices differ across the states, a useful description of circle sentencing in New South Wales is given by Marchetti and Daly:

> Participants sit in a circle, which has four community elders, the magistrate, the offender, the offender's support people, the Aboriginal Project Officer, the victim and their supporters, the defence counsel and the police prosecutor. The court is closed, and permission from the magistrate and the elders is required before observers can watch the proceedings by sitting outside the circle. The magistrate prepares a document, which describes the offence and relevant information about the offender's background. The text is elaborated orally by all participants in court, including the offender. Circle members discuss what would be an appropriate sentence plan for the offender. It reconvenes after a few months to assess the offender's progress.[9]

It is not clear that circle sentencing reduces reoffending,[10] but there are still benefits to having culturally appropriate processes that can aid rehabilitation. In a report on circle sentencing in Nowra, the Judicial Commission of NSW found that:

> The penalties imposed by the circle are no less onerous than those imposed for similar offences in conventional courts. However as the procedure is less formal, the offender is more likely to 'sit up and take notice' and appreciate the harm caused to the victim. In this regard there is generally an acceptance of responsibility as well as an apology for the offending behaviour—a platform upon which rehabilitation can be built.[11]

Outside Indigenous courts and circle sentencing, Indigenous disadvantage can be recognised as a mitigating factor in sentencing. However, courts have debated over time whether Indigenous offenders should be treated any differently to non-Indigenous offenders. This is a difficult issue to resolve given that, according to some views, recognising Indigenous disadvantage (including a history of alcohol abuse and domestic violence) could amount to racial stereotyping and discrimination.

In *R v Bugmy* (2013) 249 CLR 571, the High Court claimed there was no reason to sentence Aboriginal offenders differently to non-Aboriginal offenders, or to take into account the higher rates of Indigenous incarceration. However, the court did recognise that 'an Aboriginal offender's deprived background may mitigate the sentence … in the same way that the deprived background of a non-Aboriginal offender may mitigate that offender's sentence'. This means an Indigenous offender who has experienced significant hardship, including a history of alcohol abuse, might have a sentence reduced for that reason (as might any other, non-Indigenous offender).

What is to be avoided, however, is an assumption that all Indigenous offenders will necessarily fit into this category. As the High Court stated in ***Munda v WA*** (2013) 249 CLR 600, 'to accept that Aboriginal offenders are in general less responsible for their actions than other persons would be to deny Aboriginal people their full measure of human dignity'. The court should not engage in a practice of 'racial stereotyping' that consigns Aboriginal offenders, 'by reason of their race and place of residence, to a category of persons who are less capable than others of decent behaviour'.[12]

I. Imprisonment and parole

A convicted offender may be released under supervision earlier than the total period of imprisonment handed down by a sentencing court. Being released on conditions while serving a prison sentence is called **parole**. It is similar to probation, in that the offender is free to go about their daily life but must comply with certain requirements and obligations. These can include receiving visits from a corrective services officer, letting corrective services know if they change their job or home address, not leaving the state without permission, attending counselling and rehabilitation sessions, and being tested for drugs and alcohol. **Corrective services** is a core department in the criminal justice system that is responsible for managing prisons. It has dedicated probation and parole officers who are responsible for supervising and managing offenders who are released in the community.

Parole: when a prisoner is released on conditions while serving their sentence

Corrective services: core department in the criminal justice system that is responsible for managing prisons

If an offender breaches parole, the conditions of the order can change, or the offender may be returned to prison. In Queensland, a sentencing judge must set a parole release date for prison sentences of three years or less.[13] For more serious offences, the court can choose to set a date when the offender will become eligible. Offenders who are eligible for parole must apply to the state **Parole Board**, an independent authority that makes decisions about release and the conditions involved.

Parole Board: an authority independent to a prison, which decides whether offenders should be released on parole

In New South Wales, the ***Crimes (Sentencing Procedure) Act 1999*** (NSW) establishes standard non-parole periods for a long list of offences. A **non-parole period** (NPP) is the period of a sentence during which a prisoner is not eligible for parole. Victoria requires that a non-parole period be set for prison terms of two years or more, unless the court considers it inappropriate. Queensland takes a more limited approach by requiring courts to impose an NPP only for serious violent offences.

Non-parole period: period during a prison sentence when a convicted offender cannot be released under supervision

2. APPEALS

Appeal rights are a core aspect of due process. A convicted person can appeal against the fact that they were convicted, or the sentence they received. The prosecution can appeal against a sentence that is too lenient, or in rare circumstances against an **acquittal**.

Acquit: find that a defendant is not guilty

To **appeal** a decision means to challenge it in a higher court. Whoever does this is known the **appellant**. The other party becomes the **respondent**. (Usually, it is the defendant who becomes the appellant, and the state the respondent.)

Appeal: challenge a decision in a higher court

Appellant: person who lodges an appeal

Respondent: party arguing against the grounds of an appeal

A. Appeals and the court hierarchy

Appeals are made to a court higher than the one the case was heard in, so the process mirrors the court hierarchy explained in Chapter 3. At the bottom are the local or magistrates courts, which have no **appellate**

Appellate jurisdiction: power of a court to hear appeals from lower courts

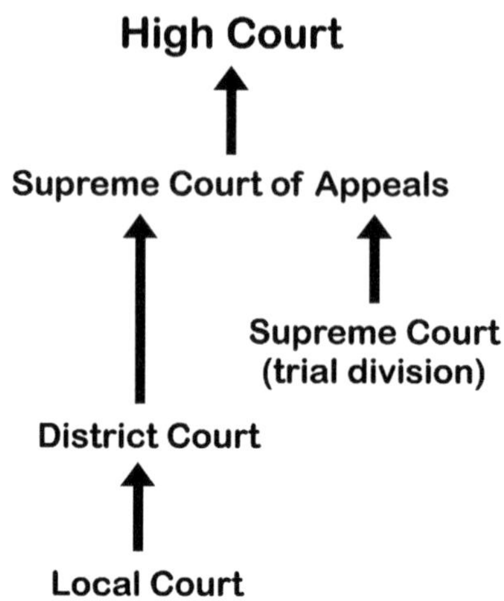

Figure 12.1 Appeals hierarchy

jurisdiction (meaning the power to hear an appeal). If an offender disagrees with a decision in the magistrates court, they can apply (usually within a short period of time) to the district court. They can challenge either the conviction or the sentence. This is the only stage of the process where an appeal functions as a complete rehearing of the evidence. The judge who hears an appeal in the district court may confirm, set aside or vary the decision of the magistrates court, or make any other appropriate order.

As a defendant moves further up the court hierarchy, the grounds for appeal become increasingly limited. If a defendant disagrees with a decision in the district or supreme court, they can appeal to the appeals division of the supreme court, which is usually called the Court of Criminal Appeal (or simply the Court of Appeal). An appeal cannot be made from the district court to the trial division of the supreme court, which hears criminal cases for the first time. You can see these pathways in Figure 12.1.

B. Appeals against conviction and sentence

A defendant can appeal against their conviction to the Court of Appeal if they can point to a **question of law** that affected the original decision. For example, the

Question of law: a legal issue that provides the basis for an appeal

judge might have made an error when allowing evidence to be admitted, or while explaining an element of the offence to the jury.

If the defendant cannot point to a legal error, they can still appeal on a question of fact (essentially, that they believe the jury got the decision wrong). However, this requires **leave** of the court (permission to have the case heard) and is not guaranteed. Appeal courts are generally reluctant to overturn the decision of a jury, as the jury members were able to hear the witnesses and see the evidence first-hand during the criminal trial. Unlike appeals in the district court, appeals in the supreme court do not involve a complete rehearing of the evidence.

Leave: permission granted by a court to hear an appeal

In an appeal against conviction, the original decision could be overturned for three possible reasons. First, the jury might have reached an unreasonable decision that could not be supported by the evidence. This is an error of fact, and is sometimes called an **unsafe and unsatisfactory** verdict. Second, the judge might have made an error of law, such as allowing prejudicial evidence to be put before the jury. Third, there could have been a **miscarriage of justice**. This essentially means there was a wrongful conviction. It overlaps with the first two grounds, but is designed to give judges a wider discretion to overturn wrongful decisions where appropriate. If the court **allows** the appeal (i.e., agrees with the defendant's arguments) it will either substitute a verdict of acquittal, meaning the defendant is not guilty and free to go, or it can order a retrial in a lower court.

Unsafe and unsatisfactory: phrase describing cases that were decided wrongly by a jury

Miscarriage of justice: a wrongful conviction

Allow: agree with the arguments in an appeal

The grounds for appealing against sentence are much more limited. Either party can appeal against sentence, but they need to seek leave of the court, and there needs to be some substantial error in the type or severity of punishment. Courts of appeal are reluctant to adjust sentences handed down by lower courts, or they would be continually tweaking every decision. They will change a sentence only if it was **manifestly excessive** (far too harsh) or **manifestly inadequate** (far too lenient).

Manifestly excessive: phrase used to describe sentencing judgments that are found on appeal to be too severe

Manifestly inadequate: phrase used to describe sentencing judgments that are found on appeal to be too lenient

C. The High Court

If a party disagrees with the decision of a Court of Appeal, they can appeal to the High Court. However, the grounds for appealing to the High Court are quite limited.

Special leave to appeal: permission to have an appeal heard in the High Court

An applicant first needs to seek **special leave to appeal**. This sets a higher bar than the permission granted by Supreme Courts of Appeal. Gaining special leave requires an issue of law that has public importance, affects the administration of justice, or would resolve disagreement between the states. These requirements are set out in s 35A of the ***Judiciary Act 1903*** (Cth). A party cannot appeal to the High Court simply because they disagree with a conviction or sentence. The rates of approval for special leave applications are very low, usually around 10%.[14]

Once an appeal has been heard by the High Court, the avenues of appeal are complete. There is no higher court for an appeal to be heard in, even if someone disagrees with the outcome. According to section 72 of the Constitution, decisions of the High Court are 'final and conclusive'.

D. Benefits and limits

This system of appeals helps to protect defendants against wrongful convictions and other miscarriages of justice. It is a core aspect of due process and enhances the rule of law.

However, the system is not perfect. Several reasons for this are explained well by Ransley and Goldsmith.[15] First, a guilty person can be let free, but the prosecution can appeal against an acquittal only in very rare circumstances. Double jeopardy laws mean the person cannot be tried again for the same crime, unless there is some significant new evidence. Second, defendants can plead guilty to an offence out of fear, ignorance, or a lack of understanding. If this happens, no trial takes place and the person cannot appeal against their conviction because they admitted their guilt. Third, even if a wrongful conviction is overturned and a person is acquitted, this can take a long time and the person may have already spent many years or even decades in prison.

When someone is wrongfully convicted, there is usually no compensation for the time they lost in their lives and the conditions they were kept in, through no fault of their own. Article 14(6) of the ***International Covenant on Civil and***

Political Rights requires that people who have been wrongfully convicted 'shall be compensated according to law'. However, research shows that less than one-third of Australians convicted for a crime they did not commit received any compensation.[16] This is yet another way that Australia is failing to meet its international human rights obligations.

KEY POINTS

- Sentencing judges must consider the purposes of punishment, principles of sentencing, and aggravating and mitigating factors, and weigh them up in a decision-making process called instinctive synthesis. This helps to arrive at appropriate punishments in individual cases.
- Mandatory minimum sentences are controversial because they reduce a sentencing judge's discretion to determine an appropriate punishment. They also undermine the separation of powers and impact disproportionately on Indigenous offenders.
- Appealing a court decision means challenging the decision in a higher court. As a case moves further up the court hierarchy, the grounds for appealing the decision become more limited. Once an appellant reaches the High Court, all avenues of appeal have been exhausted.

DISCUSSION QUESTIONS

1. Aside from imprisonment, what other types of punishments can a court impose?
2. What is the difference between the purposes of punishment and the principles of sentencing?
3. Do judges have too much or too little discretion in sentencing?
4. Do you agree that some crimes should have a mandatory minimum sentence?
5. Is the sentencing of Indigenous offenders any different to the sentencing of non-Indigenous offenders?
6. If a case begins in the local or magistrates court, what are the different pathways of appeal it can follow? Can you draw this as a diagram without looking?
7. Should all prisoners who were wrongfully convicted receive compensation when they are released?

NOTES

1 See Bandes, S.A. (2009). Victims, 'closure', and the sociology of emotion. ***Law and Contemporary Problems***, ***72***, 1-26.

2 Traynor, S., & Potas, I. (2002). Sentencing methodology: two-tiered or instinctive synthesis. ***Sentencing Trends & Issues*** (No. 25). Judicial Commission of NSW.

3 *AB v R* (1999) 198 CLR 111

4 Sentencing Advisory Council (2017). You Be the Judge. Retrieved from https://virtualjudge.sentencingcouncil.vic.gov.au/

5 Fitzgibbon, K., & Roffee, J. (2017). Mandatory minimum sentences and populist criminal justice policy do not work – here's why. ***The Conversation***, 19 April.

6 Howe, L. (2001). Mandatory sentencing: A death sentence in the Northern Territory? ***Current Issues in Criminal Justice***, ***12***(3), 376-381.

7 Tubex, H. (2016). Mandatory sentencing leads to unjust, unfair outcomes – it doesn't make us safe. ***The Conversation***, 5 January.

8 Marchetti, E., & Daly, K. (2004). Indigenous courts and justice practices in Australia (Trends & Issues in Crime and Criminal Justice, No. 277). Canberra: Australian Institute of Criminology.

9 Ibid.

10 Ibid.

11 Fitzgerald, J. (2008). Does circle sentencing reduce Aboriginal offending? ***Contemporary Issues in Crime and Justice*** (No 115). NSW Bureau of Crime Statistics and Research.

12 ***Munda v WA*** (2013) 249 CLR 600.

13 ***Penalties and Sentences Act 1992*** (Qld), s 160B

14 Stuhmcke, A., & Stewart, P. (2020). Special leave to appeal to the High Court: which applications are most likely to be granted leave? ***Precedent***, ***158***, 20.

15 Ransley, J., & Goldsmith, A. (2006). Failures of justice. In A. Goldsmith, M. Israel, & K. Daly (Eds.), ***Crime and Justice: A Guide to Criminology*** (3rd ed., pp. 465-484). Lawbook Co.

16 Meeton, P. (2020). When justice fails: wrongful convictions in Australia. ***Right Now: Human Rights in Australia***, 2 October. Retrieved from: https://rightnow.org.au/opinion/when-justice-fails-wrongful-convictions-in-australia/.

Chapter 13
Cybercrime

In this chapter, you will learn about:

- Cyber-enabled and cyber-dependent crime
- Fraud, identity theft, sexting, revenge porn and cyber-bullying
- Criminal hacking, denial-of-service attacks and ransomware

These final chapters focus on key areas in recent lawmaking. They are designed as case studies to draw together and build on what you have learned. Now that you know many legal concepts and ideas, you can apply your knowledge in these and other areas of study and interest.

These final chapters reinforce the idea that law is not simply a collection of fixed rules. Rather, laws develop over time in response to new crimes, changes in morals and values, and other events in Australian society and around the world.

This chapter teaches you about cybercrime: criminal acts involving computers. Cybercrime poses many challenges, in part because laws designed for 'real world' crimes are not always suited to online spaces.

Cybercrime can be cyber-enabled or cyber-dependent. The eSafety Commissioner plays a critical role by educating communities how to stay safe online. The office also has powers to address harmful online content.

1. WHAT IS CYBERCRIME?

Cybercrime is crime involving computers, but some crimes depend on computers more than others. A distinction is often drawn between cyber-enabled and

DOI: 10.4324/9781003433408-16

Cyber-enabled crime: more traditional crimes committed online

Cyber-dependent crime: cyber-crime that depends on technology

cyber-dependent crime.[1] **Cyber-enabled crime** refers to more traditional crimes (such as abuse and fraud) that are now easier to commit using computers. Computers enable those crimes on a much larger scale. **Cyber-dependent crime** refers to newer crimes (such as denial-of-service attacks and ransomware) that have come about since the development of computers. These crimes depend on technology and would not exist otherwise.

Revenge porn: distributing intimate images to embarrass or humiliate a person

The distinction is not perfect. Fraud is a good example of something that has long been committed in the 'real world' and is enabled on a much larger scale by technology. But something like **revenge porn** (posting or sending intimate images of someone without their consent) is also typically classed as cyber-enabled. It was never a major concern that people were doing this before smartphones by handing out printed photographs. Technology has certainly made the crime easier to commit, but it has enabled it to such a degree that technology is fundamental to the behaviour and our understanding of it.

Equally, something like malware is rightly cyber-dependent, as you cannot have malicious software without computers. But criminal hacking, typically seen as cyber-dependent, could be considered an online version of breaking and entering with theft of someone's data. Thought of in that way, even the most technically proficient cybercrime could be considered cyber-enabled, not cyber-dependent, as it has offline equivalents.

Still, the distinction has stuck, and it helps us to think about different types of cybercrime and the extent to which they rely on technology. A better way to think about it is that cyber-enabled crimes require low levels of technical skill, and cyber-dependent crimes high levels. Online harassment and abuse require only a very basic understanding of technology: how to take photos, send messages, and make posts to social media. Malware and criminal hacking, by contrast, require more specialised techniques. (These can be purchased online, through marketplaces on the dark web, but someone still needs to do it.) That is in no way a comment on the seriousness of the behaviour or its impact: online abuse is incredibly damaging to mental health, and criminal hacking can involve no immediate harm to others (for example, if someone gains access to a secure government system but does not change or steal anything). Thinking about the level of skill required merely provides another basis and clearer justification for distinguishing two commonly accepted branches of cybercrime.

However we carve it up, it is clear that cybercrime has a significant impact on Australians, their mental health, finances, and the wider economy. In 2022/23, nearly 94,000 reports of cybercrime were made to law enforcement—1 every 6 minutes—and that is only what was reported.[2] It is difficult to estimate the total financial impacts, but one expert recently estimated that cybercrime was costing the Australian economy $42 billion per year.[3]

Large numbers of Australians experience cybercrime daily. In a recent survey of nearly 14,000 computer users by the Australian Institute of Criminology (AIC), nearly half experienced cybercrime in the previous year, and more than one-third experienced a data breach that exposed personal information.[4] Most users did not seek help from authorities, mostly as they did not know that help was available or where to seek it. This suggests that the real rates of cybercrime in Australia are far higher than what is reported, and that education can play a key role in helping to improve online safety.

These impacts are experienced disproportionately by Indigenous peoples and LGBTIQA+ communities.[5] In one study, more than one-third of Indigenous people had experienced abuse online, and 21% had received direct threats from other social media users.[6] This tells us that cybercrime is not only about online environments. In addition to cybercrime's concrete impacts on people's finances and mental health, it can be closely connected to real or feared offline contact.

Enforcement remains a key problem. Cybercrime is usually transnational, meaning it crosses international boundaries and involves multiple jurisdictions. The target of an attack may be in Australia, but the offender is often sitting at a computer on the other side of the world. Cyber-criminals use many effective techniques to remain anonymous, so attributing the crime to any one person or group is incredibly difficult. In part, this is because digital evidence is 'highly volatile': it can be hard to capture and retain, and it may not exist by the time a trial takes place.[7] For these and other reasons, proving a cybercrime offence beyond a reasonable doubt in an Australian courtroom can be near impossible. Foreign governments can also sponsor and support attacks by cyber-criminals on Australian targets, so prosecuting the individual or group who committed the attack would not in any case solve the main problem. For that reason, cybercrime is not only a problem for law enforcement, but also for diplomats, the military, intelligence agencies, and international organisations including the UN.

Still, Australian parliaments have enacted many new laws to address cybercrime. These are especially important for online harassment and abuse, which do not always pose the same problems with transnational enforcement. The sections below explain the most common types of cybercrime and legal responses.

2. CYBER-ENABLED CRIME

A. Fraud

Fraud: stealing something dishonestly

As we discussed in Chapter 10, **fraud** involves stealing something dishonestly. In the 'real' world, this could involve someone posing as a salesperson. They drive around the streets in an expensive car. They knock on people's doors, wearing a suit and holding a clipboard. They tell them about a brand-new product or investment scheme that will be life-changing. But there is only limited stock left or spots available, and the neighbours have already shown interest, so the offer will not be valid for long and a deposit must be paid today, with instalments to follow. They build a relationship with the person and maintain contact for a while. Then they are gone, along with the person's life savings.

This is a stereotypical example, but it has important elements that also play out in online spaces. The car, suit and clipboard create an image of authority and legitimacy, and there is urgency to the request. The offender builds rapport and maintains contact, while commitments to the offender increase over time.

419 scam: another name for a Nigerian prince scam

This is precisely what happens with many online scams. You have probably heard of Nigerian prince scams, also known as **419 scams** because of the section of Nigerian criminal law that is designed to deal with them. In the original version of the scam, the offender sends an email to multiple targets saying he is a Nigerian prince who needs help getting his wealth out of the country. If you could just send your bank account details or pay a small fee to help him, the prince will give you a share of his glorious wealth. For every person who agrees to help, the scammer collects a small payment or steals money from a bank account. The amounts of money can increase over time as more help is requested.

These scams appear to have started in Nigeria but can come from anywhere. They use many different stories (not just the one about the Nigerian prince, especially now that most people have heard about the story). But they tend to follow this basic model and rely on a similar psychology. It might seem surprising that people still fall for the trick, but it plays on a victim's trust, vulnerability, and willingness to help others in need. The key technique is the series of escalating commitments, which is very difficult for victims to pull out of once the process starts and keeps getting worse.

A more common version of the 419 scam now happens on online dating platforms. In this version, scammers take advantage of people looking online for romantic partners. A scammer creates a fake profile, builds a victim's trust, professes love for them quickly and starts asking for money, beginning with very small amounts and progressing to much larger sums. In online dating scams, the scammer often asks for money to fund a family member's medical operation or some other made-up emergency.

In 2023, Australians lost $473 million to scams of all types.[8] More than half ($272 million) was lost to investment scams, and $34 million to romance scams. Romance scams have a disproportionate impact on older victims, with the biggest losses coming from victims aged 45 years or older. This suggests that scammers target older victims who are vulnerable due to a recent divorce, the loss of a long-term partner, or a lack of experience with technology.

Online scams can be prosecuted through existing offences for fraud, though as with all types of cybercrime, enforcing those laws remains a key problem. In the AIC's recent survey, only 2.5% of fraud or scam victims were told by police that the person had been arrested, charged or prosecuted.[9]

B. Identity theft

Identity theft is another type of cybercrime that is relatively familiar to the law. This is where an offender steals personal information—such as residential addresses, phone numbers, bank account details, credit card numbers, usernames and online passwords—and uses that information to purchase goods or steal money. Often, offenders who steal personal information do not use the information themselves; they make money by selling the information to organised criminal groups. Those groups use the information to create fake identification documents, which can facilitate acts of terrorism and other serious crimes.[10]

Identity theft: stealing personal information like usernames, passwords, bank account details and credit card numbers

Personal information is commonly stolen through **phishing** emails. These are deceptive emails that look like they come from an official organisation, such as

Phishing: deceiving a person into providing personal information (usually via email)

a bank, the tax office, or your employer. (The term phishing refers to 'fishing' for passwords and other information from the sea of victims on the internet, but is spelled with a 'ph' as this is a common substitute spelling for 'f' in hacker culture.)

A typical phishing email tells a victim there was suspicious or unauthorised activity on their account, or that they are owed some money, so they need to confirm their account details. After clicking on a link, victims type their personal information into a fake form, which the offender uses to collect their information.

Phishing emails were first noticed in Australia around 2003.[11] At that time, the emails contained lots of spelling and grammatical errors and the fake websites did not look much like the official version. Now they are much more sophisticated and can include information tailored to individual victims.

Identity theft can be prosecuted under existing laws for theft and fraud. However, new laws have also been enacted to target it directly. For example, in New South Wales, it is a crime to deal with or possess 'identification information', including bank account details and passport numbers, or to possess equipment for making fake identification documents. There are equivalent offences under federal law. Under section 192K of the ***Crimes Act 1900*** (NSW), possessing identification information with intent to commit an indictable offence attracts a maximum penalty of seven years' imprisonment. These new offences were introduced by the *Crimes Amendment (Fraud, Identity and Forgery Offences) Act 2009* (NSW) to counter these persistent threats online.

C. Sexting and revenge porn

Sexting: sending and receiving intimate images

Sexting—taking naked or partially naked photos or videos and sending them via mobile phones, email or social media—is now common behaviour. According to one study, half of young Australians aged 16 to 18 had sent a sexual picture or video of themselves, and 70% had received one.[12] In another survey, two-thirds of respondents aged 18–29 had seen a naked 'selfie' they were not meant to see.[13]

Revenge porn is where intimate images are sent to others or posted online without consent. The name comes from using sexual images to embarrass a partner after a break-up, but it now means sending or posting any intimate content without permission. Revenge porn can also include threatening to send or publish intimate content.

Most Australian states have enacted laws targeting revenge porn. In Victoria, section 41DA of the ***Summary Offences Act 1966*** (Vic) makes it a summary offence punishable by two years imprisonment to distribute an intimate image. There are exemptions for young people with more serious offences relating to child abuse material. Section 91P of the ***Crimes Act 1900*** (NSW) makes it an indictable offence punishable by three years imprisonment to record or distribute an intimate image without consent. Prosecutions against children under 16 can commence only with the consent of the Director of Public Prosecutions.

Sexting raises more difficult questions. If two people aged 16 years or older consent to taking naked photos and share those only with each other, the criminal law does not seem like an appropriate response. Both parties are considered legally capable of consenting to sexual intercourse, so there is not a strong legal case for making the conduct unlawful. When the age drops to 15 or lower, whether offences should be triggered becomes a more difficult question. There would not be much public interest in prosecuting 10–15 year-olds for sexting, but there is a stronger argument for having laws in place, because it is not clear that younger children can properly consent to the behaviour, and there are longer-term risks with other children storing the images.

For these reasons, and under laws targeting more serious online conduct, sexting by children younger than 16 can lead to very serious consequences. In Queensland, new offences for revenge porn were introduced by the ***Criminal Code (Non-Consensual Sharing of Intimate Images) Amendment Act 2019*** (Qld). It is an offence punishable by three years imprisonment to distribute intimate images or recordings without consent. However, a child under 16 is not considered capable of granting consent, so young children who send an intimate image of themselves or another child under 16 (even if they thought they were consenting) would fall foul of this law. In addition, much more serious offences apply (up to 14 years' imprisonment) where any person possesses or distributes 'child exploitation material' (CEM). CEM includes images of children under 16 in a sexual context, where this would be 'likely to cause offence for a reasonable adult'.[14] There are no exemptions for young people involved in less harmful sexting. The situation is similar under federal law. Many offences relate to 'child abuse material', which includes sexual images of children under 18.[15]

If someone is convicted of serious offences for child exploitation or child abuse material, they can be placed on a sex offenders (child protection) register. These are official, confidential lists of people who have been convicted of sexual and other serious offences against children. People listed on the register must report their personal details and whereabouts to police, and they are not allowed to work or volunteer in roles involving children. Being listed on a sex offenders register is a very serious consequence. It is not appropriate for young people who sext each other, or even those who post revenge porn maliciously.

Laws for revenge porn across Australia are well targeted, but reform is needed to ensure that young people who sext cannot be caught up in very serious offences relating to child exploitation and abuse. Those offences target some of the most serious and morally reprehensible content on the Internet, and there is no argument that the serious penalties in them are warranted—just not for young people involved in what is now very common behaviour.

D. Cyberbullying

Cyber-bullying: harassment, teasing, or other online conduct that is repeated, intentional and cruel

Cyberbullying refers to intentional and repeated behaviour that uses technology and is cruel and hurtful.[16] This can include sending abusive messages, threatening to cause physical harm, teasing and making fun of someone, posting embarrassing photos, spreading rumours, or repeated unwanted contact.

Cyberbullying can be done by people that a victim knows (like classmates) or total strangers. It can be done through SMS or instant messages, social media, email, online games, chat rooms, discussion boards, and forums. Cyberbullying can have a serious impact on mental health and wellbeing, making victims feel upset, overwhelmed, embarrassed, and angry.[17]

carriage service: any means of electronic communication (any means of electronic communication)

Cyberbullying can be a crime. Under federal law, it is a serious offence to use a **carriage service** to threaten someone's life or cause them serious harm. It is also a crime to use a carriage service in a way that is menacing, harassing or offensive. Offences under state law for stalking could also apply. For example, section 13 of the ***Crimes (Domestic and Personal Violence) Act*** *2007* (NSW) makes it an offence punishable by five years imprisonment to stalk or intimidate someone with intent to cause them fear of physical or mental harm.

eSafety Commissioner: independent office established in 2015 that promotes online safety and handles complaints about harmful online content

For other cases of online bullying, abuse and harassment, the eSafety Commissioner can become involved. The **eSafety Commissioner** is an independent, national office that was created by the *Enhancing Online Safety Act 2015* (Cth). It has many different functions relating to online safety: including education, supporting research, publishing reports and papers, and evaluating community awareness programs. The eSafety Commissioner's website provides clear, informative resources that can help all Australians understand and report harmful online content.

The *Online Safety Act 2021* (Cth) enhanced the Commissioner's original powers. The legislation defines cyber-bullying material as any digital content that would be likely to seriously threaten, intimidate, harass or humiliate an Australian child. A child or parent can make a complaint about cyberbullying material to the eSafety Commissioner. The Commissioner can then investigate the complaint and issue notices that require a social media company, internet service or hosting provider to take it down. A company that fails to comply with one of these notices faces fines of about $150,000.[18] The user who posted the content can also be required to take it down, apologise, and refrain from posting more material targeting the user who made the complaint.[19]

3. CYBER-DEPENDENT CRIME

A. Criminal hacking

Cybercrime that relies on hacking and other, more sophisticated techniques is addressed by laws that target unauthorised access of computer systems and the modification of data. For reasons explained at the start of this chapter, enforcement remains a key issue, but these laws can be used to prosecute criminal hacks that access company databases and steal or modify personal data. For example, in 2023, both Medibank and Optus were hacked by cyber-criminals overseas. Nearly ten million customer records from each company, which included personal and sensitive information, were stolen and posted on the dark web.[20]

Back in 2001, the federal parliament enacted the *Cybercrime Act 2001* (Cth) ('Cybercrime Act'). The purpose of this was to implement the Council of Europe's Convention on Cybercrime ('Cybercrime Convention') into Australian law. The Cybercrime Convention was the first international treaty for addressing cybercrime. It seeks to increase cooperation between countries, improve investigation by law enforcement, and harmonise (make consistent) different national laws.

The Cybercrime Act introduced new criminal offences into Australian law. Part 10.7 of the ***Criminal Code Act 1995*** (Cth) now contains offences that target the unauthorised access, modification or impairment of data or electronic communications. For example, section 477.2 says the following:

477.2 Unauthorised modification of data to cause impairment

1 A person commits an offence if:

(a) the person causes any unauthorised modification of data held in a computer; and

(b) the person knows the modification is unauthorised; and

(c) the person is reckless as to whether the modification impairs or will impair:

(i)access to that or any other data held in any computer; or

(ii) the reliability, security or operation, of any such data.

Penalty: ten years' imprisonment

Reading the elements of this offence, we know that a person will face a maximum penalty of ten years' imprisonment if they:

1. modify any data held in a computer (***actus reus***) AND
2. know that they are not authorised to modify that data (***mens rea***) AND
3. are reckless as to whether their actions will impair access to or otherwise compromise the data (***mens rea***).

Data is defined broadly as any information, program or part of a program. Modifying data includes adding data as well as changing it. This means the offences can apply to a wide range of cyber-dependent crime, including denial-of-service attacks and the distribution of viruses, worms or ransomware, which are all explained below.

In Chapter 10, you learned about ***mens rea*** and how it normally means intention, but can also involve rules around knowledge and recklessness. You can see in the offence above that the mental requirements do not require the offender to 'intend' something. There are other offences in Part 10.7 where intention is a required mental element. For this offence, the mental elements require that the offender 'knows' they are not allowed to modify the data, and is 'reckless' as to the consequences of their actions. **Recklessness** means the offender is aware there is a substantial risk of those consequences occurring, but continues their course of action anyway.

Recklessness: where an offender is aware of a substantial risk of harm, but continues the act anyway

Very similar offences to those at the federal level have been enacted in New South Wales and Victoria. In Queensland, there is a single offence for 'computer hacking and misuse'. This is found in section 408E of the *Criminal Code 1899* (Qld):

> **408E Computer hacking and misuse**
> 1. A person who uses a restricted computer without the consent of the computer's controller commits an offence.
>   Penalty: Maximum penalty—two years imprisonment
> 2. If the person causes or intends to cause detriment or damage, or gains or intends to gain a benefit, the person commits a crime and is liable to imprisonment for five years.
> 3. If the person causes a detriment or damage or obtains a benefit for any person to the value of more than $5,000, or intends to commit an indictable offence, the person commits a crime and is liable to imprisonment for 10 years.

A restricted computer is essentially any computer that is protected by a password.

The Queensland law establishes a tiered penalty scheme for different levels of conduct. Accessing and using a restricted computer without a victim's consent attracts a maximum penalty of two years' imprisonment. This increases to five years where the offender causes damage, or gains a benefit, or intends either of those things. That doubles to ten years where the damage or benefit is worth more than $5,000 or the person intends to commit an indictable offence.

B. Denial of service

A **denial-of-service (DoS) attack** is where a computer, server or network is over-loaded with requests to the point where it slows down substantially or stops working. The technique is commonly used to bring down government websites. To access a website, you type a Uniform Resource Locator (URL) into a web browser (or you click on a link that directs you to one). Based on the URL, the browser requests files from a

Denial-of-service (DoS) attack: a type of cyber-attack in which a computer, server or network is overloaded with requests to the point where it slows down substantially or stops working

server. A server is a big computer that is always connected to the internet and delivers files for people to view via their web browsers. The files have different types of code that make up the text (HTML), visuals (CSS) and interactive elements (Javascript) on the website. Your web browser renders that code as a website that you can read, browse and click on. For more complex websites and applications, including social media, the files include more complex coding frameworks that manage user databases, check your passwords, and interact with servers in many other ways behind the scenes.

In a denial-of-service attack, tens or hundreds of thousands of computers request a website's files at the same time, so the server cannot cope and no one can access them. If you tried to access the website, it would fail to load and you would receive an error message. (Colloquially, we could say the website 'crashed', though a denial-of-service attack makes this happen intentionally, when websites crash for many other, innocent reasons, including a lack of server capacity for a growing userbase, a flood of genuine requests from the community at the same time, or technical and maintenance issues.) Crashing a website does not sound very serious, but it can cause significant disruption to the services that governments and companies provide.

Botnet: a network of computers that have been compromised through a trojan or other malware

Bot: one compromised computer in a botnet

Spam: unwanted email messages

DoS attacks commonly employ **botnets**. These are networks of computers that have been compromised and are controlled by a central authority.[21] A single computer in the network is called a **bot** (from 'robot', because the computer is being operated automatically without the victim knowing it).

Criminal hackers create a botnet by gaining control of other computers. Beyond denial-of-service attacks, botnets are also commonly used to distribute viruses and send spam. **Spam** messages are unwanted email messages. (The term comes from the brand name of the tinned lunch meat, which is a contraction of 'spiced ham'. The word was used in a famous Monty Python sketch where a menu is full of different meals containing spam, and the customer doesn't want spam in any of them.)

Users who are part of a botnet are usually innocent and have no idea their computer has been compromised (if your computer has ever operated very slowly for no apparent reason, you might have been part of a botnet and not even known it!). One of the largest botnets was the Srizbi botnet, which harnessed the power of some 500,000 computers and was said to be responsible for up to 40% of the world's spam.[22] Where a DoS attack involves many computers attacking the same target, through a botnet or otherwise, it is called a **distributed denial-of-service (DDoS) attack**.

Distributed denial-of-service (DDoS) attack: a denial-of-service attack launched by very large numbers of computers, usually through a botnet

C. Malware

Malware is a catch-all phrase for malicious software. There are different types of malware, including trojans, viruses, worms and ransomware. These can allow an offender to access someone else's computer remotely, steal personal information, log a user's keystrokes to find out passwords, or make the device malfunction.

Malware: malicious software, including trojans, viruses, worms and ransomware

A **trojan** is a computer program that appears to be useful or harmless but damages a computer once it runs. This comes from the classical myth of the Trojan horse, in which the Greeks left a large wooden horse outside the city of Troy. Thinking it was a gift, the Trojans brought the horse inside their city walls, which were otherwise impenetrable. The horse contained Greek soldiers, who broke out of the horse at night and let in the rest of the Greek army, who conquered the city.

Trojan: a computer program that appears to be legitimate but causes harm once it runs

Viruses and **worms** are self-replicating code that spread from computer to computer. They can be introduced through trojans, phishing emails, email attachments, or infected websites. The major difference between a virus and a worm is that viruses work by attaching themselves to a 'host' file or program, and worms are standalone programs that operate independently.[23]

Virus: self-replicating computer code that attaches itself to a host file or program

Worm: self-replicating computer code that operates independently of other files and programs

Some worms are designed simply to keep replicating over and over, without causing additional harm. This does not sound so bad, but they can severely disrupt computers and networks by taking up memory and bandwidth. **Memory** (also known as Random Access Memory or RAM) refers to how much information a computer can store temporarily to process multiple

Memory: how much information a computer can store temporarily to perform multiple tasks at the same time

tasks at the same time. This is usually expressed in gigabytes, with most consumer computers having between 4 and 16 gigabytes of RAM. **Bandwidth** refers to how much data can be transferred over a system in a fixed amount of time. This is often expressed in megabits per second or Mbps (your internet connection might have a bandwidth of 50 Mbps, or 100 if you are lucky). As computing becomes more complex, the amount of memory and bandwidth that individuals, companies and governments have available to them can determine the operations they are able to perform, and how quickly they can perform them.

Bandwidth: the amount of data that can pass through a computer system in a fixed amount of time

More sophisticated worms can cause serious damage to **critical infrastructure**. Critical infrastructure refers to computer networks, engineering systems and facilities needed to deliver essential services to a population, including gas, water, transport, electricity, telecommunications and nuclear power.

Critical infrastructure: computer networks, engineering systems and facilities needed to deliver essential services (like gas, water and electricity) to a population

A famous example of this was **Stuxnet**. Stuxnet was a worm that caused substantial damage to Iran's nuclear power program. It exploited multiple vulnerabilities in computer code to interfere with gas centrifuges in a nuclear power plant. While no one claimed responsibility for the attack, most sources agree that it was the product of a joint US–Israeli intelligence operation.[24]

Stuxnet: a very sophisticated computer worm that caused substantial damage to the Iranian nuclear power program

Worms can operate subtly in the background, but ransomware makes itself known. **Ransomware** is malware that locks down a computer until the user pays a fee to unlock it. It can hijack your computer with a full-screen warning telling you that all your files are encrypted, and you need to pay up before everything is deleted. In 2017, ransomware known as **Wannacry** spread globally through computers running Microsoft software. The attackers demanded US$300 in **Bitcoin** to decrypt each user's files. The ransomware spread to 150 countries and infected more than 230,000 computers. A major victim was the UK's National Health Service (NHS), with computers in its many hospitals and medical centres infected. The attack cost the NHS up to £100 million and led to 19,000 medical appointments being cancelled.[25]

Ransomware: a type of malware that locks a user out of a computer system and demands money to regain access

Wannacry: sophisticated ransomware that spread through more than 230,000 computers and substantially impacted the United Kingdom's hospital system

Bitcoin: a type of digital currency

Ransomware is an increasingly common method used by cyber-criminals against Australian targets. It is also common for ransom demands to be made separately after criminal hackers steal data, with threats to release the information on the dark web unless the money is paid (this happened with both the Medibank and Optus hacks). This can happen to any individual, company, government department or the court system. In early 2024, Victorian courts were hit by a ransomware attack that targeted audio-visual archives, including recordings of witness testimony in highly sensitive cases.[26] Beyond the significant disruptions and immediate privacy invasions, these sorts of attacks undermine our trust in the ability of companies and governments to keep our private information safe over the long-term. They pose serious, ongoing threats to Australia's **cyber-security**: our ability to stay safe from malicious threats online.

Cyber-security: the extent to which computer systems and networks are protected from malicious acts and actors

KEY POINTS

- Cyber-enabled crimes include romance scams, identity theft, revenge porn and cyber-bullying. Cyber-dependent crimes include criminal hacking, denial-of-service attacks, and ransomware.
- The eSafety Commissioner plays an important role by promoting online safety and investigating complaints about revenge porn, cyberbullying, and other harmful online content.
- Criminal hacking and ransomware that targets Australian interests and institutions will be major ongoing threats to Australia's cyber-security.

DISCUSSION QUESTIONS

1. What is the difference between cyber-enabled and cyber-dependent crime?
2. Do you think sexting should be a crime? Does it matter whether the person sent or received a message? What if the person is 10, 14, 16, or 18 years of age?
3. When is cyber-bullying a crime, and when should it be?
4. What other offences are found in Part 10.7 of the *Criminal Code Act 1995* (Cth)? What are the elements (*mens rea* and *actus reus*) of each?
5. What else can you find out about Stuxnet and Wannacry? Can you identify any other major malware attacks that have happened in recent years, in Australia or around the world?

6. To what extent should we be responsible for protecting our personal information online, compared to companies and governments? What are some steps we could all take to improve our cyber-security?

NOTES

1 Voce, I., & Morgan, A. ***Cybercrime in Australia 2023*** (Statistical Report 43). Australian Institute of Criminology.
2 Australian Signals Directorate (2023). ***ASD cyber threat report 2022-2023***. Australian Government. Retrieved from: https://www.cyber.gov.au/about-us/reports-and-statistics/asd-cyber-threat-report-july-2022-june-2023.
3 UNSW Sydney (2021). Cybercrime an estimated $42 billion cost to Australian economy, ***News***, 6 December. Retrieved from: https://www.unsw.edu.au/news/2021/12/cybercrime-an-estimated--42-billion-cost-to-australian-economy.
4 Voce & Morgan, n 1.
5 Ibid.
6 Carlson, B., & Frazer, R. (2019). We need to do more about cyberbullying against Indigenous Australians. ***The Conversation***, 9 May.
7 Maurushat, A. (2010). Australia's accession to the Cybercrime Convention: is the Convention still relevant in combating cybercrime in the era of botnets and obfuscation crime tools? ***University of New South Wales Law Journal***, ***33***(2), 431-473.
8 National Anti-Scam Centre (2024). ***Scamwatch: scam statistics***. Australian Government. Retrieved from: https://www.scamwatch.gov.au/research-and-resources/scam-statistics.
9 Voce & Morgan, n 1.
10 United Nations Office on Drugs and Crime (2019). ***Economic fraud and identity-related crime***. Retrieved from https://www.unodc.org/unodc/en/corruption/identity-related-crime.html
11 Zetter, K. (2015) Hacker lexicon: What is phishing? ***Wired***, 7 April.
12 Lee, M., Crofts, T., McGovern, A., & Milivojevic, S. (2015). Sexting among young people: perceptions and practices. ***Trends & Issues in Criminal Justice*** (No. 508). Australian Institute of Criminology.>
13 Triple J Hack (2018). ***Young, smart, and kinda broke: What we learnt from our Census for Young People***. Retrieved from https://www.abc.net.au/triplej/programs/hack/whats-up-in-your-world-the-census-for-young-people/10051266.
14 ***Criminal Code 1899*** (Qld) s 207A.
15 See, eg, ***Criminal Code Act 1995*** (Cth) s 474.22.

16 Legal Aid Queensland (2016). ***Cyber bullying, sexting and Facebook: know the law, know your rights.*** Retrieved from: https://www.legalaid.qld.gov.au/files/assets/public/v/1/publications/criminal-justice/cyber-bullying-sexting-and-facebook-guide-3.pdf.
17 eSafety Commissioner (2024). ***How to look after yourself if you are cyberbullied***. Australian Government. Retrieved from: https://www.esafety.gov.au/key-topics/cyberbullying/how-to-look-after-yourself-if-you-are-cyberbullied.
18 ***Online Safety Act 2021*** (Cth) s 67.
19 ***Online Safety Act*** 2021 (Cth) s 70.
20 Taylor, J. (2023). Medibank class action launched after massive hack put private information of millions on dark web. ***The Guardian***, 16 February; Smith, P. (2022). Inside the Optus hack that woke up Australia. ***Financial Review***, December 2022.
21 Kaspersky (2024). ***What is a botnet?*** Retrieved from: https://usa.kaspersky.com/resource-center/threats/botnet-attacks.
22 Thomson, I. (2008). Spam levels to rise as Srizbi botnet returns. ***iTnews***, 28 November.
23 Kaspersky (2024). ***What's the difference between a virus and a worm?*** Retrieved from: https://www.kaspersky.com/resource-center/threats/computer-viruses-vs-worms.
24 Nakashima, E., & Warrick, J. (2012). Stuxnet was work of U.S. and Israeli experts, officials say. ***The Washington Post***, 2 June.
25 Palmer, D. (2018). This is how much the WannaCry ransomware attack cost the NHS. ***ZDNet***, 12 October.
26 Knight, B., & Tippet, H. (2024). Cyber attack on Victoria's court system may have exposed recordings of sensitive cases. ***ABC News***, 2 January.

Chapter 14
Counter-terrorism

In this chapter, you will learn about:

- Australia's legal responses to terrorism
- Preparatory offences and terrorist organisations
- Control orders, PDOs and citizenship stripping

Like many other countries, Australia faces an ongoing threat of terrorism. The Australian government has responded to this threat by enacting nearly 100 pieces of legislation.[1] These laws have created new criminal offences and expanded the powers of police and intelligence agencies. The laws impact on many human rights, including those to liberty, privacy, freedom of speech and a fair trial.

This chapter explains Australia's legal responses to terrorism and identifies some key lessons. It is critical that governments enacting counter-terrorism laws scrutinise those laws properly while protecting human rights and press freedom.

1. AUSTRALIA'S LEGAL RESPONSES TO TERRORISM

On 11 September 2001, 19 hijackers flew two planes into New York's World Trade Center towers. They flew another into the Pentagon building, which houses the United States Department of Defense. A fourth plane, United Airlines Flight 93, crashed into a field in Pennsylvania, killing all passengers on board. The 9/11 attacks killed nearly 3000 innocent people and injured more than 6000. The hijackers were members of the terrorist organisation al-Qaeda, led at that time by Osama bin Laden.

On 7 July 2005, four suicide bombers detonated bombs on London's underground rail network and a double-decker bus in Tavistock Square. The 7/7 bombings, as

DOI: 10.4324/9781003433408-17

they came to be known, killed 52 people and injured more than 700. The attackers were four young British men who built the bombs out of inexpensive and readily available materials.

On 29 June 2014, Abu Bakr al-Baghdadi, then leader of the terrorist organisation Islamic State declared a caliphate over territory covering a large part of Iraq and Syria. A **caliphate** is a state ruled under strict Islamic law by a leader known as a **caliph**. By making the declaration, al-Baghdadi told the world he was a descendant of the prophet Muhammed with absolute power over that territory. At the peak of its power, there were up to eight million people living in the territory claimed by Islamic State.

Caliphate: a state ruled under Islamic law

Caliph: the ruler of a Caliphate

On 15 March 2019, an Australian gunman walked into two mosques in Christchurch, New Zealand, killing 51 Muslim worshippers and seriously injuring many more. He live-streamed the shootings on Facebook. While it was quickly taken down, the footage was broadcast for 17 minutes and viewed all around the world. Immediately before the shooting, he posted a **manifesto**: a long document outlining his ideology and motivations for the killing. His manifesto was called **The Great Replacement**. This is the name of a **conspiracy theory**, closely associated with right-wing extremism, which falsely claims that western governments are allowing their countries to be taken over by Muslims. **Right-wing extremism** is an ideology based in white supremacy and neo-Nazi beliefs. Many right-wing extremist groups believe they are continuing the goals of the Nazi Party from World War II.

In the last two decades, there have been many tens of thousands of terrorist attacks around the world.[2] However, these four key moments—9/11, 7/7, the creation of the IS caliphate and the Christchurch massacre—have done the most to shape counter-terrorism laws in Australia and around the world. In response to these events, Australia and many other countries introduced new offences and powers which help police and intelligence agencies prevent terrorist attacks.

Manifesto: a long document stating a terrorist's ideology and motivations

The Great Replacement: conspiracy theory that falsely claims Western governments are allowing their governments to be taken over by Muslims

Conspiracy theory: explanation that falsely claims a small group of powerful people are secretly controlling events in society

Right-wing extremism: extreme ideology based in white supremacy and neo-Nazi beliefs

Since the 9/11 attacks, Australia has enacted nearly 100 laws in response to these threats.[3] Of these, 44 were enacted under the Liberal Howard government between 2002 and 2007.[4] This meant the federal parliament was passing a new counterterrorism law every 6.7 weeks.[5] The rates slowed down after that, but counter-terrorism is still a common topic of law reform in Australia.

Five Eyes: intelligence network comprising Australia, Canada, New Zealand, the United States and the United Kingdom

Australia's counter-terrorism laws far exceed the number enacted by our closest allies in the '**Five Eyes**' network: Canada, New Zealand, the United States and the United Kingdom. Kent Roach, one of the world's leading experts on counterterrorism laws, has described Australia's approach to counter-terrorism as 'hyper-legislation'.[6] By this, he means not only that Australia has enacted many more laws, much faster than other countries, but also that the 'relentless pace' has reduced the time available to scrutinise the laws properly in parliament.[7] Clive Walker, another leading expert on counter-terrorism law from the University of Leeds, called most of Australia's counter-terrorism laws 'panic legislation',[8] meaning they are more about politicians responding quickly to world events than taking the time to craft the best possible laws.

2. WHAT IS TERRORISM?

Australia's counter-terrorism laws depend on a legal definition of terrorism. This was introduced in 2002 with Australia's first national counter-terrorism laws. Before then, Australia had no federal or state laws against terrorism. This was not surprising, given that Australia did not have the same history of terrorism as many other countries.

Before 2002, committing a terrorist attack in Australia was still illegal: someone who let off a bomb in public could be charged with murder and many other offences. However, having specific counter-terrorism laws means that many different types of conduct, beyond committing a terrorist act or attempting to commit one, are now criminal. This includes, for example, preparing an act of terrorism and being a member of a terrorist organisation. Based on those offences, police and intelligence agencies have also been given special powers to investigate and prevent terrorism.

Australia's legal definition of terrorism is found in section 100.1 of the ***Criminal Code Act 1995*** (Cth) ('Criminal Code'). Defining terrorism is a notoriously difficult task because countries have very different views on what should be included or not. What one country considers to be terrorism, another might consider to be legitimate political protest. Some countries even fund or support terrorism. Because of these and other reasons, there is no internationally agreed definition of terrorism in a treaty or declaration.

However, at the time of the 9/11 attacks, the UK already had a legal definition of terrorism in its ***Terrorism Act 2000*** (UK). That legislation consolidated temporary and emergency powers that addressed threats of terrorism in Northern Ireland. Australia and many other countries essentially copied this UK definition. This was partly because, on 28 September 2001, the United Nations (UN) Security Council issued Resolution 1373. **Resolution 1373** required UN member states to enact new laws targeting the preparation and financing of terrorism within 90 days.

Resolution 1373: resolution issued by the United Nations Security Council on 28 September 2001, which required member states to enact laws targeting the preparation and financing of terrorism

Australia's definition in section 100.1 defines a terrorist act as any conduct, or the threat of conduct, which satisfies three elements. First, the conduct or threat must be designed to advance a political, religious or ideological cause. This is often referred to as a **motive requirement**. It is the key feature separating terrorism from other types of crime.

Motive requirement: requirement found in legal definitions of terrorism, which requires that an act of terrorism be designed to advance a political, religious or ideological cause

Ordinarily, the reason why a person committed a crime (like murder or assault) is irrelevant to determining whether the person is guilty. Motive can be considered in a sentencing hearing, but the only issue at trial is whether they intended to do a criminal act. For example, if somebody steals money because they have a large gambling debt, or for any other reason, the only relevant question at trial is whether they stole the money and intended to steal it. The 'why' is not part of the crime. With terrorism, however, the 'why' becomes a core, defining element. To count as terrorism, the conduct must be designed to advance a religious, political, or ideological cause.

Second, the conduct or threat must be intended to intimidate a government or a section of the population. This is a more typical *mens rea* requirement. Third, the conduct must cause one or more specific types of harm. The list of harms includes serious physical harm, serious damage to property, or death, endangering life, creating a serious risk to health or safety, or seriously interfering with or disrupting an electronic system. The last of these is designed to address the risks of **cyber-terrorism**, which could involve criminal hacking against critical infrastructure.

Cyber-terrorism: terrorism that involves cyber-attacks against electronic systems

Exception: rule in legislation that excludes certain conduct from the scope of a criminal offence

A final aspect of the definition of terrorism is an exception for legitimate political protest. An **exception** (or exemption) is a rule in legislation that excludes certain conduct from the scope of a criminal offence. (This is similar to the defences that we talked about in Chapter 10, but slightly different, as it excludes the conduct from the start.) If an act or threat is advocacy, protest, dissent or industrial action and is only intended to cause serious property damage, the terrorism laws will not apply.

3. OFFENCES

Australia's counter-terrorism laws have introduced many new offences. In several different ways, these go beyond the scope of the traditional criminal law.

A. Preparatory offences

Preparatory offences: offences in division 101 of the *Criminal Code Act 1995* (Cth) which target the preparation of terrorist acts

A defining feature of Australia's counter-terrorism laws is a series of offences that target the preparation of terrorist acts. These were introduced in 2002 and are found in division 101 of the Criminal Code. They are known as **preparatory offences** because they go beyond the ordinary law of attempt.

In Chapter 10, we discussed what it means to be found guilty of attempting to commit a crime. Attempted murder means a person tries to commit murder but failed for some reason (like missing the target, or the gun misfiring). Preparing to commit murder—for example, by purchasing a gun—is not unlawful.

Because of special offences introduced in response to terrorism, preparing to commit terrorism is a crime. The key offence is found in section 101.6, which makes it a crime to do any act in preparation for terrorism.

Other sections in division 101 make it a crime to:

- provide or receive training connected with terrorism (section 101.2)
- possess things connected with terrorist acts (101.4)
- collect or make documents likely to facilitate terrorist acts (101.5)

These offences target **ancillary conduct**, meaning activities that are related to preparing a terrorist act, whereas section 101.6 targets preparation directly.

Ancillary conduct: conduct that is related to the preparation of terrorist acts, like training and support for terrorism

Instead of punishing a person for committing an act, these offences address the risk of a terrorist act occurring. There is an offence (found in section 101.1) for committing a terrorist act, but in practice this is rarely used.

This undermines the **harm principle** we talked about in Chapter 4. Ordinarily, the criminal law punishes an offender for causing harm to someone else, or for attempting to cause harm. Australia's counter-terrorism laws are triggered at a much earlier stage, when an offender is preparing to commit a crime. The crime may or may not happen at some unspecified future time and location. For this reason, counter-terrorism laws in Australia and other countries have been called a form of '**pre-crime**'.[9] The laws punish a person for what they are likely to do in the future, rather than something they have already done.

Harm principle: principle attributed to the British philosopher John Stuart Mill, which says the law should only prohibit conduct that is harmful

Pre-crime: term used to describe many counter-terrorism laws because they punish people for something they are likely to do in the future

B. Terrorist organisations

Another feature is a series of offences relating to terrorist organisations. These are found in division 102 of the Criminal Code. They depend on a legal definition of a 'terrorist organisation' and a power to proscribe (ban) those organisations.

According to section 102.1(1), an organisation is a **terrorist organisation** if it is 'directly or indirectly engaged in, preparing, planning, assisting in or fostering the doing of a terrorist act', or if it advocates terrorism. Advocating terrorism means to counsel, promote, encourage or urge the doing of a terrorist act, or provide instruction on how to commit one. This is similar to the idea of accessorial liability we looked at in Chapter 8, but it extends beyond that to include 'promotion'. This could include, for example, posting general statements of support for terrorism online.

Terrorist organisation: an organisation that is involved in the preparation or planning of a terrorist act

Proscribed organisation: an organisation formally listed by the Australian government as a terrorist organisation

Proscription regime: a scheme for banning terrorist organisations

Proscribe: ban an organisation

Under division 102, the Governor-General can also make regulations that list prohibited terrorist organisations. This is often called a **proscription regime**. To **proscribe** an organisation means to ban or prohibit it. If an organisation is proscribed in the regulations, the fact that the organisation is a terrorist organisation does not need to be proven in court.

In early 2024, 29 organisations were listed as proscribed terrorist organisations.[10] They include Islamic State, several different branches of al-Qaeda, Jemaah Islamiah (which was responsible for the 2002 Bali bombings) and many others. More recently, three right-wing terrorist groups were added: Sonnenkrieg Division, The Base, and National Socialist Order.

When a group is a terrorist organisation, this triggers a series of offences. These are:

- directing the activities of a terrorist organisation (section 102.2)
- membership of a terrorist organisation (section 102.3)
- recruiting for a terrorist organisation (section 102.4)
- training involving a terrorist organisation (section 102.5)
- getting funds to, from or for a terrorist organisation (section 102.6)
- providing support to a terrorist organisation (section 102.7)
- associating with terrorist organisations (section 102.8).

Being a member of a terrorist organisation is a 'status' offence because it does not require the person to actually do anything: simply being a member of the organisation is sufficient to attract a maximum penalty of ten years imprisonment. In other words, the offence targets something about the person, rather than something they have done.

Under section 102.8, a person can be put in prison for three years if they intentionally associate on two or more occasions with another person who they know is a member of a terrorist organisation. This does not require preparation for terrorism or other harmful behaviour—it simply requires that two people met each other multiple times, where the meetings are intended to support the organisation in some way.

C. Declared areas

In 2014, the federal government introduced a series of new counter-terrorism laws in response to the threat from Islamic State.[11] One of the most extraordinary offences introduced at this time was a declared area offence, which is found in section 119.2.

This offence provides a maximum penalty of ten years imprisonment where a person enters or remains in a declared area. A declared area is any area of a foreign country which the Minister for Foreign Affairs declares a 'no-go' zone. Two areas were designated in this way: the city of Mosul in Iraq and the Raqqa province in Syria. Those were the two main strongholds of the Islamic State. The designations are no longer current, and since then, no other areas have been declared.

Any person who enters or remains in a declared area is subject to the maximum penalty, regardless of whether they become involved in terrorism. There are no other elements to the offence, beyond entering or remaining in the area. This means a person can be put in prison for a long time simply for 'being' somewhere. The prosecution does not need to prove that an offender caused or intended to cause any harm.

It is a defence for an accused person to show that they entered or remained in the area 'solely for a legitimate purpose'. This conflicts with the presumption of innocence because it requires the defendant to establish their innocence, rather than requiring the prosecution to prove something harmful. The legislation presumes the person must have done something criminal if they were in a declared area.

The legislation sets out a list of legitimate reasons for being in a declared area. These include providing humanitarian aid, producing official news reports and making genuine family visits. However, the list does not include many other reasons why innocent people may enter or remain in conflict zones, such as helping friends, conducting business, or producing unofficial news and human rights reports.

D. Advocating terrorism

The offence of advocating terrorism, found in section 80.2C, was also introduced in 2014. Under this section, it is a crime to **advocate** terrorism where the offender is reckless as to whether another person will engage in

Advocate: to counsel, promote, encourage, urge, praise or promote the doing of a terrorist act

terrorism as a result. Advocating terrorism means to counsel, promote, encourage or urge the doing of a terrorist act or terrorism offence.

Like the grounds for proscribing terrorist organisations, this is broader than the concept of accessorial liability we discussed in Chapter 8. It includes 'promotion', and does not require an offender to encourage, support or assist a specific terrorist act.

E. Hate symbols

At the end of 2023, the federal Parliament enacted laws targeting the public display of symbols used by right-wing extremist groups and other terrorist organisations. It is an offence punishable by 12 months in prison to publicly display the Nazi swastika, the 'SS' symbol, or a symbol used to identify any terrorist organisation.[12] It is also an offence to perform a Nazi salute in public or trade in goods that display any of these symbols.

These laws were designed mainly to address threats from right-wing extremism. They added to a patchwork of similar laws targeting Nazi symbols across the country.[13]

4. POWERS

In addition to creating new criminal offences, Australia's counter-terrorism laws have given significant new powers to police, intelligence agencies and courts.

A. Control orders

Control order: court order that imposes restrictions and obligations on a person for the purpose of preventing a terrorist act, or preventing the support or facilitation of terrorism

In 2005, in response to the 7/7 London bombings, the Australian government introduced two major police powers. Control orders were based on UK legislation and are found in division 104 of the Criminal Code. A **control order** is a court order that imposes restrictions and obligations on a person for the purposes of counter-terrorism. The orders are issued by judges of the state supreme courts on application by a senior member of the Australian Federal Police (AFP).

Section 104.5(3) sets out a long list of restrictions and obligations that can be made under a control order. Among other things, a control order can require a person to abide by a **curfew** (be at home at specified times of the day and night), report to police stations at regular intervals, and wear an electronic monitoring bracelet. It is an offence punishable by five years in prison to breach any of these conditions.

Curfew: requirement in a control order that a person must be at home during specified times of the day and night

Control orders are similar to bail, probation and parole, but there is a major difference. Bail, probation and parole are all parts of the criminal justice system. They apply to people charged or convicted of a criminal offence. Control orders are issued by a court but they are separate from the criminal justice process. They are issued under civil law and can be imposed for a wide range of reasons, including to prevent a terrorist act or support for terrorism. This means a person subject to a control order need not be suspected of committing a terrorism offence, or being involved in terrorism.

B. Preventative detention orders

Australia's other major response to the London bombings was to introduce **preventative detention order** (PDO) powers. These are found in division 105. Under a PDO, a person may be detained by the AFP for up to 48 hours—and up to fourteen days under state legislation—for the purpose of preventing an 'imminent' terrorist attack or to preserve evidence of a recent attack. As with control orders, the person need not be suspected of a criminal offence.

Preventative detention order: power that allows police to detain a person for up to two weeks to prevent an imminent terrorist act, or to preserve evidence about a recent attack

There are significant restrictions on a detainee's contact with the outside world. A detainee may contact a family member and their employer, but only to say they are 'safe but not able to be contacted for the time being'. If they reveal anything about their detention, they face a criminal offence punishable by five years in prison.

PDOs are an extraordinary power not available in similar countries such as the United Kingdom, Canada or the United States. In 2013, a committee appointed by the Council of Australian Governments (COAG) examined these and other counterterrorism powers. Justice Whealy, a former New South Wales Supreme Court judge who chaired that review, wrote the following about the PDO powers in the committee's final report:

> The concept of police officers detaining persons 'incommunicado' without charge for up to 14 days, in other than the most extreme circumstances, might be thought to be unacceptable in a liberal democracy. There are many in the community who would regard detention of this kind as quite inappropriate. To some, it might call to mind the sudden and unexplained 'disappearances' of citizens last century during the fearful rule of discredited totalitarian regimes.[14]

Incommunicado: when a detained person cannot contact anyone

To detain someone **incommunicado** means the person is not able to contact anyone while they are being detained, or even explain their disappearance. Despite many recommendations that the PDO powers be repealed, they remain current law.

C. ASIO questioning warrants

ASIO: the Australian Security Intelligence Organisation, Australia's domestic intelligence organisation that is responsible for protecting national security

The Australian Security Intelligence Organisation (**ASIO**) is Australia's domestic intelligence agency. It has responsibility for preventing terrorist acts and other forms of politically motivated violence. It has many secretive powers, including to intercept communications, inspect mail, and place tracking devices on vehicles. ASIO officers also conduct undercover operations, using agents to pose as members of terrorist organisations and other groups.

In 2003, ASIO was given a power to detain non-suspects for questioning. A person could be questioned in eight-hour blocks up to a maximum of 24 hours where this would 'substantially assist the collection of intelligence that is important in relation to a terrorism offence'. They could be detained for up to a week for this purpose. In 2020, that detention power was repealed. The current powers are still found in Part III Division III of the ***Australian Security Intelligence Organisation Act 1979*** (Cth) ('ASIO Act'). They allow police to apprehend (essentially, arrest) a person for questioning by ASIO. Anyone who refuses to answer one of ASIO's questions faces five years in prison.

D. Special intelligence operations

In 2014, in response to the threat of terrorism from Islamic State, new laws created a special intelligence operations regime. A **special intelligence operation** (SIO) is a special undercover operation approved by the Attorney-General in which ASIO officers are granted immunity from civil and criminal liability. **Immunity** means that ASIO officers who commit a crime or do some other unlawful act during an SIO cannot be punished by a court. Immunity cannot be granted for conduct that would cause death or serious injury, constitute torture, cause serious property damage, or involve the commission of a sexual offence.

Special Intelligence Operation: undercover operation that has been specially approved by the Attorney-General, in which ASIO officers are granted immunity from civil and criminal liability

Immunity: protection from legal liability

One of the biggest controversies surrounding SIOs relates to section 35P of the ASIO Act. Section 35P provides a maximum penalty of five years imprisonment where a person discloses any information about an SIO and the disclosure will endanger health or safety or 'prejudice' (undermine the success of) the operation. An initial version of the offence did not require any harm to be caused by disclosing the information. This caused significant controversy over the impact it would have on journalists reporting on national security matters.[15]

E. Metadata

Amendments to the ***Telecommunications (Interception and Access) Act 1979*** (Cth) made in 2015 mean that all communications service providers (CSPs) must retain metadata for two years. CSPs are businesses, like Telstra and Optus, which provide mobile phone, email and other communication services.

Metadata is a popular term used to describe data about a communication, other than its substance or content. In other words, metadata captures the time, date, location and other information about a phone call, email or SMS message, but not the content of these communications. CSPs must retain this data about all

Metadata: data about communications, including the time, location and length of phone calls between devices

our communications for two years. This poses a risk to privacy, as metadata can reveal significant information about our lives: who we talk to, how long we talk to them for, where we spend our days and how long we spend travelling to and from work.[16]

Under these laws, metadata may be accessed by 'enforcement agencies' without a warrant. A request can be made where accessing the metadata would be reasonably necessary to enforce the criminal law, enforce a monetary fine, or find a missing person. Enforcement agencies include police and other investigative agencies such as the Independent Commission Against Corruption (ICAC). However, a much longer list of agencies have accessed metadata under the laws, including local councils.[17] This is concerning because it suggests that data about people's whereabouts and private communications is being accessed to enforce minor fines and infringements. In addition, the use of this data is not subject to the same legal protections (such as the laws of evidence) that are available in a criminal court.

F. Encryption

When the threat from Islamic State was at its highest, it became widely known that terrorist organisations used encrypted messaging services—such as WhatsApp and Telegram—to hide their communications from authorities. Because of this, in 2018, the federal Parliament enacted laws that allow police and intelligence agencies to request or require technology companies to provide them with technical assistance. Federal and state police commissioners can request voluntary assistance from technology companies or require it with a 'technical assistance notice'. There are fines for companies that fail to comply. With approval from the Attorney-General, they can even require a company to develop a new capability.

The main purpose of enacting the laws was to allow terrorist communications to be decrypted, but the powers extend far beyond that, and can require technology companies even to change part of the services they provide. The laws apply to almost any technology company in the world, including Meta, Apple and Microsoft. They were heavily criticised by technology companies, both locally and globally. Mozilla went so far as to say the laws could do 'significant harm to the Internet'.[18]

G. Citizenship stripping

Under the *Australian Citizenship Act 2007* (Cth), courts can strip the Australian citizenship of dual citizens involved in terrorism and other serious offences, including espionage and treason. The person will be left only with the citizenship of another country, and so they can be deported. The power cannot be used where a person only has Australian citizenship, as they would be left stateless (not be a citizen of any country). These powers can be used against dual citizens as young as 14.

These powers were first introduced in 2015, but at that time they gave the power to the Minister for Home Affairs. Those laws were eventually found to be unconstitutional for breaching the separation of powers.[19] In two important decisions, the High Court found that stripping someone's citizenship amounted to a form of punishment, which only courts can hand out.

5. LESSONS

Australia's experience with counter-terrorism laws suggests several important lessons.

A. Scrutinise laws properly

Australia's counter-terrorism laws confirm the need for parliaments to spend sufficient time examining laws before they are enacted. With the exception of ASIO's questioning and detention warrant powers, most of Australia's counter-terrorism laws have been passed with no more than a few days' scrutiny in parliament.

A key example was the legislation introduced in 2014 to address the threat from **foreign fighters**: people who travelled to Iraq and Syria to join and fight with Islamic State. The Bill was 160 pages long and made hundreds of detailed, complicated amendments to more than 25 pieces of legislation. A committee inquiry by the Parliamentary Joint Committee on Intelligence and Security (**PJCIS**) allowed only eight days for law reform organisations and members of the public to make submissions. Following that process, the Bill was given just three days' scrutiny in parliament. Debate in the House of Representatives lasted just two days.

Foreign fighters: people who travelled to Syria and Iraq to fight with the terrorist organisation Islamic State

Another concerning trend is for the federal parliament to enact laws that it knows are problematic and then to review the legislation after it is enacted. This happened in 2014 with the legislation that created the SIO regime, and again with the encryption laws. It was seen previously under the Howard government, when controversial laws were passed on the understanding that they would be reviewed immediately by the Australian Law Reform Commission.

Passing laws so quickly through the federal parliament when they are lengthy, complex, go beyond laws enacted by other countries, and clearly impact on human rights is not adequate for an advanced liberal democracy like Australia. Enacting laws that our elected representatives know are problematic, and expecting to review those laws later, is bordering on a dereliction of duty by parliament. It also undermines the separation of powers by giving too much power to the executive branch of government. In theory, parliament should decide on the laws that the executive gets to use. In counter-terrorism, the executive often demands new powers to address a security threat, and parliament does not act as an effective check and balance, because no political party wants to be seen as undermining counter-terrorism efforts. In our democratic system, parliament is a representative forum where every piece of legislation should be appropriately and thoroughly reviewed, to ensure we have the best possible laws in place.

B. Protect human rights

Australia's counter-terrorism laws impact on many human rights. These include the rights to freedom of movement, freedom of speech and opinion, privacy, liberty, a fair trial, and freedom from arbitrary detention. The PDO powers, which allow a person to be detained incommunicado, are the clearest example.

Right to silence: requirement that people do not need to answer questions put to them by police

There are many others. ASIO's questioning warrants, which include an offence for failing to answer ASIO's questions, undermine the **right to silence**. This normally requires that a person is not required to answer questions put to them by law enforcement.

Presumption of innocence: principle that everyone is considered innocent until they are found guilty in a court of law

The declared area offence undermines the **presumption of innocence** because it assumes that any person in a declared area is guilty of some harmful conduct. It requires an accused person to provide evidence that they were in the declared area solely for a legitimate reason.

These and other laws would not be possible in a country with stronger human rights protection. If Australia had constitutional protection for human rights, the laws could be struck down using the High Court's power of judicial review. Without those protections, a court cannot strike down legislation on human rights grounds. A law might be invalidated on some other ground (for example, because it breaches the separation of powers or does not fall under a head of power in section 51). This happened with the original version of the citizenship-stripping laws. But there is simply no basis for making an argument in an Australian courtroom that counter-terrorism laws breach human rights.

The Parliamentary Joint Committee on Human Rights examines legislation for its impact on human rights, but this process did not exist when most of Australia's counter-terrorism laws were enacted. In any case, the committee can only make recommendations to the Commonwealth parliament; it cannot prevent a Bill from becoming law. The committee has little effect in the face of political and community pressure to respond strongly to threats of terrorism. Many Bills that clearly impact on human rights have been enacted with little scrutiny or substantive change.

C. Protect media freedom

A final concerning trend is that counter-terrorism laws undermine the ability of journalists to report on national security matters. There are many different disclosure offences attached to the SIO regime, PDO powers and ASIO's questioning warrants, and these do not have exceptions or defences for reporting in the public interest.

These offences prevent journalists from reporting freely on the use of the powers, even if they did so responsibly on topics that the Australian community ought to know about. For example, journalists would be prohibited from revealing that ASIO officers physically mistreated a suspect during questioning under a warrant.

The metadata laws also pose a risk to journalists, because the powers can be used to reveal a journalist's confidential sources. The legislation now requires that enforcement agencies seek a 'journalist information warrant' to request access to a journalist's metadata. However, journalists cannot challenge these warrants and they are not even notified that a warrant has been issued.

The federal government has maintained that it will not use counter-terrorism laws to prosecute journalists for 'doing their job'.[20] However, guarantees like these depend on goodwill, not the law, and they are not sufficient to protect freedom of the press in Australia. Freedom of the press means that media organisations can decide what they publish and are able to criticise government agencies without fear of retribution. It means that journalists should be free to publish information that is in the public interest, even if that information embarrasses government or exposes wrongdoing. Indeed, it is precisely those circumstances involving government wrongdoing that are important for journalists to report.

Of course, to protect Australia's national security, there are many things about counter-terrorism that should not be reported in the press. Journalists should not be able to disclose details about intelligence agencies' sources, methods, ongoing operations, or anything else that would harm national security. However, the legislation does not adequately account for situations where journalists working for official media organisations reveal significant information in the public interest—such as criminal conduct, corruption, or other major wrongdoing done in the name of national security. In a submission to a PJCIS inquiry, a coalition of Australia's largest media organisations wrote that 'fair scrutiny and public interest reporting is increasingly difficult and there is a real risk that journalists could go to jail for doing their jobs'.[21]

KEY POINTS

- The federal parliament has enacted nearly 100 pieces of legislation in response to the threat of terrorism. These laws have created many new criminal offences and significantly expanded the powers of police and ASIO, Australia's domestic intelligence agency.
- Australia has some of the most far-reaching, controversial counter-terrorism laws in the world. These laws are possible because the Constitution does not protect human rights.
- Criminal offences for disclosing information and metadata laws restrict the ability of journalists to report significant information in the public interest.

DISCUSSION QUESTIONS

1. What is terrorism in Australian law?
2. How do preparatory offences differ from the ordinary law of attempt?

3. What terrorist organisations are currently proscribed by the Australian government? What can you find out about these organisations (such as their motives, tactics, and recent attacks)?
4. How does the declared area offence undermine the presumption of innocence?
5. Should it be a crime to post material online that advocates terrorism?
6. How do control orders differ from bail, probation and parole?
7. To what extent do the metadata laws impact our right to privacy? How much private information can metadata reveal about our lives?
8. How could Australia's counter-terrorism laws be amended to provide greater protections for journalists and freedom of the press?

NOTES

1 Hardy, K. & Williams, G. (2022). Two decades of Australian counterterrorism laws. ***Melbourne University Law Review*, *46***(1), 34-81.

2 See University of Maryland (2022). ***START: Global Terrorism Database***. Retrieved from: https://www.start.umd.edu/gtd/.

3 Hardy & Williams, n 1.

4 Williams, G. (2011). A decade of Australian anti-terror laws. ***Melbourne University Law Review*, *35***, 1136-1176.

5 Ibid.

6 Roach, K. (2011). ***The 9/11 Effect***. Cambridge University Press.

7 Ibid.

8 Walker, C. (2006). Clamping down on terrorism in the United Kingdom. Journal of International Criminal Justice, ***4***, 1137-1151.

9 Zedner, L. (2007). Pre-crime and post-criminology? ***Theoretical Criminology*, *11***(2), 261-281.

10 Australian National Security (2024). ***Listed terrorist organisations***. Retrieved from: https://www.nationalsecurity.gov.au/what-australia-is-doing/terrorist-organisations/listed-terrorist-organisations.

11 Hardy, K., & Williams, G. (2016). Australian legal responses to foreign fighters. ***Criminal Law Journal*, *40***(4), 196-212.

12 ***Criminal Code Act 1995*** (Cth) ss 80.2H, 80.2HA.

13 See Hardy, K. (2023). Legal in one state, a crime in another: laws banning hate symbols are a mixed bag. ***The Conversation***, 26 October.

14 Council of Australian Governments (2013). ***Council of Australian Governments review of counter-terrorism legislation***. Australian Government.

15 Hardy, K., & Williams, G. (2016). Special intelligence operations and freedom of the press. ***Alternative Law Journal*, *41***(3), 160-164.

16 Ockenden, W. (2015). What reporter Will Ockenden's metadata reveals about his life. ***ABC News***, 24 August.

17 Anderson, S. (2016). List of agencies applying for metadata access without warrant released by government. ***ABC News***, 18 January.

18 Hardy, K. (2020). Australia's encryption laws: practical need or political strategy? *Internet Policy Review*, *9*(3), 1-16.

19 ***Benbrika v Minister for Home Affairs*** [2023] HCA 33; ***Alexander v Minister for Home Affairs*** [2022] HCA 19.

20 Taylor, L. (2014). George Brandis: Attorney general must approve prosecution of journalists under security laws. ***The Guardian***, 30 October.

21 Media, Entertainment & Arts Alliance (2018). ***Joint media organisations submission on National Security Legislation Amendment (Espionage and Foreign Interference) Bill 2017.*** Retrieved from: https://www.meaa.org/mediaroom/joint-media-organisations-submission-on-national-security-legislation-amendment-espionage-and-foreign-interference-bill-2017.

Glossary of key terms

419 scam: another name for a Nigerian prince scam

ABC: the Australian Broadcasting Corporation, one of Australia's public broadcasters

ABC Charter: section of legislation setting out the ABC's legal functions to produce diverse, independent and educational content

Abstain: decline formally to vote for or against a proposal

Above the line: approach to Senate voting where voters indicate their preference of political parties

Access to justice: the ability of people to source legal advice and representation, and to use the court system

Accession: when a state ratifies a treaty that was earlier negotiated and signed by other states

Accessorial liability: extended criminal liability that applies to people who aid, abet, counsel or procure the commission of a crime

Acquit: find that a defendant is not guilty of a crime

Act: a piece of legislation

Act of indecency: sexual act done in front of another person without their consent

Actual bodily harm: harm that is real but not trivial

***Actus reus*:** physical or conduct elements of a crime (means 'guilty act')

Ad hoc tribunal: court set up for a time-limited purpose, usually to prosecute individuals for war crimes

Administer: use laws in practice

Admission: when somebody makes a statement that suggests they are guilty

Adversarial system: court system where two parties oppose each other

Advisory opinion: judicial statement of legal advice

Advocate: to counsel, promote, encourage, urge, praise or promote the doing of a terrorist act

Affirmative consent: rules that requires people participating in a sexual act to check that the other person is consenting

AFP: Australian Federal Police

Aggravated assault: assault with an additional element involving greater likely harm, which attracts a higher maximum penalty

Aggravating factor: any piece of information that suggests a sentence should be more severe

Allow: agree with the arguments in an appeal

Amend: to change a law

Anarchy: a state of disordered conflict

Ancillary conduct: conduct that is related to the preparation of terrorist acts, like training and support for terrorism

Appeal: challenge a decision in a higher court

Appellant: person who lodges an appeal

Appellate jurisdiction: power of a court to hear appeals from lower courts

Armed robbery: an aggravated version of robbery where a weapon is used

Arraignment: when a judge or magistrate reads out a criminal charge to the defendant

Arrest: to take a person into police custody to investigate a crime or have a court determine whether they committed one

Article: a section of a treaty or other international law document

ASIO: the Australian Security Intelligence Organisation, Australia's domestic intelligence organisation that is responsible for protecting national security

Assault: unlawful contact with another person

Assimilation: government policy that said other cultures should reject their heritage and become part of the white community

Attempt: when someone starts committing a crime but fails to complete the *actus reus*

AustLII: the Australasian Legal Information Institute, an online database of legislation and case law

Australian Electoral Commission: independent body responsible for running elections

Authoritarian system: system of government where power is highly centralised and populations are often controlled by fear and coercion

Bail: the conditional release of a person after they are charged and before the criminal trial

Balance of power: the deciding votes in a house of parliament

Balance of probabilities: civil standard of proof, which favours the stronger case

Bandwidth: the amount of data that can pass through a computer system in a fixed amount of time

Barrister: specialist advocate who represents clients in court
Battery: contact with another person without their consent
Below the line: approach to Senate voting where voters indicate their preference of candidates
Bench: the central, elevated platform in a courtroom where the judge or magistrate sits
Beyond a reasonable doubt: standard of proof in criminal proceedings
Bias: tendency to produce content that favours one side or viewpoint unfairly
Bicameral: having two chambers
Bilateral: between two states
Bill: a proposal for legislation
Bill of Rights: part of a country's constitution that provides legal protection for human rights
Binding precedent: rules from previous judgments that courts must follow
Bipartisan support: when a proposal is supported by both major political parties
Bitcoin: a type of digital currency
Body corporate: committee that manages a property on behalf of all owners in a strata title scheme
Bot: one compromised computer in a botnet
Botnet: a network of computers that have been compromised through a trojan or other malware
Breach: fail to meet a legal requirement
Burden of proof: the responsibility to prove something in court
By-laws: rules made by body corporates that say what people can and cannot do on common property in a strata title scheme
Cabinet: meeting of senior Ministers with responsibility over important portfolios like defence, finance and education
Caliph: the ruler of a Caliphate
Caliphate: a state ruled under Islamic law
Carriage service: any means of electronic communication
Case: legal dispute between two parties in court
Case law: collection of judgments published by courts
Case note: academic summary of a judgment, which often includes critical analysis
Catchwords: collection of key words at the start of a judgment that summarise what the case is about
Caution: when police inform a person of the right to silence, and also an official warning issued by police
Cede: to surrender, give up or hand over
Centralisation: when a national government acquires greater lawmaking powers, at the expense of those held by state or regional governments

Centrist: a person who falls between left- and right-wing political views

Chamber: a large room where legislation is debated

Charge: an administrative decision to prosecute a person in court

Charter: in relation to public broadcasters, a section of legislation that sets out their functions and obligations to the community

Chief Minister: the equivalent of a state premier in the territories

Circle sentencing: a mediation process based on traditional Indigenous practices

Civil liberty: the sphere of protected freedom we gain under the social contract

Civil liberties: individual rights we gain as citizens living under a government, including privacy and freedom of speech

Class action: legal claim where at least seven people are affected by the same circumstances, and one or more people pursue the claim on behalf of a larger group

Closing statement: final speech made by a lawyer to the court, which sums up their major evidence and arguments

Closing the Gap: national agreement that sets out 19 targets across 17 areas to help reduce gaps in outcomes between Indigenous and non-Indigenous Australians

COAG: forum made up of leaders from the three levels of government (now replaced by National Cabinet)

Coalition: agreement between political parties to vote together in parliament

Code of ethics: for journalists, a document containing agreed rules and standards to maintain integrity in the profession

Coercive federalism: when the federal government dominates or unfairly influences the state governments

Collective responsibility: principle that says members of Cabinet must publicly support decisions reached by Cabinet as a whole

Commit: to send a case to a higher court

Committal hearing: initial proceedings held in a local court to determine whether a criminal case should be heard in a higher court

Common law: another name for case law

Commonwealth Parliament: the Australian Parliament in Canberra

Community legal centres: independent community organisations that provide legal advice and services to communities

Community service order: order issued by a court that requires a convicted offender to complete a specified number of hours volunteering in the community

Compensation: the payment of money to repair harm

Complicity: liability for assisting, providing instruction in or otherwise facilitating the commission of a crime

Compulsory voting: system that penalises people for not voting at elections

Concurrent powers: lawmaking powers held by the federal and State governments

Conditional: when a person's release is subject to restrictions and obligations, like reporting to a police station

Conduct elements: another name for the physical elements of a crime

Conference: in restorative justice, a meeting between the offender, victim and other people which provides a safe place to talk about the crime

Confession: when somebody admits to committing a crime

Confirmation bias: tendency to seek out information that confirms what you already think or feel

Conflict of laws: another name for private international law

Conquer: to take a country by force

Conscience vote: when members of a political party can vote according to their individual views and not party politics

Consent: when a person understands what something involves and agrees to it

Conservative: reluctant to accept significant social or economic change

Consideration: the legal value that each party promises to exchange in a legally binding contract

Consistency: principle that sentencing judges should treat similar cases in a similar way

Consolidated Acts: the current and complete version of legislation

Conspiracy: where two or more people agree to commit a crime

Conspiracy theory: explanation that falsely claims a small group of powerful people are secretly controlling events in society

Constitution: Australia's founding legal document, which came into force 1 January 1901

Constitutional conventions: meetings held in the 1890s to debate and draft the text of the Constitution

Constructive possession: principle that says an owner of goods can still be in possession of them, even if they are held by another person

Contract: legally binding agreement

Contract law: area of the law that governs agreements between individuals

Control order: court order that imposes restrictions and obligations on a person for the purpose of preventing a terrorist act, or preventing the support or facilitation of terrorism

Convention: another name for a treaty

Conventions: unwritten, traditional ways that things are done in a system of law and government

Cooperative federalism: when the federal and state governments work well together

Coordinative federalism: when the federal and state governments have clearly defined responsibilities

Corrective services: core department in the criminal justice system that is responsible for managing prisons

Councillors: elected representatives to local governments

Councils: another name for local governments, and the chambers where councillors meet

Crime: conduct that causes harm or is morally wrong and attracts a penalty of imprisonment under the law

Crimes against humanity: systematic criminal acts against civilian populations during armed conflict

Crimes of aggression: when one country invades another contrary to international law

Criminal justice system: collection of institutions and processes that impose penalties on people for committing crimes

Criminal law: area of law that tells us when someone breaches the rules of society and should be punished

Critical infrastructure: computer networks, engineering systems and facilities needed to deliver essential services (like gas, water and electricity) to a population

Cross-bench: minor parties and independents who often hold the balance of power

Cross-examination: when lawyers ask questions to undermine the accuracy of testimony presented by a witness who was called by the opposing side

Crown: government that is prosecuting the defendant in a criminal case

Curfew: requirement in a control order that a person must be at home during specified times of the day and night

Customary international law: fundamental rules based in state practice rather than treaty law

Cyber-bullying: harassment, teasing, or other online conduct that is repeated, intentional and cruel

Cyber-dependent crime: cybercrime that depends on technology

Cyber-enabled crime: more traditional crimes committed online

Cyber-security: the extent to which computer systems and networks are protected from malicious acts and actors

Cyber-terrorism: terrorism that involves cyber-attacks against electronic systems

Damage control: public relations strategies designed to minimise the impact of mistakes and controversies

Damages: payment awarded by a court as compensation

Declaration: a non-binding treaty

Declaration of incompatibility: statement issued by a court under a human rights act which says a piece of legislation is incompatible with human rights
Defamation: when someone harms another person's reputation by publishing false information about them
Defence: a specific legal argument that excuses or partially justifies a crime
Defendant: the accused person in a criminal trial
Delegated legislation: another name for regulations
Democracy: political system where governments are elected by the people
Denial-of-service (DoS) attack: a type of cyber-attack in which a computer, server or network is overloaded with requests to the point where it slows down substantially or stops working
Denunciation: declaring that conduct is morally wrong
Deontology: branch of philosophy that focuses on ethics and the inherent morality of different choices
Deregulate: change or remove rules to make something legal
Derogate: suspend or interrupt a legal obligation
Deterrence: signalling to an individual or the community that committing a crime will attract punishment, to encourage them not to offend
Dialogue model: model of human rights protection in which courts can declare legislation incompatible with human rights
Dictatorship: system of government ruled by a leader with absolute power
Direct democracy: hypothetical system of government in which people contribute to every decision
Disclosure: pre-trial process where the prosecution informs a defendant of the evidence against them
Discretion: the ability to choose between multiple courses of action that are lawfully available
Disinformation: false or inaccurate content spread intentionally to deceive or manipulate an audience
Dissent: minority opinion of a court
Dissolve: to dismiss an entire house of parliament and re-elect its membership
Distinction: principle of international humanitarian law which says that military attacks must distinguish between military and non-military targets, and between combatants and civilians
Distributive justice: when resources, outcomes and opportunities are distributed fairly across society
Distributed denial-of-service (DDoS) attack: a denial-of-service attack launched by very large numbers of computers, usually through a botnet
District court: court on the second tier of the court hierarchy
Division: a group of sections in legislation

***Doli incapax*:** presumption that children aged 10-13 years do not have the maturity to be considered criminally responsible

Double dissolution: special election in which both houses of parliament are dissolved

Double majority: requirement that changes to the text of the Constitution must be approved by a majority of Australians overall, and a majority of people in a majority of States

Due process: requirement that everyone should receive a fair hearing of their case in court

Duty of care: an obligation not to cause foreseeable harm to others

Easement: a right to use part of someone's land for a specific purpose without owning it

Electoral roll: register of all voters in Australia

Electorate: defined geographical area that elects one member to the House of Representatives

Elements: the components or ingredients of legal tests

Empanel: to select and enrol the members of a jury

Enact: to make a Bill into law

Enlightenment: historical period following the Middle Ages and Renaissance which saw a move away from religion towards scientific and rational thinking

Enter a plea: when a defendant claims to the court that they are guilty or not guilty of the crime

Equal suffrage: principle that says every person's vote should be worth the same value

Equality: distributing things equally

Equity: redistributing things to address inequality

eSafety Commissioner: independent office established in 2015 that promotes online safety and handles complaints about harmful online content

Evidence-in-chief: initial statement of witness testimony

Exception: rule in legislation that excludes certain conduct from the scope of a criminal offence

Exclusive possession: sole right to live on and use land, to the exclusion of all others

Exclusive powers: lawmaking powers belonging to only one level of government

Executive: branch of government that administers (uses) laws in practice

Expert evidence: opinion evidence given by a suitably trained and experienced expert

Explanatory memorandum: document accompanying a Bill that explains what the Bill contains

Extraterritoriality: doctrine that applied in early Australian law, which said that Australian Parliaments could not legislate outside their borders

Extrinsic materials: materials separate to legislation that can be used to determine its purpose or the meaning of a word or phrase

Fact-checking: where journalists or a dedicated organisation verify the accuracy of claims made in public content

Faction: semi-organised grouping in a political party that strategise and vote together

Fault elements: another name for the mental elements of a crime

Federal parliament: the Australian parliament in Canberra

Federal system: system of government that shares lawmaking powers between a national government and several state or regional governments

Federalism: ideas and theories relating to federal systems of government

Federate: join together in a federal system of government

Federation: the moment on 1 January 1901 when the Constitution came into force and the colonies joined together as states to form the Commonwealth of Australia

Five Eyes: intelligence network comprising Australia, Canada, New Zealand, the United States and the United Kingdom

Foreign fighters: people who travelled to Syria and Iraq to fight with the terrorist organisation Islamic State

Foreign interference: when one country seeks to manipulate political events and outcomes in another

Foreperson: a jury member appointed as its leader and spokesperson

Fourth estate: phrase used to describe the media because of the important role it plays in holding governments accountable

Fraud: stealing something dishonestly

Freehold title: full legal ownership that applies to most privately held and residential land

Full defence: a defence that fully justifies a criminal act, meaning the defendant is acquitted

General Assembly: the UN's main representative forum, in which all member states deliberate on issues affecting world peace and security

General deterrence: signalling to community members that committing a crime will attract punishment, to encourage them not to offend

Geneva Conventions: series of 4 treaties and 3 optional protocols that protect non-combatants in armed conflict

Genocide: attempts to destroy, in whole or part, a national, ethnic, racial or religious group

Golden rule: common law rule that said judges could substitute another meaning of a word if the literal rule led to an absurd or inconsistent result

Good behaviour bond: order issued by a court that requires an offender to promise they will not commit another crime

Governor-General: the King's representative in Australia

Government: political party with a majority of seats in the House of Representatives

Grassroots campaigns: where community members volunteer and mobilise around a political cause

Green politics: political views that typically support environmental conservation, renewable energy, animal rights, non-violence and social justice

Greens: influential minor party that advocates for the protection of the environment

Grievous bodily harm: very serious harm that causes disfigurement, disablement, or would endanger the victim's life if they did not receive medical treatment

Guideline judgment: judgment that explains the typical punishment for an offence

Hansard: transcripts of parliamentary proceedings

Harm principle: principle attributed to the British philosopher John Stuart Mill, who said the law should only prohibit conduct that is harmful

Head of state: the highest representative of a sovereign state

Heads of power: sub-sections in section 51 of the Constitution which list the federal Parliament's lawmaking powers

Heard summarily: when an indictable offence is heard by a magistrate in the local court

Hearsay: statements that are heard second-hand

Held: decided by a judge or judges

High Court: the highest court in Australia

Homicide: the unlawful killing of another person

House: chamber in a parliament

House of Representatives: lower house of the federal parliament

Human rights: core freedoms that all human beings should be afforded to respect their dignity and wellbeing

Human rights act: piece of legislation that allows courts to declare legislation incompatible with human rights

Hung parliament: when neither major party wins a majority in the lower house

Identity theft: stealing personal information like usernames, passwords, bank account details and credit card numbers

Immunity: protection from legal liability

Impartiality: requirement that judges are independent and do not have conflicts of interest

Implement: recreate a treaty provision in domestic legislation

Implied rights: rights that are not expressly protected, but the High Court has developed by interpreting other words in the Constitution

Inalienable: not able to be taken away

Incapacitation: putting a person in prison to protect the community from further harm

Inchoate liability: legal responsibility for attempt and conspiracy (means 'not fully formed or developed')

Incommunicado: when a detained person cannot contact anyone

Indecent assault: unwanted contact with sexual connotations

Independent: elected representative who is not a member of a political party

Indictable offence: a more serious offence that attracts a penalty of three years imprisonment or more

Indigenous Land Use Agreements: binding legal contracts between traditional owners of land and a corporate or government interest

Individualised justice: principle that a punishment should be fair in all the circumstances of an individual case

Infringement notice: ticket that requires payment of money as a fine

Insanity: defence that can be made out where an offender could not understand what they were doing, could not control their actions, or could not understand right from wrong

Instinctive synthesis: overall process followed by sentencing judges, in which they weigh up all relevant factors

Institutional sovereignty: the legal and political power of institutions like Parliament

Instrument of ratification: signed statement deposited with the United Nations which confirms a government's intention to be bound by a treaty

International armed conflict: war between two countries

International Court of Justice: the United Nation's main court

International Criminal Court: international court established under the Rome Statue which hears cases on genocide, war crimes, crimes against humanity and crimes of aggression

Investigative journalism: news reporting that involves deeper inquiries into matters of public importance, typically presented in longer articles and documentary-style TV programs

Joint committee: a parliamentary committee made up of members from both houses

Joint judgment: when two or more judges write their opinions together

Journalist: someone involved in the profession of reporting news

Judge: experienced lawyer who is appointed to preside over trials and resolve legal disputes

Judgment: published statement of reasons that explains a judge's decision and how they arrived at it

Judicial review: power of the High Court to strike down legislation that is incompatible with the Constitution

Judiciary: technical term for the court system

Jurisdiction: the geographical area in which laws operate and a court's authority to hear different types of cases

Jurists: highly qualified and esteemed international law scholars

Jury trial: criminal trial held in district or supreme court, where a jury decides the defendant's guilt

***Jus ad bellum*:** laws of war

***Jus in bello*:** laws in war

Justice: a complex concept which captures ideas many different ideas relating to fairness and equality

Justice reinvestment: when governments redirect funds from prisons to community-based strategies which address the underlying causes of crime

Labor Party: a centre-left political party and one of two major political parties in Australia

Larceny: another name for stealing

Law: a body of rules found in legislation and case law that regulate behaviour

Law reform: when laws are proposed and made by parliaments

Law reports: volumes of judgments

Leadership spill: when a vote is held to contest the leadership of a political party

Lease: agreement that governs the relationship between a tenant who lives in a property and a landlord who owns it

Leave: permission granted by a court to hear an appeal

Left-wing: to have political views which are more progressive

Legal Aid: government-funded offices which provide free legal advice and services to people in need

Legal fiction: principle with legal force based on something that is factually inaccurate

Legal representation: having a lawyer to contest your case in court

Legislation: a document containing legal rules that were approved by a parliament

Legislature: a technical term for Parliament used when discussing the separation of powers

Legislative instruments: regulations, rules and determinations made by Ministers

LexisNexis: database of case law accessible through university libraries

Liable: legally responsible for

Liberal democracy: a system of government that combines principles of liberalism and democracy

Liberal Party: a centre-right political party and one of two major political parties in Australia

Liberalism: political philosophy that emphasises individual freedom from government

Literal rule: common law rule that said judges should prefer the ordinary or dictionary meaning of a word

Lobby: when an individual or group petitions a political party to change law or policy

Local court: lowest court on the court hierarchy

Local governments: the lowest level of government in Australia

Lower house: another name for the federal House of Representatives

Magistrate: judge in a local court

Magistrates court: another name for the local court

Majoritarian system: a system of government dominated by two political parties

Majority verdict: a decision that 11 out of 12 jury members agree on

Makarrata Commission: a truth-telling commission that would help to overcome previous harm and symbolise the restoration of peace

Malware: malicious software, including trojans, viruses, worms and ransomware

Mandatory minimum: minimum penalty set in legislation for a criminal offence

Manifestly excessive: phrase used to describe sentencing judgments that are found on appeal to be too severe

Manifestly inadequate: phrase used to describe sentencing judgments that are found on appeal to be too lenient

Manifesto: a long document stating a terrorist's ideology and motivations

Manslaughter: the accidental or negligent killing of another person

Mass media: group of publishing and broadcasting companies that communicate to a very large audience

Material facts: the most important facts from a judgment that are relevant to precedent

Mayor: head of a local government

Media: broadcasting and publishing companies that communicate information to the public

Medium-neutral citation: a simplified, less official citation that is often used for judgments found online

Members: politicians elected to the House of Representatives

Memory: how much information a computer can store temporarily to perform multiple tasks at the same time

***Mens rea*:** the mental or fault elements of an offence (means 'guilty act')

Mental elements: elements that describe the offender's state of mind

Merits: how likely a legal case is to succeed in court

Metadata: data about communications, including the time, location and length of phone calls between two devices

Minister: senior member of government with responsibility over a specific policy area

Minor parties: political parties other than the Labor, Liberal and National parties

Minority government: a government that achieves a majority in the lower house by securing support from the cross-bench

Miscarriage of justice: a wrongful conviction

Mischief rule: common law rule that said judges could consider the problem legislation was designed to prevent

Misinformation: false or inaccurate content that unintentionally misleads an audience

Mitigating factor: any piece of information that suggests a sentence should be less severe

M'Naghten's rules: common law rules relating to the defence of insanity

Monarch: King or Queen

Motive requirement: requirement found in legal definitions of terrorism, which requires that an act of terrorism be designed to advance a political, religious or ideological cause

MP: abbreviation for Member of Parliament

Multilateral: between three or more states

Multinational: a large, often powerful company that operates in multiple countries

Murder: the intentional or reckless killing of another person

National Cabinet: meeting of the Prime Minister, Premiers and Chief Ministers

National Party: centre-right country party that forms a Coalition with the Liberal Party

National Redress Scheme: scheme established to provide compensation for victims of institutional child sexual abuse

Native title: right to use lands and waters which derives from the traditional laws and customs of Indigenous people

Natural justice: another name for due process

Negligence: acts that cause harm to someone by breaching a duty of care

Neoliberalism: theory of government which favours free economic markets and privatisation of public services

News Corp: international media organisation owned by the Murdoch family, which is widely recognised as favouring right-wing viewpoints

Non-derogable: not able to be suspended

Non-international armed conflict: war within a country

Non-parole period: period during a prison sentence when a convicted offender cannot be released under supervision

Notice: requirement that everyone should know the case and evidence against them

Notice to appear: order issued by police that requires a person to attend court at a later date

Numbered Acts: legislation listed by the year it was enacted

***Obiter dicta*:** things a judge says which are not part of the *ratio decidendi* but may be relevant to a future case (means 'by the way')

Ombudsman: office that investigates complaints against members of government departments

Open court: a court that is open for everyone to see

***Opinio juris*:** intention to be bound by a rule, which forms part of customary international law

Opinion: another name for a judgment, or in evidence law, a belief that something was likely to happen

Opposition: the political party with the second highest number of seats in the House of Representatives

Optional protocols: additional agreements that relate to a primary treaty

Organ: word used to describe the six main parts of the UN

Original jurisdiction: a court's power to hear a case for the first time

Parity: principle that multiple offenders should receive a similar sentence for the same crime

Parliament: a lawmaking forum made up of elected politicians

Parliamentary committee: group of members or senators who meet separately to examine Bills in detail

Parliamentary Joint Committee on Human Rights: parliamentary committee that examines whether legislation complies with human rights

Parole: when a prisoner is released on conditions while serving their sentence

Parole Board: an authority independent to a prison, which decides whether offenders should be released on parole

Parsimony: favouring the least severe sentence that is appropriate in the circumstances

Part: a group of divisions in legislation

Partial defence: defence that reduces a charge from murder to manslaughter

Party: one of the sides in a legal dispute

Peremptory challenge: when the prosecution or defence challenges the enrolment of a juror without giving a reason

Persuasive precedent: rules from previous cases that are not binding on courts, but may be considered

Phishing: deceiving a person into providing personal information (usually via email)

Physical elements: elements that describe the offender's conduct

Plea: declaration by the defendant that they will or will not contest the charges

Plenary power: unrestrained lawmaking power

Police prosecutor: a police officer with legal training that pursues criminal charges in court

Political party: an organisation with a set of beliefs, values and goals that puts forward members for election to parliament

Popular sovereignty: the inherent lawmaking power of the people

Populism: decisions that favour the interests and values of most people

Portfolio: area of government policy that a Minister is responsible for

Possess: have physical control over something

Preamble: opening statement to a constitution or international law instrument

Precedent: core principle of law which says the rule and reasoning used in a previous judgment must be used again when similar cases come before a court

Pre-charge detention: the limited time available for police to question a suspect after arrest and before charge

Pre-crime: term used to describe many counter-terrorism laws because they punish people for something they are likely to do in the future

Preference deal: negotiated agreements between political parties to allocate preferences other than the primary vote

Preferential voting: voting system used in the House of Representatives which is based on candidates winning a 50% majority of the vote from an electorate

Prejudice: discrimination towards groups in society, especially on the grounds of race, religion or ethnicity

Prejudicial evidence: evidence that would unfairly suggest the defendant is guilty

Preparatory offences: offences in division 101 of the *Criminal Code Act 1995* (Cth) which target the preparation of terrorist acts

Press gallery: group of around 250 journalists and other media staff who work in Parliament House

Presumption of innocence: principle that everyone is considered innocent until they are found guilty in a court of law

Preventative detention order: power that allows police to detain a person for up to two weeks to prevent an imminent terrorist act, or to preserve evidence about a recent attack

Primary vote: the 'number 1' vote cast on a ballot paper

Prime Minister: the leader of the government

Principle of legality: judicial presumption that parliament did not intend to interfere with fundamental rights and freedoms

Principles of sentencing: general rules that explain how a judge should arrive at an appropriate sentence

Private international law: rules that help to resolve disputes between companies and citizens in different countries

Private law: area of law that governs relationships between individuals

Privatisation: the selling of publicly owned assets, industries and services to private companies

Privilege against self-incrimination: right that means suspects can refuse to answer police questions that would reveal information suggesting they are guilty

Probation: when a convicted offender is released on conditions, such as reporting to a correctional services officer at regular time

Probative value: relevance to a rational assessment of whether the defendant is guilty

Problem question: common exam type given in university law schools, where students determine likely outcomes in hypothetical cases

Procedural fairness: another name for due process

Procedural justice: when processes are fair

Procedural justice policing: when police officers engage respectfully with communities and give people an opportunity to have their voices heard

Produce: in relation to drug offences, to manufacture, prepare or package illegal drugs

Progressive: in favour of social or economic change

Property law: area of law that governs usage and ownership rights

Property offences: crimes that involve stealing things or fraudulently acquiring them

Proportional voting: voting system used in the Senate that requires candidates to reach a quota

Proportionality: in sentencing, the principle that punishments should be appropriate in type and severity to the crime committed, or in international law, that military attacks must not be excessive compared to the military advantage sought

Proscribe: ban an organisation

Proscribed organisation: an organisation formally listed by the Australian government as a terrorist organisation

Proscription regime: a scheme for banning terrorist organisations

Prosecution service: office of lawyers working for the government who pursue criminal charges in court

Prosecutor: government lawyer that pursues charges against a defendant in court

Provocation: a partial defence to murder, where a person kills someone after being provoked and losing self-control

Public broadcaster: taxpayer-funded media organisation with a legal duty to produce diverse, independent and educational content

Public international law: system of rules that states must abide by when interacting with each other, and to protect their own citizens

Public law: area of law that tells us about Australia's system of law and government

Public order offences: offences involving harmful conduct done in public, such as loitering, urinating in public, or using offensive language

Public service: government departments and agencies

Publicity: requirement that court proceedings should be open for everyone to see

Purposes of punishment: reasons why courts punish offenders, which are considered while sentencing them

Purposive rule: another name for the mischief rule

Question of law: a legal issue that provides the basis for an appeal

Question time: a regular, dedicated time in Parliament when ministers must answer questions without notice

Questions without notice: questions in parliament that ministers are not told about in advance, so they cannot prepare an answer

Quota: defined percentage of a vote

Races power: head of power in section 51(xxvi) of the Constitution, which says that the federal Parliament can make special laws for the people of any race

Radical title: land ownership acquired by Britain upon colonisation, which is subject to valid native title claims

Ransomware: a type of malware that locks a user out of a computer system and demands money to regain access

Ratify: confirm intention to be bound by a treaty

***Ratio decidendi*:** the key rule or reasoning from a judgment that must be applied as precedent (means 'the reason for the decision')

Read down: when the High Court interprets a section of legislation so it is consistent with the Constitution

Reading: stage of parliamentary debate on a Bill

Recidivism: when people reoffend after being released from prison

Recklessness: where an offender is aware of a substantial risk of harm, but continues the act anyway

Records of the Australasian Federal Conventions: transcripts of the constitutional conventions

Recuse: when a judge steps down from a case due to a conflict of interest

Re-examination: the final stage of questioning a witness, when the side that called the witness asks questions to reinforce the testimony

Referendum: national vote on whether to change the text of the Constitution

Referendum Council: body appointed in 2016 to make recommendations on how Indigenous peoples could be recognised in the Constitution

Referendum machinery Bill: Bill introduced into the federal Parliament containing a proposal for constitutional change, which will be voted on by the Australian people

Regulate: to guide and restrict behaviour

Regulations: legislation made by Ministers

Rehabilitation: helping an offender address the underlying reasons why they committed a crime

Remand: when somebody is held in prison after they are charged and before the criminal trial

Remedy: a court order designed to offset harm or loss

Reparations: compensation payments

Repeal: to remove or revoke a law

Representative government: system of government where politicians are elected by the people and make decisions on their behalf

Republic: a system of government with a head of state that represents the people

Repugnancy: doctrine that applied in early Australian law, which said Australian Parliaments could not legislate inconsistently with British law

Reservation: exception or qualification to the articles of a treaty

Reserved powers doctrine: principle that the federal Parliament has specific lawmaking powers, while the rest is left to the states

Resolution: statement of opinion or intention by the United Nations General Assembly or Security Council

Resolution 1373: resolution issued by the United Nations Security Council on 28 September 2001, which required member states to enact laws targeting the preparation and financing of terrorism

Respondent: party arguing against the grounds of an appeal

Responsible government: a system of government where Ministers sit in Parliament, which blurs the executive and legislative branches

Restorative justice: alternative means of resolving cases, usually through mediation and other dispute resolution processes

Retribution: punishment inflicted as repayment for a harmful act

Retrospective legislation: laws that apply from a prior date so that a person can be punished for something that was not a crime when they did it

Revenge porn: distributing intimate images to embarrass or humiliate a person

Right to silence: requirement that people do not need to answer questions put to them by police

Right-wing: to have political views that are more conservative

Right-wing extremism: extreme ideology based in white supremacy and neo-Nazi beliefs

Robbery: stealing something with force of violence

Rome Statute: treaty that established and governs the International Criminal Court

Royal assent: when the Governor-General signs a Bill into law

Royal commission: the highest level of public inquiry in Australia, usually chaired by a former judge

Rule: a statement, principle or instruction that says what someone can, cannot or must do, or how something must be done

Rule of law: a principle that says laws should be publicly accessible and clearly written, and that everyone should be treated equally under the law

SBS: the Special Broadcasting Service, one of Australia's public broadcasters

Secondary legislation: another name for regulations

Second reading speech: Minister's speech in parliament which outlines the purpose of a Bill and what it contains

Section: an individual rule in legislation

Security Council: UN organ with primary responsibility for maintaining international peace and security

Self-defence: when a person reasonably believes another person will kill or seriously harm them, and responds with reasonably necessary force

Self-determination: human right for communities to freely determine their political status and future development

Senate: upper house of the federal parliament

Senators: politicians elected to the Senate

Sentencing advisory council: state body that conducts research, produces advice and educates communities about sentencing

Separation of powers: principle that says power should be divided between the legislature, executive, and judiciary

Sexting: sending and receiving intimate images

Settle: agree to resolve a legal dispute out of the courtroom, often by one side paying money to the other as compensation

Settlement: doctrine from colonial law that allowed a country to claim unoccupied land

Sexual assault: penetrating another person's bodily orifices without their consent

Small government: idea that governments should interfere minimally in business and the lives of their citizens

Social contract: the hypothetical agreement we enter into as citizens living under a government, which grants us civil liberties

Social justice: efforts to address inequalities in society

Solicitor: lawyer who briefs barristers on cases, but can also represent clients in court

Solicitor-General: lawyer for the Commonwealth and second highest law officer in Australia after the Attorney-General

Solitary confinement: when prisoners are held separately to other detainees under stricter conditions

Sovereign: a ruler with absolute power over a given territory, often used interchangeably with King or Queen

Sovereign state: an internationally recognised government that has legal and political power over its citizens within a defined territory

Sovereignty: absolute legal and political power over a defined territory

Spam: unwanted email messages

Speaker: member of parliament chosen to preside over proceedings

Special leave to appeal: permission to have an appeal heard in the High Court

Special Intelligence Operation: undercover operation that has been specially approved by the Attorney-General, in which ASIO officers are granted immunity from civil and criminal liability

Specific deterrence: signalling to an offender that their actions will be treated severely, to encourage them not to reoffend

Standard of proof: requirement that court cases be proven to a specified level of certainty

Standing orders: rules that specify how parliaments are run

***Stare decisis*:** Latin name for the doctrine of precedent (means 'to stand by things decided')

State: term used in political philosophy that refers to the national government of a country

State of nature: term used by the philosopher Jean-Jacques Rousseau to describe a state of anarchy before we lived under governments

Statute: a piece of legislation

Statutory functions: the purposes of an organisation and the tasks it performs, as set out in legislation

Statutory interpretation: methods used by judges to determine the meaning of words and phrases in legislation

Stayed: when a court case is delayed by a judge's order

Stealing: taking something from another person without their consent, with an intention to permanently deprive them of the thing

Stolen Generations: successive generations of Indigenous who were forcibly taken from their families and taught to adopt white culture

Stop and search: power that allows police to stop somebody on the street and search them for illegal materials

Strata title: a shared ownership arrangement commonly used in apartment blocks

Stuxnet: a very sophisticated computer worm that caused substantial damage to the Iranian nuclear power program

Subordinate legislation: another name for regulations

Subsidiary: a company owned by a parent company

Substantial impairment: defence that can be made out where the offender was operating under an abnormality of mind

Substantive justice: when outcomes are fair

Sue: bring a civil action against someone in court

Summary offence: a less serious offence punishable by two years imprisonment or less

Summary trial: criminal trial in the local court, which is decided by magistrate alone

Summons: order issued by police that requires a person to attend court at a later date

Supply: the passage of money Bills so a government can pay for its policies

Supreme court: the highest court in a State

Surplus votes: votes for a candidate in excess of the quota required to win a senate seat

Suspended sentence: a prison term that is not served immediately but can be triggered if the offender commits another crime

Sustainable Development Goals: 17 goals developed by the UN Economic and Social Council to create a better world by 2030

Swing: a shift in voter preferences, either towards or away from a party

Table: formally submit a document into the parliamentary record

Tabloid: a newspaper associated with sensationalist content and celebrity news

Taking out the trash: when governments release information that makes them look bad at a time when fewer people are likely to notice it

Teal independents: group of independent candidates loosely aligned on issues relating to climate change, anti-corruption and gender equality

Technology-enabled crime: crime that is easier to commit because of the Internet, but is relatively familiar to the law

Tenterfield Oration: speech given in 1889 by Sir Henry Parkes which made the case for Federation

***Terra Nullius*:** legal fiction that allowed Britain to settle Australia (means 'land belonging to no one')

Terrorist organisation: organisation that is involved in the preparation or planning of a terrorist act

Testimony: formal statement made by a witness to the court, which explains their interpretation of events

The Great Replacement: conspiracy theory that falsely claims western governments are allowing their governments to be taken over by Muslims
Theft: another name for stealing
Therapeutic jurisprudence: court processes that promote the wellbeing of offenders and victims
Title: ownership rights over something
Torrens title: sole registered ownership of land and property to the exclusion of all others
Tort: an unlawful but non-criminal harm
Totality: principle that a sentence for multiple crimes should be fair overall
Trade unions: organisations that represents workers' rights
Trafficking: supplying drugs on a large scale
Transfer value: reduced value of surplus votes when redistributed to other candidates
Transparency: when governments communicate information openly with their citizens
Treaty: a formal, written agreement between two or more countries that is governed by international law
Tribunal: quasi-court that is part of the executive branch of government
Trojan: a computer program that appears to be legitimate but causes harm once it runs
UDHR: Universal Declaration of Human Rights, the founding document of the Human Rights movement, published in 1948 by the UN General Assembly
Uluru Statement from the Heart: statement on Indigenous rights and recognition published in 2017 by the Referendum Council
Unanimous: agreed or supported by every member in a group
UNDRIP: the United Nations Declaration on the Rights of Indigenous Peoples, a comprehensive instrument that recognises, protects and promotes Indigenous rights, including to self-determination
Unicameral: having one chamber
United Nations: international organisation dedicated to international peace, security, and human rights
Unlawful imprisonment: tort where someone is detained against their will
Unsafe and unsatisfactory: phrase describing cases that were decided wrongly by a jury
Upper house: another name for the federal Senate
Utilitarian: approach to decision-making designed to maximise happiness for the most people
Valedictory speech: a final, farewell speech given by a serving member of parliament who has decided to resign or not contest their seat at the next election

Veil of ignorance: thought experiment designed by philosopher John Rawls, where we imagine what a society would look like if we did not know our place in it

Verdict: magistrate or jury's decision whether a person is guilty or not guilty

Vertical fiscal imbalance: an imbalance in public revenue, where the federal government has most of the money and the States do not collect enough to deliver their key services

Veto: power to prevent a law being enacted or a resolution being issued

Victim impact statement: prepared statement presented to a court that explains the impact of a crime on a victim or their family

Virus: self-replicating computer code that attaches itself to a host file or program

Voice to Parliament: proposed representative body that would allow representatives of First Nations communities to advise the Parliament and executive government

Wannacry: sophisticated ransomware that spread through more than 230,000 computers and substantially impacted the United Kingdom's hospital system

War crimes: acts committed by individuals against international law during armed conflict

Warrant: an order issued by a judge that allows police to use a special power

Whistleblower: someone working for an organisation or government department who exposes misconduct, corruption or criminal behaviour

Witness: a person who presents testimony to the court

Worm: self-replicating computer code that operates independently of other files and programs

Wounding: when a blade or other instrument cuts the interior layer of a person's skin

Index

Note: Page numbers in *italics* indicate figures.

7/7 bombings 252–253
9/11 attacks 252–255

Abbott, T. 63, 68, 76, 83, 173
ABC *see* Australian Broadcasting Corporation (ABC)
abstain 15
accession 157, 158
accessorial liability 196
acquit 194, 229
act 20, 172–174; of indecency 185
ACT *see* Australian Capital Territory (ACT)
actual bodily harm 188
actus reus 194–196, 223, 244
ACT v Commonwealth (1992) 141
ad hoc tribunals 162
administer 70, 105
admission 205
adversarial system 36, 121
advisory opinion 160
AEC *see* Australian Electoral Commission (AEC)
affirmative consent 190
AFP *see* Australian Federal Police (AFP)
aggravated assault 190
aggravating factor 221–222
AHRC *see* Australian Human Rights Commission (AHRC)
AIC *see* Australian Institute of Criminology (AIC)
Albanese, A. 63, 66, 150
allow 231
al-Qaeda 252
amend 20
anarchy 94
ancillary conduct 257
appeal 229–233; benefits of 232–233; court hierarchy and 229–230, *230*; High Court, to 232; limits of 232–233; meaning 39, 122, 229; special leave to 41
appeal against conviction and sentence 230–231
appellant 229
appellate jurisdiction 40–41, 229–230
armed robbery 191
arraignment 211
arrest 6, 205–206
article 165
ASIO *see* Australian Security Intelligence Organisation (ASIO)
ASIO Act, section 35P 263
ASIS *see* Australian Secret Intelligence Service (ASIS)

assault 12, 187–190; aggravated 190; 'assault causing death' 255; indecent 188; sexual 188
assimilation 133
ATO *see* Australian Taxation Office (ATO)
attempt 195
AustLII (Australasian Legal Information Institute) 25–27, 41, *45*
Australian Broadcasting Corporation (ABC) 73, 76–77; Charter 74; Four Corners program 80, 82; Q&A program 80, 83
Australian Capital Territory (ACT): Human Rights Act 2004 173; unicameral legislature 22
Australian Communist Party v Commonwealth (1951) 109
Australian Electoral Commission (AEC) 52
Australian Federal Police (AFP) 82, 261
Australian Human Rights Commission (AHRC) 172–173
Australian Institute of Criminology (AIC) 237, 239
Australian Law Reform Commission 266
Australian Secret Intelligence Service (ASIS) 161
Australian Security Intelligence Organisation (ASIO) 205, 265, 266; questioning warrants 262–263
Australian Taxation Office (ATO) 105
authoritarian system 79

bail 208–210; conditional 209
balance of power 60
balance of probabilities 121
bandwidth 248
barrister 125
battery 187
Bell, V. 108
bench 36
Bentham, J. 117
beyond a reasonable doubt 121, 193
bias: confirmation 83; meaning 83; media 83–85
bicameral parliament 22
bilateral 157
Bill of Rights 155, 168
bills: approval process 22–24, *24*; committee stage 24–25; explanatory memorandum 26; meaning 21; readings 22
binding precedent 37–38
bipartisan support 150
Bitcoin 248
body corporate 12
bot 246
botnet 246
Brandis, G. 150
breach 5
Brennan, F. 176
burden of proof 121, 211
by-laws 12, 13

Cabinet: meaning 69; National 104; *see also* government
caliph 253
caliphate 253
Canavan, *Re* (2017) 50
carriage service 242
case 36
case law 35–47; catchwords 44; citation 42–44, *43*; court hierarchy 38–40, *38*; finding 41–42; jurisdiction 40–41; material facts 44–47; meaning 7, 35–37; precedent 37–38; ratio 44–47; reading 42–47
case note 47
catchwords 42, 44
caution 204, 207

cede 138
CEM *see* child exploitation material (CEM)
centralisation 103
Centre for Innovative Justice, RMIT University 123
centrist 62
chambers 22
Channel 10 75
charge 206–207
Charlesworth, H. 161
charter 74
Chief Minister 80
child exploitation material (CEM) 241
Chisholm, R. 120
Churchill, W. 96
circle sentencing 123–124, 226–227
citation: case law 42–44, *43*; legislation *23*, 27; medium-neutral 43, *43*
citizenship stripping 265
civil law 9
civil liberties 95
class action 81
CLCs *see* community legal centres (CLCs)
Clinton, H. 87
closing statement 215–216
Closing the Gap 132–133
COAG *see* Council of Australian Governments (COAG)
coalition 65
Coco v The Queen (1994) 172
code of ethics 73
coercive federalism 104
Coe v Commonwealth (No 2) (1993) 136
collective responsibility 69
committal hearing 211
common law *see* case law
Commonwealth (Cth) 99; Acts Interpretation Act 1901 32, 33; Australia Act 1986 141; Australian Broadcasting Act 1983 74; Australian Citizenship Act 2007 265; Australian Human Rights Commission Act 1986 172; Australian Security Intelligence Organisation Act 1979 28–30, *29*; Charter of the United Nations Act 1945 160; Commonwealth Electoral Act 1918 52, 140–141; Criminal Code Act 1995 183, 244, 254, 256; Cybercrime Act 2001 243; Enhancing Online Safety Act 2015 243; Human Rights (Parliamentary Scrutiny) Act 2011 173; Judiciary Act 1903 41, 232; Migration Act 1958 105; Native Title Act 1993 143; Online Safety Act 2021 243; Racial Discrimination Act 1975 173; Special Broadcasting Act 1991 74; Telecommunications (Interception and Access) Act 1979: 263
Commonwealth of Australia Constitution Act 1900 (Imp) 140
communications service providers (CSPs) 263, 264
community legal centres (CLCs) 126–127
community service order 219
compensation 114
complicity 196
compulsory voting 52
concurrent powers 99
conditional bail 209
conduct elements *see* physical elements
conference 123
confession 205
confirmation bias 83
conflict of laws 156
conquer 138

conscience vote 15
consent 189; affirmative 190
conservative 61
consideration 10–11
Consolidated Acts 26
conspiracy 195–196
conspiracy theory 253
Constitution xvii, 8, 41, 50, 52, 95, 96, 99–101, 107, 140, 145–147, 148–149 168–171, 193, 232
constitutional conventions 139–140
constructive possession 13, 191
contract 4; law 10; social 94, 135
control orders 260–261
conventions 51, *see also* treaty
Conversation, The 88
cooperative federalism 104
coordinative federalism 104
corrective services 228
councillors 102
Council of Australian Governments (COAG) 104, 262
Council of Europe: Convention on Cybercrime ('Cybercrime Convention') 243–244
councils 102
counter-terrorism 252–268; ASIO questioning warrants 262–263; citizenship stripping 265; control orders 260–261; declared areas 259; encryption 264; examining laws before enactment 265–266; hate symbols 260; human rights protection 266–267; media freedom, protection of 267–268; metadata 263–264; offences 256–260; powers 260–265; preparatory offences 256–257; preventative detention orders 261–262; special intelligence operations 263; terrorist organisations 257–258; *see also* terrorism
courts: district 39; hierarchy 38–40, *38*, 230; local 38–39; open 120; supreme 39
Cowdery, N. 186
crimes: of aggression 162; cyber-dependent 236, 243–249; cyber-enabled 236, 238–243; defences 196–198; guilty of 193–199; against humanity 162; meaning 183; types of 187–193; war 162; young offenders 199
Criminal Code, division 102 257, 258
criminal hacking 243–245
criminal justice system 201; stages of *202*
criminal responsibility 183–199
criminal trial 210–216; closing statement 215–216; evidence 214–215; jury trials 212–213; pre-trial 210–211; summary trials 211–212; witnesses 215–216
critical infrastructure 248
cross-bench 60
cross-examination 215
crown 36
CSPs *see* communications service providers (CSPs)
Cth *see* Commonwealth (Cth)
curfew 261
customary international law 158
cyberbullying 242–243
cybercrime 235–249; 419 scams 238–239; meaning 235–238
cyber-dependent crime 236; criminal hacking 243–245; DoS attack 245–247; malware 247–249
cyber-enabled crime 236; cyberbullying 242–243; fraud 238–239; identity theft 239–240; revenge porn 240–242; sexting 240–242
cyber-security 249
cyber-terrorism 255

damages 11, 208; control of 78
Davis, K. C. 201–202
DDoS *see* distributed denial-of-service (DDoS) attack
declaration 158
declaration of incompatibility 174
Declaration of the Rights of Man and of the Citizen 95
defamation 11–12
defences 196–198; full 197; insanity 198; meaning 196–197; partial 197, 198; provocation 197–198; self-defence 197; substantial impairment 198
defendant 36, 210
delegated legislation 8, 33
democracy 95–98; accountability of politicians 97; direct 96; equal suffrage 97; features of 96; liberal 93; populism, tend towards 96–97; representative government 96
denial-of-service (DoS) attack 245–247; distributed 247
denunciation 219–220
deontology 118
deregulate 76
derogate 167
deterrence: general 219, 220; meaning 219, 220; specific 219, 220
dialogue model 174
Dicey, A. V. 109
dictatorship 79, 80
direct democracy 96
discretion 201–203
disinformation 86–87
dissolve 55
distributed denial-of-service (DDoS) attack 247
distributive justice 115
district court 39
doli incapax 199
Don Dale Royal Commission 199
DoS *see* denial-of-service (DoS) attack
double dissolution 54–55
double majority 144–145, 175
Douzinas, C. 156
Downer, A. 161
drug offences 191–192; constructive possession 191; possessing 191; producing 192; trafficking 192
due process 120–122
Dutton, P. 64
duty of care 11

easement 13
electoral roll 52
electorate 51
elements 193; fault 194; mental 194; physical 194
empanel 212
employment, law and 16–17
enact 20
enter a plea 212
environmental offences 192
equality 115, 116, *116*
equal suffrage 97
equity 115, 116, *116*
eSafety Commissioner 243
European Convention on Human Rights 168
evidence: expert 214–215; hearsay 214; opinion 214; prejudicial 214; sentencing 222–224
evidence-in-chief 215
exception 256
exclusive possession 143
exclusive powers 101
executive 69, 70, 105
expert evidence 214–215
Expert Panel on Recognising Aboriginal and Torres Strait Islander Peoples in the Constitution ('Expert Panel') 146–148

explanatory memorandum 26
extraterritoriality 141
extrinsic materials 32, 33

fact-checking 88
faction 62
Fairfax Media 75
Family Court of Australia 39–40
fault elements 194
Federal Circuit 39–40
federal government: heads of power 99; shared lawmaking powers 99–101; *see also* government
federalism 19, 20, 98–104, 139–141; advantages of 102–104; centralisation 103; challenges of 102–104; coercive 104; concurrent powers 99; cooperative 104; coordinative 104; exclusive powers 101; local government, role of 101–102; meaning 98; plenary power 101; reserved powers doctrine 103; vertical fiscal imbalance 103
First Nations National Constitutional Convention 149
First Nations Peoples 131–151; 1967 referendum 145–146; assimilation policy 133; Closing the Gap 132–133; constitutional recognition 144–151; Expert Panel 146–148; Federation 139–141; justice 131–134; *Mabo* decision 141–144; native title 141–144; settlement 138–139; sovereignty 134–137; *terra nullius*, doctrine of 138–139, 142, 143; Uluru Statement from the Heart 137; Voice to Parliament 144, 148–151
'Five Eyes' network 254
foreign fighters 265
foreign interference 87
foreperson 213
fourth estate: media as 77–83
fraud 191, 236, 238–239
freedom of expression 77
freehold title 12, 143
full defence 197
Fuller, L.: *Morality of Law, The* 109–110

general deterrence 219, 220
Geneva Conventions 163
genocide 162
Gillard, J. 63, 67, 146
golden rule 32
good behaviour bond 219
government: executive branch of *68*; justice, contribution to 127–128; levels of *102*; local 101–102; meaning 21, 51; minority 67; representative 96; responsible 107–108; small 64; *see also* Cabinet; federal government
Governor-General 23, 55, 105
grassroots campaigns 86
Grattan Institute 98
Great Replacement, The 253
Greens 65–66
grievous bodily harm 188
guideline judgments 224

hansard 25
Hanson, P. 66
harm principle 94, 95, 257
hate symbols 260
Hawke, B. 62
head of state xix, 23
heads of power 99
heard summarily 193
hearing, committal 211
hearsay 214
held 37
High Court: appeal to 232; appellate jurisdiction 40–41; judicial review, power of 99, 170–172;

meaning 39; original jurisdiction 40; special leave to appeal 41, 232
homicide 21, 187
honesty 119
house 22
House of Parliament 50–61
House of Representatives 51–53; ballot paper *53*; meaning 22, 50; Senate, comparison to *54*; *see also* Senate
Howard, J. 52, 60, 64, 148, 173
human rights xviii, 155, 164–168; act 173–174; models for change 174–176; protection, in Australian law 168–176, 266–267; statutes 172–174; treaties 165–166
hung parliament 67

ICAC *see* Independent Commission Against Corruption (ICAC)
ICC *see* International Criminal Court (ICC)
ICCPR *see* International Covenant on Civil and Political Rights (ICCPR)
ICESCR *see* International Covenant on Economic, Social and Cultural Rights (ICESCR)
ICJ *see* International Court of Justice (ICJ)
identity theft 239–240
IHL *see* international humanitarian law (IHL)
ILUAs *see* Indigenous Land Use Agreements (ILUAs)
immunity 263
impartiality 121–122
implement 158
implied rights 169–170
imprisonment 228–229; unlawful 12
inalienable 167
incapacitation 220
inchoate liability 195
incommunicado 262
indecent assault 188
Independent Commission Against Corruption (ICAC) 264
independents 67–68
indictable offence 193
Indigenous Land Use Agreements (ILUAs) 143
individualised justice 221
infringement notice 207
insanity 198
instinctive synthesis 224–225
institutional sovereignty 136
instrument of ratification 157
international armed conflict 163
International Court of Justice (ICJ) 160–161
International Covenant on Civil and Political Rights (ICCPR) 77; article 14(6) 232–233
International Covenant on Economic, Social and Cultural Rights (ICESCR) 137; article 1 167
International Criminal Court (ICC) 162
international humanitarian law (IHL) 163
international law 8–9, 155–164; branches of 156–159; customary 158; private 156; public 156–157; sources of 156–159
investigative journalism 75
Islamic State 253, 259, 263, 264, 265

Jacqui Lambie Network 67
joint committee 24
joint judgment 36–37
journalist 73
judges: meaning 7, 36; reading of legislation 31–33
judgment 36; joint 36–37
judicial review 99, 170–172

judiciary 106
jurisdiction: appellate 40–41; meaning 9, 20, 40; original 40
jurists 159
jury trials 212–213
jus ad bellum 163
jus in bello 163
justice 113–128, 131–134; access to 124–127; compensation 114; distributive 115; due process 120–122; equality 115, 116, *116*; equity 115, 116, *116*; government, role of 127–128; individualised 221; meaning 113; miscarriage of 231; natural 120; procedural 115; reinvestment 124; restorative 123; retribution 113–114; social 115; substantive 115; utilitarian perspective 117–118

Kant, I. 118
Kelly, C. 67, 86
Kerr, Sir J. 62

Labor Party 61, 62–63, 97
Lambie, J. 67
larceny *see* stealing
law: branches of 9–14, *10*; elements of 30–31; and employment 16–17; meaning 5–7; question of 230; reform 14–15; reports 43; rule 5–6; and society 14–16; sources of 7–9
Law Council of Australia 125
leadership spill 63
lease 3–4
leave of court 231
left-wing 61
Legal Aid 126
legal fiction 138–139
legality, principle of 33, 109–110, 172
legal representation 122
legislation 19–34; bills approval process 22–24; citation *23*, 27; committee stage 24–25; delegated 8, 33; divisions 28–30, *28*, *29*; elements of law 30–31; finding 25–27; formation of 21–25; judge's reading of 31–33; meaning 7, 19; parts 28–30, *28*, *29*; reading 27–33; regulations of 33–34; retrospective 110; secondary 8; sections 28–30, *28*, *29*; structure of 28–30, *28*, *29*; subordinate 8
legislative instruments 8
legislature 105
LexisNexis 41
liable 184
liberal democracy 93
liberalism 64, 93–95
Liberal Party 61, 63–64, 97
Lincoln, A. 96
literal rule 32
lobby 97
local court 38–39
local government 101–102

Mabo decision 13, 37, 44, *45*, 131, 136, 141–144
magistrate 36
magistrates court *see* local court
majoritarian system 53
majority verdict 213
Makarrata Commission 150
malware 247–249
mandatory minimums 225–226
manifesto 253
manslaughter 20–21, 30–31; by criminal negligence 187; by unlawful and dangerous act 187
Marbury v Madison (1803) 171
mass media 72
material facts 44–47; meaning 45
mayor 102

McBride, D. 82–83, 161
media 72–88; bias 83–85; as fourth estate 77–83; mass 72; meaning 72; ownership 72–77; social 85–88
media freedom, protection of 267–268
Medibank 243
medium-neutral citation 43, *43*
Members of Parliament (MPs) 51
Members of the Yorta Yorta Aboriginal Community v Victoria (2002) 135
memory 247–248
mens rea 194, 195, 199, 223, 244, 255
mental elements 194
Menzies, Sir R. 63
metadata 4, 263–264
Minister for Immigration and Ethnic Affairs v Teoh (1995) 172
ministers 8, 21–22, 69–70
minority government 67
minor parties 66–67
miscarriage of justice 231
mischief rule 32
misinformation: meaning 86; social media and 85–88
mitigating factor 222
M'Naghten's rules 198
monarch 134
Montesquieu: *Spirit of the Laws, The* 106
Morrison, S. 64, 108
motive requirement 255
MPs *see* Members of Parliament (MPs)
multilateral 157
multinational 74
Munda v WA (2013) 228
murder 20–21, 30–31, 184
Murray, L. 147
National Cabinet 104
National Human Rights Consultation 176
National Party 65
National Redress Scheme 114
native title 13, 141–144
natural justice 120
negligence 11
neoliberalism 76
News Corp 74, 76, 83
New South Wales (NSW): bail laws 209–210; Constitution Act 1902 101; Crimes Act 1900 20–21, 27, 193, 225, 240, 241; Crimes (Sentencing Procedure) Act 1999 229; Crimes (Domestic and Personal Violence) Act 2007 242; Crimes Amendment (Fraud, Identity and Forgery Offences) Act 2009 240; Criminal Procedure Regulation 2017, regulation 39 226; Evidence Amendment (Evidence of Silence) Act 2013 (No 9) 205; Law Enforcement (Powers and Responsibilities) Act 2002 204; New South Wales Act 1823 139; proportional voting 55
New Zealand (NZ): Bill of Rights Act 1990 175
Nigerian prince scams (419 scams) 238–239
Nine Entertainment Network 75–76
non-derogable 167–168
non-international armed conflict 163
non-parole period (NPP) 229
non-refoulement 159
Northern Territory (NT): Royal Commission into the Protection and Detention of Children in the Northern Territory 81; unicameral legislature 22
notice 120; to appear 206; infringement 207

NPP *see* non-parole period (NPP)
NSW *see* New South Wales (NSW)
NT *see* Northern Territory (NT)
Numbered Acts 26
NZ *see* New Zealand (NZ)
NZYQ v Minister for Immigration, Citizenship & Multicultural Affairs (2023) 171

obiter dicta 46
O'Brien, K. 83
occupational health and safety offences 192
ombudsman 208
open court 120
Operation Sovereign Borders 64
opinio juris 158, 159
opinion 36, 214
opposition 51
optional protocols 163
Optus 243
organ 159
original jurisdiction 40

Palmer United Party (PUP) 66–67
parity 221
parliamentary committee 24
Parliamentary Joint Committee on Human Rights (PJCHR) 173, 175
Parliamentary Joint Committee on Intelligence and Security (PJCIS) 265, 268
parole 228–229; meaning 229
Parole Board 229
parsimony 221
partial defences 197, 198
party 36
paternalistic offences 192
PDO *see* preventative detention orders (PDO)
Pearson, N. 150
peremptory challenge 212
persuasive precedent 40
phishing 239–240
physical elements 194
PJCHR *see* Parliamentary Joint Committee on Human Rights (PJCHR)
PJCIS *see* Parliamentary Joint Committee on Intelligence and Security (PJCIS)
plea 211; enter a 212
plenary power 101
police powers: arrest 205–206; charge 206–207; misuse of 207–208; questioning 204–205; searches 203–204; stop and search power 204
police prosecutor 207
political parties 7, 50, 61–68; centrist 62; conservative 61; faction 62; Greens 65–66; independents 67–68; Labor Party 61, 62–63; leadership spill 63; left-wing 61; Liberal Party 61, 63–64; meaning 50; minor parties 66–67; National Party 65; progressive 61; right-wing 61; swing 63
popular sovereignty 136
populism 96–97
portfolios 69
possess 13, 191
Potter v Minahan (1908) 172
precedent 37–38; binding 37–38; meaning 37; persuasive 40
pre-charge detention 206
pre-crime 257
preference deal (Senate) 59
preferential voting 51, 52–53, 63
prejudice 72
prejudicial evidence 121, 214
preparatory offences 256–257
press gallery 77–78
presumption of innocence 121, 211, 266
pre-trial disclosure 210–211

preventative detention orders (PDO) 261–262
primary vote 53
Prime Minister 51
private international law 156
private law xxi, 9, 12
privatisation 76
privilege against self-incrimination 205
probation 219
probative value 214
problem question 46
procedural fairness 120
procedural justice 115
Productivity Commission 126, 132
progressive 61
property law 12
property offences 190–191
proportionality 163–164; sentencing 220, 221
proportional voting 55–56
proscribe 258
proscribed organisation 258
proscription regime 258
prosecution service 207
prosecutor 207
provocation 197–198
public broadcaster 73–74
public international law: branches of 156–157; meaning 156
publicity 120
public law xx, 9
public order offences 185, 192
public service 105
punishment: purposes of 219–220; types of 218–219
PUP *see* Palmer United Party (PUP)
purposes of punishment 219–220
purposive rule 32, 33

Queensland (Qld): Criminal Code 1899 183–184, 245; Criminal Code (Non-Consensual Sharing of Intimate Images) Amendment Act 2019 241; Human Rights Act 2019 173; Penalties and Sentences Act 1992 223; unicameral legislature 22
question of law 230
questions without notice 108
question time 108
quota 55

races power 145
radical title 142
'Raise the Age' campaign 199
ransomware 248, 249
rape *see* sexual assault
ratify 157
ratio decidendi 46
Rawls, J.: *Theory of Justice*, *A* 119
read down 170
reading: case law 42–47; legislation 27–33; meaning 23
recidivism 122
recklessness 188–189, 245
Records of the Australasian Federal Conventions 140
recuse 122
re-examination 215
referendum xviii, 144, 175; 1967 145–146
Referendum Council 149–150
regulate 5, 6
regulations 7, 33–34
rehabilitation 219
remand 208–209
remedy 5
reparations 82
repeal 20
representative government 96
republic xix
repugnancy 141
reservation 157–158
reserved powers doctrine 103
resolution 159
respondent 229

responsible government 107; question time 108
restorative justice (RJ) 123
retribution 113–114, 219
retrospective legislation 110
revenge porn 236, 240–242
right to silence 205, 266
right-wing 61; extremism 253
RJ *see* restorative justice (RJ)
Roach v Electoral Commissioner (2007) 169
road traffic offences 192
robbery 183–184, 191; armed 191; meaning 184; punishment of 184
Rome Statute 162
Rousseau, J-J. 94; *Social Contract, The* 96
royal assent 23
royal commission 80–81
Royal Commission into Institutional Responses to Child Abuse 114
Rudd, K. 63, 133, 134, 176
rule of law 108–110
Rule of Law Index 110
R v Bugmy (2013) 228
R v Singh (2012) 198

same-sex marriage 15
Sandel, M. J.: *Justice: What's the Right Thing to Do?* 119
SBS *see* Special Broadcasting Service (SBS)
SDGs *see* Sustainable Development Goals (SDGs)
secondary legislation 8
second reading speech 23
section 20
self-defence 197
self-determination 137, 167
Senate: above the line (voting) 56, *57*; accountability 59–61; ballots 56–59; below the line (voting) *58*, 59; House of Representatives, comparison to *54*; meaning 22, 50; preference deal 59; proportional voting 55–56; staggered elections 54–55; voting procedures 56–59; *see also* House of Representatives
senators 19, 54
sentencing: advisory council 225; aggravating factor 221–222; appeals against 230–231; circle 226–227; consistency 221; evidence 222–224; guideline judgments 224; Indigenous offenders 226–228; individualised justice 221; instinctive synthesis 224–225; mandatory minimums 225–226; mitigating factor 222; parity 221; parsimony 221; principles of 220–221; proportionality 220, 221; suspended 219; totality 221; victim impact statement 223–224
Sentencing Advisory Council 225
separation of powers 104–108, *106*; administer 105; blurring of powers 106, 107; executive 105; judiciary 106; legislature 105; meaning 105
settlement 11, 138–139
Seven Media Holdings 76
sexting 240–242
sexual assault 188
shared lawmaking powers 99–101
SIO *see* special intelligence operations (SIO)
small government 64
small-l liberals 64
social contract 94, 135
social justice 115
social media, and misinformation 85–88
society, law and 14–16
solicitor 125
Solicitor-General 108
solitary confinement 81

sovereign: meaning 134; state 94, 95, 135
sovereignty 134–137, 149; institutional 136; meaning 135; popular 136
spam 246
Speaker 22–23
Special Broadcasting Service (SBS) 73; Charter 74
special intelligence operations (SIO) 263
special leave to appeal 41
specific deterrence 219, 220
staggered elections (Senate) 54–55
standards of proof 121
standing orders 23
stare decisis 38
status offence 258
statute *see* act
statutory functions 74
statutory interpretation 32
stayed 122
stealing 191
Steggall, Z. 68
Stolen Generations 133
stop and search power 204
strata title 12
Stuxnet 248
subordinate legislation 8
subsidiary 75
substantial impairment 198
substantive justice 115
sue 11
Sue v Hill (1999) 141
summary offence 193
summary trials 211–212
summons 206
supply 68
supreme court 39, 40, 46, 230
surplus votes 56
suspended sentence 219
Sustainable Development Goals (SDGs) 161
swing 63
table 25
tabloid 74–75
taking out the trash 78
teal independents 68
Ten Network Holdings 75
Tenterfield Oration 139
terra nullius, doctrine of xviii, 37, 138–139, 142, 143
terrorism: advocating 259–260; Australia's legal responses to 252–254; cyber-terrorism 255; exception 256; meaning 254–256; motive requirement 255; *see also* counter-terrorism
terrorist organisations 257–258
testimony 215
Thabo Meli v R (1954) 195
theft *see* stealing
therapeutic jurisprudence (TJ) 122–123
TJ *see* therapeutic jurisprudence (TJ)
Torrens title 12, 143
tort 11, 208
totality 221
trade unions 97
trafficking 192
transfer value 56
transparency 78
treaty 9, 51, 157; bilateral 157; multilateral 157
tribunal 8, 40
trojan 247
Trump, D. 87
Turnbull, M. 64, 68, 75, 80, 150

UAP *see* United Australia Party (UAP)
UDHR *see* Universal Declaration of Human Rights (UDHR)
UK *see* United Kingdom (UK)
Uluru Statement from the Heart 137
UN *see* United Nations (UN)
unanimous verdict 213

UNDRIP *see* United Nations Declaration on the Rights of Indigenous Peoples (UNDRIP)
UNHRC *see* United Nations Human Rights Committee (UNHRC)
unicameral legislature 22
United Australia Party (UAP) 66
United Kingdom (UK): Human Rights Act 1998 175; National Health Service (NHS) 248; Statute of Westminster 1931 (Imp) 141; Terrorism Act 2000 255
United Nations (UN) 157–164; Economic and Social Council 161; Secretariat 162; Sustainable Development Goals 161; Trusteeship Council 162
United Nations Charter 1945 (UN Charter) 159–160; section 51 163
United Nations Convention on the Rights of Refugees: article 33 159
United Nations Declaration on the Rights of Indigenous Peoples (UNDRIP) 176
United Nations General Assembly 135, 159, 160, 165
United Nations Human Rights Committee (UNHRC) 171, 173
United Nations Security Council 159, 160, 162; Resolution 1373 255
Universal Declaration of Human Rights (UDHR) 158, 165, *166*; article 1 165; article 23 167; article 27 167; preamble 165
unlawful imprisonment 12
unsafe and unsatisfactory verdict 231
utilitarian 117–118

valedictory speech 64
Veen (No 2) (1988) 220
veil of ignorance 119–120
verdict: majority 213; meaning 213; unanimous 213; unsafe and unsatisfactory 231
vertical fiscal imbalance (VFI) 103
veto 160
VFI *see* vertical fiscal imbalance (VFI)
victim impact statement 114, 223–224
Victoria: bail laws 210; Sentencing Advisory Council 225; Summary Offences Act 1966 241; Victorian Charter of Human Rights and Responsibilities Act 2006 173; 'You Be the Judge' program 225
viruses 247
Voice to Parliament xviii, 134, 144, 148–151
voting 70; compulsory 52; conscience 15; preferential 51, 52–53, 63; primary 53; proportional 55–56; Senate *see* Senate; surplus 56

WA *see* Western Australia (WA)
Wannacry 248
war crimes 162
warrant 203–204
Western Australia (WA): Criminal Investigation Act 2006 204
whistleblower 67, 82–83
Whitlam, G. 62
Wik Peoples v Queensland (1996) 136
Williamson v DPP (1999) 210
Williams v R (1986) 206
witness 215
WorkChoices legislation 60
World Justice Project 110
worms 247
wounding 188

young offenders 199

For Product Safety Concerns and Information please contact our EU representative GPSR@taylorandfrancis.com
Taylor & Francis Verlag GmbH, Kaufingerstraße 24, 80331 München, Germany

www.ingramcontent.com/pod-product-compliance
Ingram Content Group UK Ltd.
Pitfield, Milton Keynes, MK11 3LW, UK
UKHW020153200926
475702UK00016B/2691
9781032560205